Betty
lots of love
Christmas 2003
Tom (& Rosie)
xxx
x

Dedication

for James Raistrick
my beloved father
and
Theo Cowan
my dearest friend

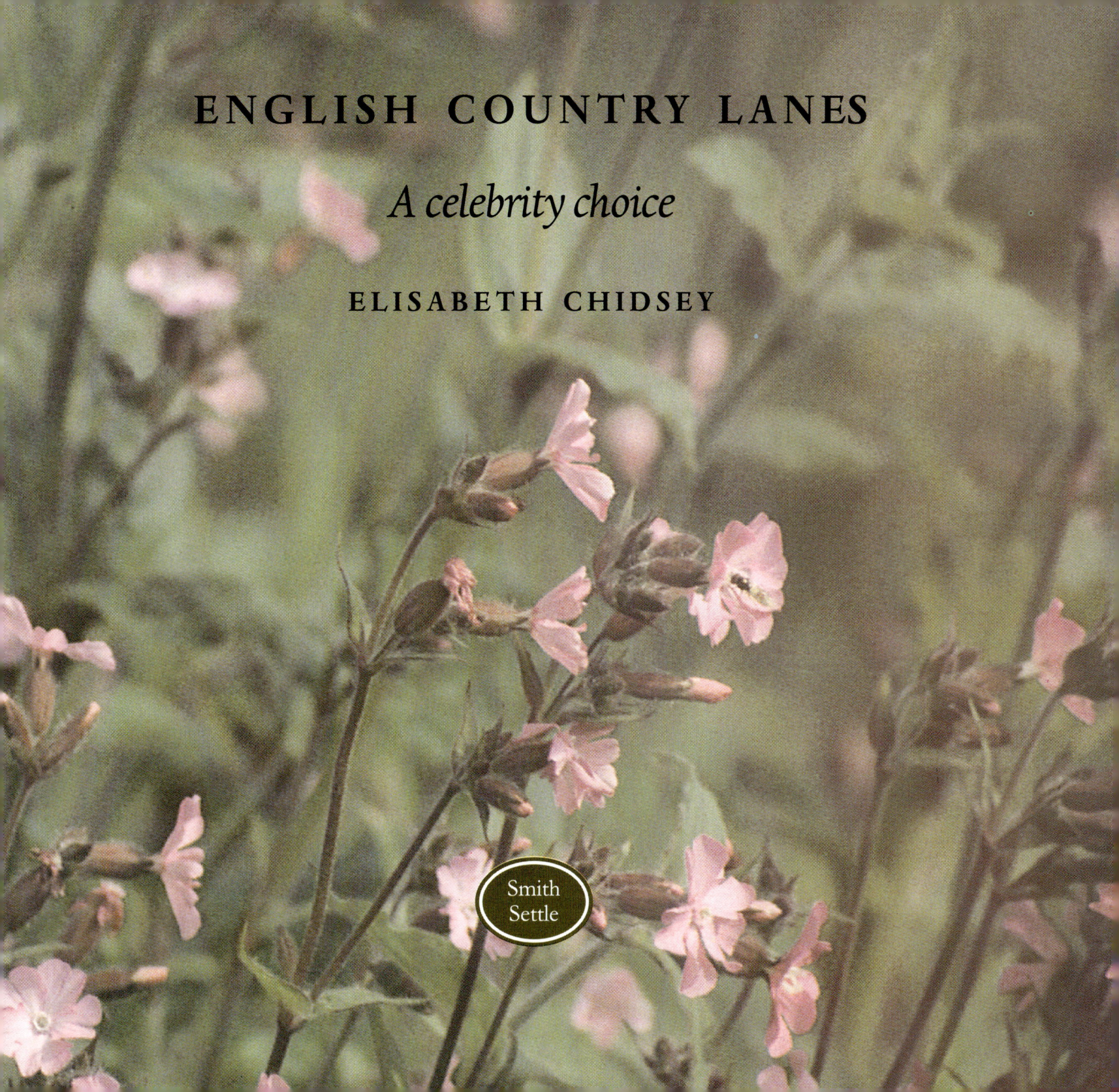

First published in 2002 by
Smith Settle Ltd
Ilkley Road
Otley
West Yorkshire
LS21 3JP

Text © Elisabeth Chidsey 2002
Photographs © Elisabeth Chidsey 2002
Maps © Christine Denmead 2002
Drawings © Neil Carter 2002
Decorated Initials © Brian Partridge 2002

All rights reserved. No part of this book may be reproduced,
stored or introduced into a retrieval system, or transmitted
in any form or by any means (electronic, mechanical,
photocopying, recording or otherwise) without the
prior permission of Smith Settle Ltd.

The right of Elisabeth Chidsey to be identified
as the author of this work has been asserted
by her in accordance with the Copyright,
Designs and Patents Act 1988.

ISBN Paperback   2 85825 155 9
Hardback   1 85825 156 7

Set in Monotype Dante

Designed, printed and bound by
SMITH SETTLE
Ilkley Road, Otley, West Yorkshire LS21 3JP

CONTENTS

Acknowledgements iv
Foreword – Sir Michael Caine v
Introduction – Elisabeth Chidsey vii

1. West End Lane, Hertfordshire – Dame Barbara Cartland 2
2. The Street, Oxfordshire – Jeremy Irons 20
3. Peddars Way, Norfolk – HRH Duchess of Kent 40
4. Marly Lane, Kent – David Jacobs 60
5. Crummack Lane, North Yorkshire – Clare Francis 80
6. Castle Lane, Northamptonshire – Dudley Moore 100
7. Chiddenbrook Lane, Devon – Dame Margot Fonteyn 120
8. Rookery Lane, West Sussex – Sir Patrick Moore 138
9. Coombe End, Oxfordshire – Sir Michael Caine 158
10. Millfield Lane, London – Lord Menuhin 178

Bibliography 198

ACKNOWLEDGEMENTS

The research, photography, preparation and writing of my book have been made much easier because of the help of many people.

First and foremost, the late Theo Cowan who provided the initial impetus, James and Edna Raistrick and Simon Chidsey, my staunchest supporters, Ken Smith, my publisher, for his kindness, sensitivity and unwavering belief in my book, Mark Whitley for the careful and considered editing of my work, John Walton for his good sense and sound advice, Chris and Alan Bassford, my computer wizards, Craig Steele for keeping my van on the road, Colin Marsland for turning the key, Lynne and Grahame Preston, Hazel and Colin Wilman, Peter Holmans, Janet and Gladys Gelder, Elsie Johnson, Jo Jefferson and Brenda Spence for their unflagging encouragement at times of self-doubt, Maria Ricketts in West Harting; Paul Coppi in Bishops Stortford, and Christiane and Alan Turney and family in Aldbury, for food, warmth, friendship and accommodation on demand, Bob and Betty Coath in Devon for their kindness and consideration, Dorothy Cowan and Jane Harker and Bill and Pat Petty for always being there, all the many, many people who have helped, and last, but not least, enormous thanks to Dr Madeleine Haag, friend, mentor and critic, who gave her valuable and much-appreciated advice and constant help in the preparation of the manuscript, looking after my animals, and listening to and believing in my ideas.

ELISABETH CHIDSEY
APRIL 2002

It's easy to understand why the most popular song sung over the radio during the war was: 'There'll always be an England while there's a country lane'. As well as being such peaceful, beautiful places, country lanes are a precious part of our heritage and a comforting link with both the past and the future.

Yet the lanes that meander through the English countryside are so different from one another. Some are overgrown and almost hidden; others sunken between high banks with trees meeting overhead; yet more, open and laid on the land like richly coloured ribbons. And each season holds so many things to enjoy, like the hot smell of nettles, the musk of hawthorns, and the heady perfume of wild roses and honeysuckle you often find winding around trees and bushes; the song of the wren in spring, the contented sound of the blackbird and the collared dove in summer, and the winter carolling of the robin. It's fascinating, too, to see the way the ladybirds, crickets, frogs and other little inhabitants of the lanes go about their business unconcerned with human lives, loves and traumas. One experience that still gives me a thrill whenever I think of it was seeing a hundred butterflies dancing in the shafts of sunlight through the trees in a secluded lane where I walked alone one early morning.

Trying to pin down the deep-rooted appeal of the English country lane has always intrigued me. More than likely it's a combination of things, like knowing the paths have been made by our ancestors and have been trodden before us by others in every kind of mood and situation. Some of the events that have taken place in country lanes, as the book tells, have even changed the course of English history.

Every time I walk down an English lane, I expect to find at the end of it some forgotten land, perhaps the very heart of England itself. Whenever I'm filming overseas, I have a kind of longing for the fields, the trees, the lanes and the changing seasons of home, and I was very lucky to have had a lovely old house in Oxfordshire. I hoped that by planting new hedgerows and making a freshwater lake where wild things can grow, and find peace and protection, that I was able to return something to the countryside for all the pleasure it has given me. All around our house were the country lanes of Oxfordshire and Berkshire, each one with its own character, its own flora and fauna — and I took great pleasure in discovering as many of them as time allowed.

The lanes in this book are only a minute sample of the enchanting and unique country lanes we still have in England. I wish you many joyous hours using them.

SIR MICHAEL CAINE

Many years ago there was a country lane which meandered down a hill not far from my home. A deep, sunken lane, folding into the natural contours of the land, edged with sombre stone walls made from millstone grit — Yorkshire stone — darkened and blackened by the smoke and grime of Bradford, the city far away across the valley, but softened by the branches of hawthorn trees tumbling over the wall tops. To me, as a child, it was an exciting place, full of magic. Each time I went there I found something new — some strangely shaped snail's shell, or pink and white hawthorn blossom mixed on the same branch, red and black ladybirds, shining green beetles, or the delicate, creamy, florets of elderberry flowers floating down the wind like summer snow carried on clouds of yellow pollen through shafts of sunlight filtering through the dense green cover of the trees meeting overhead.

Then, there was the careful exploration of every dim opening in the stone walls looking for spiders, insects, beetles, daddy-long-legs, field mice, frogs and other fascinating creatures that made the uneven cavities their home and whose colours, shapes and habits held me spellbound. I was familiar with the grasses, the nettles, the dock leaves, the bluebells and the foxgloves growing on the banking, taller than I was at that time. The lane was always bubbling with excited busy living and every season brought different discoveries.

In spring the lane was a fairy grotto with the haze of bluebells along the verges and then hedge parsley, and hawthorn blossom tumbled over the stone walls and exuded a musky perfume which was like no other. Birds were all around me in the bushes and trees — so close to me that I could see the feathers on their tiny throats moving as they sang. I could watch them building their nests and lay their eggs, and I can remember waiting in anticipation for the chicks to hatch and peep over the nest, mouths gaping, fluffy down at each side of their beaks, and my joy at watching them fly away. Summer had wild roses, honeysuckle, elderberries, foxgloves and campion, and autumn brought changing colours, falling leaves and rich earth smells. Then the hawthorns on the wall tops became dark, twisting and angular, the branches spangled with raindrops and shining red berries.

When I was small, the environment of this lane seemed to me to be the whole world — a secret world filled with wonder. Here was the richness and diversity of nature — the everyday life of myriads of creatures — their world as valuable and as important as the human world to me. I was too young to know about the classification of flora and fauna, or to understand about the history and development of country lanes. I only knew that my lane was an incredibly beautiful and exciting place. A place to play, explore, discover. A place I dearly loved.

When I was eleven, my parents took me to Scotland for a holiday. When I returned, my lane was gone. The authorities had seen fit to fill it in with waste and rubble, to level it out and flatten it, and make it uniform with the rest of the uniformity they think we all need. On top of the rubble they put a concrete sloping path at a difficult angle which made walking up or down it precarious, especially in the wet, snow or ice. To one side of the concrete path they had laid wide concrete slabs to make steps; one had either to take two small steps on each slab, or one large one and risk knocking the back of one's heels. In the middle of this path they placed a metal handrail, they tore out the trees and rebuilt the wall with council bricks. Soon the handrail was bent and rusty, the steps crumbled and cracked. The path was dangerous, slippery and extremely ugly. My lane, with its beauty and individuality was gone forever — along with all the life within its walls.

The lane is now static, dead; ugly to look at — nothing grows, nothing can be moved or altered or played with. There is nothing to look at, to wonder about. No birds nest there or sing there; no bees visit. To lose this unique, harmless area of peace and loveliness along with all its wildlife was horrifying, and the sense of loss I experienced as a child is still vivid in my mind to this day.

The obliteration of this lane was somebody's idea of 'progress'. The value of this interesting lane with its intimacy and its familiarity to the community was not considered. The workman hours it must have taken to fill it in and replace the lane with such ugliness, and the price of materials that were needed for such a job, must have been expensive for the taxpayers. There seemed to be no justification for altering the lane in any way at all. This country lane was serving people quite adequately as a by-way and only needed the undergrowth cutting back and the leaves sweeping up each year.

In offering us this constant conformity — related always, it appears, to the minimum of cost — our concept of the worth of individuality and beauty is becoming dulled. Serve children with environments like these, or any other faceless, uniform places, then we can expect them to act accordingly and not value the world in which they grow up.

When I grew up, I came to live in a country lane that runs down the edge of the Yorkshire moors to the River Aire in West Yorkshire. I found I was still fascinated by country lanes, their verges, their hedgerows and their history. I started to keep a journal of all the wonderful flora and fauna I saw each day as I walked down the lane with my dog, Sam. The curlew on a fine spring morning, coming down from the moor tops, calling its bubbling mating call, circling low over the lane; lapwings moving through the morning air with throbbing wings, tumbling to the ground, turning upwards at the last moment; skylarks hovering high in the sky; blackbirds in the branches of the trees, singing so beautifully; tiny wrens bursting forth with tremendous songs; lambs in the fields; and, at night, huge harvest moons over Hope Hill looking over the lane. Barn owls on the wall tops and bats flying about made evening in the lanes just as exciting as the day. For me there was still magic in a country lane.

I began to wonder about the significance of English country lanes, their history and development and their place in the English landscape. English country lanes seem, somehow, to be part of the the English consciousness. There are so many hymns, songs, poems, sayings and paintings about them both old and new. John Constable painted a well-known picture called *A Country Lane*, there is a racehorse called Top o' the Lane, and some of the sayings about country lanes have become symbolic of life: 'It's a long lane without any turning', 'Down Lover's Lane'. 'Glad for the country lanes and the fall of dew' is from the hymn 'Glad that I live am I', and

'I'll walk down the lane with a happy refrain' is from the song 'Singing in the Rain'. There are many other songs about lanes: 'Walk down Heartbreak Lane' by Robin Gibbs; 'Lover's Lane' by Cole Porter from *Miss Otis Regrets*; 'We'll Walk Together Down an English Lane' from the song 'We'll Gather Lilacs'; 'Down the Lane', a line in the song 'Julia' by the Eurythmics; 'Down Featherbed Lane' from the show *East Side of Heaven* and many more. After Lord Neville Chamberlain announced on the radio that Britain was at war with Germany in 1939, there was silence and then the announcer's voice said 'We will now play you a gramophone record entitled 'Flowers from a leafy lane'; and during the First World War, one of the most popular songs sung over the radio was 'There'll always be an England while there's a country lane'.

Why should this be? What is it about the country lane which is so nostalgic and imprints itself so deeply on our minds that we have to sing and speak about them and in times of crisis refer to them? Is the answer so simple as to be a mere trick of the landscape which captures our hearts? Instead of a single hedgerow edging a field, a country lane has hedgerows at each side of a lane, focusing the vision and the attention into a long tunnel of greenery through which we have to pass in very close and continuing contact with the plants growing at either side — this is an experience which is unusual.

Or is it perhaps knowing that the places we are walking have been developed over the centuries by our ancestors? Others, who, like us, have strolled there, maybe deep in thought or conversation, have kissed, loved and laughed and cried along the way; and often, more profound events have taken place in country lanes. Some have even changed the course of English history. Do we, when we walk a country lane, feel a kind of connection with them?

On the other hand, it may be the way a country lane folds easily into the landscape, not jarring the senses, reminding us of the ancient and symbiotic relationship between man and the land, and how satisfying and unobtrusive that relationship can be if carried out with understanding and caring. Perhaps it is a subtle combination of all these things which give us this peculiar sensitivity we seem to have when we think of English country lanes.

A lane is, by definition, a narrow, often rural way, path or street running between fields, hedges, fences or buildings, initially joining isolated communities. Lanes have been an integral part of our landscape for many centuries. They developed as animals made paths through the forests and early man followed them. When man had learned how to make tools, trees could be cut and paths made to the nearest water supply or most sheltered place to live. These followed the most convenient way.

Prehistoric paths kept to high ground where wild animals, enemies and boggy ground could be avoided. Many of these ancient tracks can still be walked in sections in various parts of Britain.

By the time of the Celts, lanes and roads with verges, as we know them, came into being. They had to be wide enough for carts and chariots to pass along. These lanes and paths stayed close to the natural contours of the land, folding into the landscape in a perfect blend of form and need, and this was also the beginning of a new kind of habitat for wildlife. Some of the banks and hedgerows in country lanes have not been disturbed for hundreds of years, and this continuation of habitat is almost unique and of special interest. As farming developed and people multiplied, lanes and roads had to take note of land ownership and land tenure. Boundaries were marked by ditches and high bankings, and the convoluted lanes with dog leg curves and bends are evidence of this. Only Roman roads cut straight through the landscape and went the shortest route between two points for military efficiency. Over the years, the ecology of each lane has developed, and the history, folklore, songs, poems, sayings and stories about the characters connected with them has added spice to their individuality and essence.

To look at an English lane as a total environment is a rewarding experience and I thought that it would be exciting to discover, photograph and write about country lanes in other areas of the English countryside and put them into a book. I believed that many people have a favourite country lane somewhere in their memory and wondered if they shared my continuing appreciation of them, so I wrote to people whom I admired, and who have given so much pleasure and interest to the general public through their talent and often relentless and demanding work, to ask them if they would tell me about their own favourite lane so that I could research, photograph and write about them in a celebration of English country lanes. The response was overwhelming and I received enthusiastic letters of support from everyone I approached.

The ten lanes in this book have been chosen, over a period of time, by celebrities, all of whom are aware of the splendour and value of English country lanes. Some of the lanes I have included as a tribute to celebrities who are no longer with us, in remembrance of the places that meant a great deal to them — places of refuge and peace which they often returned to, and to show their preferences to you and reveal a part of their life which had a private richness and satisfaction.

The rest of the lanes have been chosen by celebrities who took time out of their busy schedule to write to me, speak on the telephone or meet me. HRH the Duchess of Kent graciously gave her permission for me to write about her favourite lane in Norfolk, Dame Margot Fonteyn wrote from her farm in Panama just before she died to tell me of a perfect lane in Devon, Dudley Moore wrote to me from California and Michael Caine took me out to a magnificent lunch at Langans, his restaurant in London — an experience never to be forgotten. Patrick Moore welcomed me into his lovely thatched home on the South Coast, sat me down on his sofa with a drink and a cake, and played his piano and his xylophone for me as it was my birthday. Then he and I set off in his immaculate classic car and he drove me all around the country lanes of Sidlesham and Selsey. That too was a wonderful time.

Writing this book has been, for me, the beginning of a journey, at times a very long and hard journey in between trying to make a living and having to overcome the difficulties of the English weather in the weekends I had available to complete the photographs for my book. Also there were problems with cameras — like the time I spent three idyllic days in Norfolk photographing the ancient hawthorns in Peddars Way, HRH the Duchess of Kent's favourite lane in Norfolk, only to find that my camera had broken. I returned the week after to retake the shots but it had rained the whole week and the hawthorns were over.

I had to wait a whole year to return to the lane and retake the photographs.

But the journey has been rewarding and extremely satisfying. Not only have I discovered along the way some incredibly beautiful country lanes in a landscape to cherish, I have met many people who have helped me on my journey and made it possible for me to finish this book — all of whom appreciated what I was trying to do and who love country lanes as much as I do.

At a time of new beginnings in a new century, we should realise that our truly wonderful land has much to celebrate and that country lanes are a part of our heritage which have been around us, in a close relationship with us, for over 1,000 years. Plants and animals have shared with us this long journey through time, and now the undisturbed areas of greenery in country lanes are becoming vital places of refuge for our wildlife.

It is my hope that, wherever you are, and in whatever part of the country you live, you may be able to discover an English lane, walk down or up or along it and make it your own, and that you will enjoy the flora and fauna, the visual appearance, get to know the history and find out about the people who have walked there before you, and that perhaps by sharing the enjoyment of the enchanting English lanes in this book you will come to appreciate their compelling beauty and importance. In doing so, I am sure that you will become aware of their true value to us, to our wildlife and to our countryside, and as a result become concerned for the care and conservation of these unique English treasures.

ELISABETH CHIDSEY
APRIL 2002

West End Lane, Wild Hill, Hertfordshire

Dame Barbara Cartland

Mid-spring

'… the country lanes, the hedgerows filled with flowers and birds of every kind have given me pure contentment and tranquillity …'

West End Lane is a scintillating, voluptuous and seductive place. Decked out in every spring colour available, it wanders through an exquisite, exuberant paradise, bending and turning beneath blossom-filled banking and moving, as if intoxicated, past ravishing, herb-rich meadows, potent old oak trees and luscious rushing streams. The whole of it bustles with new life: tree branches, grass verges, cottage gardens, stone ledges, holes in chimney pots, nooks and crannies — everywhere is crammed with flowers flaunting themselves and filling the air with their provocation. Birds trill and flute, dogs bark, donkeys bellow, hens argue, geese hoot, sheep rejoice and a whole host of other impatient animals quicken the sky with their bubbling, bursting song. Here is everything that Solomon ever sang about.

Dame Barbara Cartland lived at Camfield Place, a beautiful house set in 400 acres (160ha) of rich arable farmland, which, along with the home farm, is on the east side of West End Lane, Wild Hill, Hertfordshire.

'I love my house, Camfield Place', she wrote, 'set above the fields in the gently rolling countryside of Hertfordshire. The house, the surrounding landscape, the country lanes, the hedgerows filled with flowers and birds of every kind have given me pure contentment and tranquillity, and the power and perfect loveliness surrounding this place has given me the energy and inspiration to write many, many books — over 700 now —

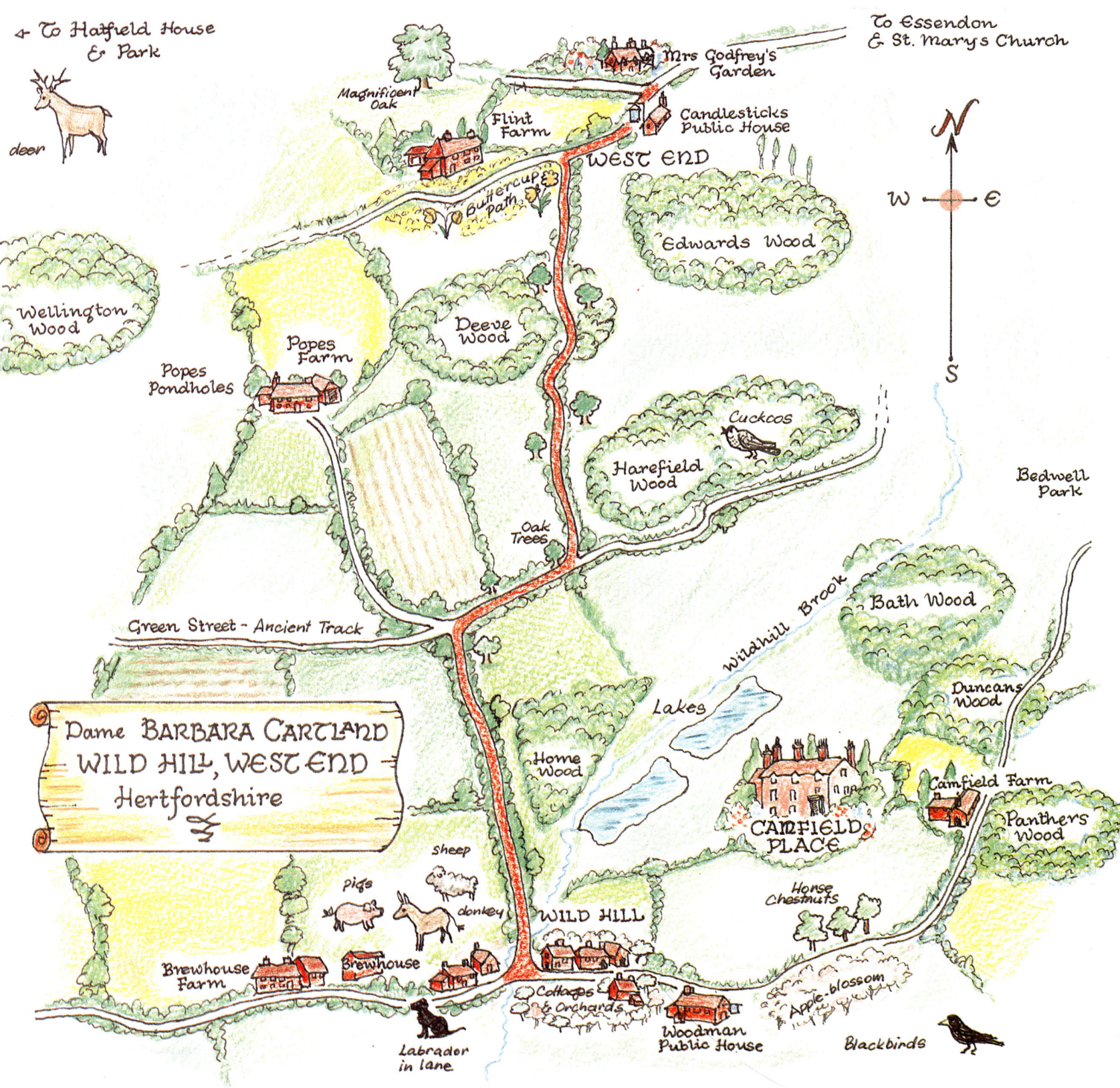

which have been translated into all the languages of the world. My books have, I hope, given people happiness and pleasure, and helped them to see that genuine, loving affection, decency and respect are values worth having and perhaps, by my efforts, I may have given them the encouragement to change their lives for the better. That is all that matters to me. I came to live at Camfield Place a long time ago when I was married to Hugh McCorquodale and have lived here ever since. In time of trial and tribulation Camfield is always there — my spiritual home.'

Camfield Place is a wonderful, evocative place set high on rich sloping meadows amongst curving, voluptuous and splendid country lanes. Stately and harmonious, it stands quite tall in the fields. The gardens and grounds are laid out above clear blue lakes and tumbling waterfalls, and reflect Barbara Cartland's dazzling personality.

There are sweeping lawns with thousands of daffodils which she planted, stunning groups of trees and woodlands, and every possible corner and space around the house and up the drive as far as the impressive wrought-iron gates — painted Nile blue with lodge houses at either side — is filled with coral-pink geraniums, breathtaking and immensely pretty.

Capability Brown landscaped the parkland in the eighteenth century, and later Lord Queensborough extended the shrubbery, filling it with rhododendrons and azaleas. They shade from rich amethyst, through scarlet, to the palest peach. In the shrubbery is an oak tree planted by Elizabeth I in 1550 when she was held prisoner at Hatfield House, half a mile (0.8km) away across the fields to the west side of the lane. This is also believed to be the spot where Elizabeth shot her first stag. The descendants of Elizabeth's own herd of deer still roam the parkland at Hatfield.

'There is so much history attached to Camfield House and surrounding this area', Dame Barbara continued. 'The kings and queens of England have ridden in the fields and lanes that I can see from my windows or have proceeded in state along the lanes nearby going up to London, and ministers and statesmen have come to Hatfield by carriage going along the lanes hereabouts. And there is the vivid image I have of Queen Elizabeth I riding her pony as a girl of ten along with her brother, Edward VI, across the fields and around the park, already troubled by the machinations of the court. At Camfield Place in the year 1275, a knight called Camville had the house. In 1611, Sir William Brocket, a knight to King James I, lived here and later, in 1861, the grandfather of Beatrix Potter, who wrote the Peter Rabbit books, bought the house and turned it from a Tudor-style house with latticed windows into the yellow-brick Victorian mansion house it is today. A wonderful place to live!'

West End Lane leads northwards from Wild Hill, a tiny hamlet which lies west off the B158 from Brookmans Park to Essendon. It dips down past the cottages, rises up through fields, has a dog-leg curve to the east, passes Green Street, the ancient road, climbs up to the Candlesticks public house then ends by St Mary's Church, Essendon. A distance of 2½ miles (4km).

At the start of Wild Hill leading to West End Lane are some cottages built in old red brick with pantiled roofs. Honeysuckle covers the walls and spirals up the chimneys; masses of rosebuds, unopened, climb around wooden trellis work and rustic arches, and in the orchard surrounding the houses are the fruit trees and bushes: plum, pear, peach, cherry, apple, blackcurrant, redcurrant, apricot, gooseberry, greengage and quince — most were tinged with pale pinks or creams, but some were white. Pale beech leaves like soft green silk hung on the low hedges all around. In front of the cottage gates at either side of the lane are glorious grass verges. A cross between a lawn and a meadow, they are filled with flowers: oxeye daisies, pink clover, blue speedwell, dandelion, yellow beaked hawksbeard and the tallest buttercups imaginable — the sun shone on them, lighting up every pulsing green vein in the yellow petals.

Here, a Labrador dog sat in the middle of the lane, warming itself on the concrete surface, yawning and watching a huge red cockerel as it waltzed out of a garden gate pursuing a hen. It was a magnificent Rhode Island Red. It strutted about, arching its shimmering green tail-feathers, raising its ruff around its neck, holding one wing down low and arrogantly fixing the female with an hypnotic eye. She ran away. Other hens appeared. A black and white Plymouth Rock, three black Austrolops, a Light Sussex with a fat, blonde body and some more Rhode Island Reds. The cockerel changed his affections and went for them. He paused, unable to choose which one he wanted, and they scooted off under the hedge, shaking their combs and complaining.

Beyond the grass is Wild Hill Brook. Natural woodland rises up on the east side of the lane, and the waterfalls at

Camfield Place feed into the brook and send it under the lane and into the fields at the other side. The trees are willow and common alder; the ones by the brook shadow its edges. Kingcups grow in the damp soil under the bridge crossing the lane, and lords and ladies are thronged and bursting on the banks of the stream — their curling, crumpling leaves turning back on themselves, folding and unfolding like sensuous tongues as they wrap around the strong brown stamens poking up inside.

The lane begins to rise steeply. The hedgerow closes in. Hedge parsley, bugloss and stitchwort freckle the shaggy, grassy banks, and the tender star-of-Bethlehem grows out quite far from the lane edge. A large oak tree, the first of many, towers above the lane on the left and further up on the east side is an iron gate painted blue. Over the top I could see Camfield Place hidden in the trees.

In the 1860s, Beatrix Potter, the writer of the Peter Rabbit books, spent a lot of time with her grandparents who owned Camfield Place. She would sit on the floor by the table leg in the dining room, hidden by her grandmother's black silk dresses, listening to her conversations about the home farm, the gardens and the latest behaviour of Spriggins, the flirtatious young servant girl who 'wore ribbons in her hair' and lived at a pretty cottage halfway down Wild Hill. Or she would sit and paint butterflies at the library table, and sometimes she would spend hours gazing out of the high windows watching the foxes on the ridges of the fields, the hedgehogs in the gardens or the toads by the ponds. Her journal of 1884 records that Camfield was 'the place she loved best in the world'. While she was staying at Camfield Place she began writing the story of Peter Rabbit. The Elizabethan walled garden, the locked door in the wall, the goldfish pond where the white cat sat twitching its tail, the pottery shed where Peter Rabbit hid from Mr MacGregor and the geranium pots he knocked over are still here, exactly the same. Even the rows of French beans, radishes and parsley which, 'feeling rather sick', he ate, still grow in the same place.

Much of the land to the north of Camfield Place on the east side of the lane belongs to Lord Essendon, and on the west side of the lane, beyond the fields belonging to Brewhouse Farm and Flint Farm, is Hatfield Park and Hatfield House which belongs to Robert Cecil, the sixth Marquis of Salisbury. Hatfield House was originally the twelfth-century palace of the bishops of Ely which was seized by

7 • WEST END LANE – DAME BARBARA CARTLAND

ENGLISH COUNTRY LANES • 8

Henry VIII. Elizabeth I lived at Hatfield Palace as a child and then later as a young woman when she was detained there by Queen Mary. James I gave Hatfield Palace to Robert Cecil, the first earl of Salisbury, who rebuilt the palace in 1611 with the existing Jacobean mansion house, Hatfield House.

Hatfield House is a magnificent building which has been the home of powerful men and women who have ruled England over the centuries. The house is built in rose-coloured brick faced with stone, and has central façades of paler stone ornamented with crests and trophies and multitudes of mullioned windows. There is a pillared cupola with a clock tower. Hatfield House is a spacious, sumptuous house with vast expanses of parkland and elegant formal gardens crammed with flowers, surrounded by pleached lime trees and topiary. A large pool is filled with water lilies and a sculptured fountain. Inside the house is a marble hall with a grand staircase, marble floors, spacious rooms hung with portraits of kings and queens, and enormous gilded rooms kept especially for state occasions. Lord David Cecil, who lived at Hatfield, wrote that as a child he was 'penetrated by the spirit of the place. The complex, pervading, evocative smell of washed stone, varnished panelling and floors polished with beeswax and smoke from generations of wood fires.' The smell of ages — the smell that Queen Elizabeth I must have known when she lived here as a child.

The palace of Hatfield was extremely important in the life of Elizabeth I because it was here she made herself ready for the triumphs and disasters in her life which were like a Jacobean tragedy — 'sensational, gorgeous and blood-stained'. England in the sixteenth century was a time of great change. The established order was overthrown and a medieval country was transformed into a modern one. Tudor times were turbulent times and Elizabeth grew up in a constant atmosphere of treasonous rebellion, deceit, plots and counter-plots, grave threats to her life, and religious and fanatical fervour and division — the Catholic Church against the rise of the Protestant faith and the constant threat of invasion from across the Channel. Through her shrewdness, courage, diplomacy and majestic show of loyalty to her people and her country, she was able to overcome all obstacles put in her way and unite the nation against invaders.

Queen Elizabeth was an 'heroic woman' who ruled her country alone and was her own prime minister in war and peace for forty years. She was the absolute ruler of England at perhaps the most crucial period in its whole history. Highly educated in matters of state — politics, religion, philosophy — she had the wisdom and perception to choose the correct policy for her country and the adroitness to put it into practice. Elizabeth had an immense sense of her role as regent of God on Earth. She was a strongly individual woman, quick-witted and serious, with pale, high-bred features, long hands and fingers, an intellectual brow and a hard unwavering

facing page   Hatfield House.

glance. Often she told lies for amusement and her conduct was unpredictable and although she was regarded as someone who showed a cool and calculating face to the world, from time to time she had passionate outbursts of emotion that showed she was far from an unfeeling woman. She had learned at a very early age to hide her true feelings and confide in no one.

In 1553, Princess Elizabeth, three months old, arrived at Hatfield along with her household servants governed by Lady Bryan. Already Elizabeth was caught up in political intrigue. Although she was daughter to King Henry VIII, by the time she was three years old her father had beheaded her mother, Anne Boleyn, and declared his daughter to be a bastard.

At the age of ten, Elizabeth was still at Hatfield, living with her half-brother Edward, prince of Wales, later Edward VI, sharing his lessons and his company. They had a rigorous education under distinguished tutors such as Roger Ascham, the Cambridge humanist and educationalist. They studied classical languages, history, rhetoric, moral philosophy, politics and theology. Elizabeth was fluent in Greek, Latin, French and Italian, and she enjoyed her lessons, but she had other diversions to balance her studies — dancing, hunting and hacking through the woods and lanes around Wild Hill (then named Wyldehille), West End and the open countryside that surrounded the little town of Hatfield. She was a competent rider and looked every bit her best on horseback. At this period in her life, Elizabeth was happy and peaceful, living with people she liked.

After the death of her father and her frail young half-brother, Mary, her older sister and Roman Catholic zealot, came into power in 1553. Although Elizabeth paid lip service to Catholicism, at heart she was a true Protestant who, given the chance, would restore England to the Anglican Church. Mary suspected Elizabeth of spying for Sir Thomas Wyatt in the rebellion of 1554 and sent her to the Tower of London, where she narrowly escaped death. Cleared of the charge, she was released and placed under house arrest for a year at Woodstock in Oxfordshire. Then in October 1555, she returned to her beloved Hatfield. As she drove back up through the lanes and woods to the small town, the church bells rang out in a great welcome and her people cheered for her, happy at her return to the great house in the park at Hatfield.

Once again she was in her own palace, leading the life of a royal princess with her own household, musicians and horses, but under the guardianship of Sir Thomas Pope, who later founded Trinity College in Oxford. She was a prisoner only in the sense that she could not leave Hatfield without permission. Her own tutor, Roger Ascham, returned to help her finish her studies. But, once again, life was not all study, and at times she forgot the Puritan mannerisms she had assumed for diplomacy's sake. She went out stag hunting in the woods near here, attended on one day, it is said, by a procession of twelve ladies clothed in white satin and twenty gentlemen in green, and met by fifty archers with scarlet boots and yellow caps, one of whom presented her with a silver-headed arrow wound round with peacock feathers.

facing page   Wild Hill going from West End Lane.

As Queen Mary lay dying, in 1558, childless and alone — for King Philip of Spain, her husband, had deserted her — the roads and lanes to Hatfield were already crowded with important people, both English and foreign, hurrying here to pay homage to the future queen.

One day as she was sitting under an oak tree in Hatfield Park reading a Greek text, her ministers came to tell Elizabeth that she was the queen of England. She was twenty-five years old. At once she held her first council and chose her ministers. On the 17th November 1558 she rode into London with full pageantry and display, dressed in a fabulous gown and wearing rich jewels, putting on a dazzling show of wealth and magnificence for her great coronation. She was greeted with bells and bonfires, and cheering demonstrations of patriotism. Her coronation procession was a masterpiece of public relations showing her ultimate strength and power. Her people loved her and shouted 'Long live the Queen'.

Elizabeth chose as her chief minister William Cecil, Lord Burghley. He was appointed principal secretary of state on the morning of her accession at Hatfield, and he served his queen with wisdom and skill for forty years. He was a man who could be trusted in the matters of highest policy. He fought corruption, and made the Tudor economic and political system work. He set up censorship and propaganda, and began an intelligence network at home and abroad. Cecil was skilled in the control of the royal household, and of military and naval establishments. His handling of royal finances and justice was honourable and scrupulous. Elizabeth came to rely on his wise counselling, friendship and judgement more and more throughout her life, and when he died in 1598 she could not hear his name mentioned without bursting into tears.

In 1571 she created him Lord Burghley and later Knight of the Garter.

Sir William Cecil was a hard worker and began working promptly at four o'clock every morning. He had risen from an ordinary background — a good marriage with high connections, a member of parliament quite early on in life, and a justice of the peace — and he found favour with Henry VIII because of his ability to argue in Latin. Henry took him into his service and sent him to watch over Elizabeth at Hatfield. William Cecil, through hard work and diligence, had achieved his ambition to make the Cecils one of the first families in England. He was slight of build, soberly dressed and always seemed to have a worried look on his face. Most of his life he was surrounded by the vicious side of political life, but he loved to build fine houses: Burghley House, Cecil House in the Strand in the centre of London, and Theobolds House in Hertfordshire. In the summer evenings when he was at Hatfield, he would walk in the gardens to clear his mind and regenerate his spirit with the flowers and the scent of the roses. He was a sensuous man in that he loved fine silks and multi-coloured tapestries, the smell of amber, and the sight of silver plate and statues from Venice. He was also a family man, and took deep delight in his wife and children. But his foremost loyalties were to Queen Elizabeth, whom he had first encountered at Hatfield.

After his death, William Cecil's son, Robert, first marquis of Salisbury, became Elizabeth's principal secretary, and was as loyal and steadfast to her as his father had been. He was a very different character from his father, deformed and sensitive, and this, it is said, set him apart. He became a member of parliament at the age of

eighteen, and in 1586 the queen required him to prepare a pamphlet giving her reasons for not wanting to execute Mary, Queen of Scots. Robert Cecil was the man who discovered the Catholic conspiracy to blow up James I — the Gunpowder Plot of the 5th November 1605 — and the man who made the peaceful change, after the death of Elizabeth, from the Tudors to the Stuarts with the accession of James I of Scotland.. Robert Cecil made Hatfield the true home of the Cecils by rebuilding it, adding to it and filling the house with many treasures. He is buried at Hatfield House. The Cecils of Hatfield had a lasting influence on the history of England. Robert Cecil, the sixth marquis of Salisbury, resides at Hatfield in the present day.

All around the lane are ancient woods and coppices with unusual names: Hoppets Wood, Panthers Wood, Harefield Wood, Deeve Wood, Wellington Wood, Edwards Wood, Duncans Wood, Bath Wood, Home Wood, Panshanger Wood and more.

Once this area was a huge forest of oak trees, and then in the Middle Ages it became an area of managed woodland called Hatfield Great Wood, with royal foresters caring for every tree. Trees were highly valued in those days — so much so that, in 1346, Edward III would only allow the rector of Essendon one single log for his hearth each year at Christmas. There are still many of the original oak trees growing in the lane marking the route of the lane as it rises up to Essendon village. Some are exceedingly old and stag-headed, others are younger and in greater glory.

The oak tree is England's traditional tree and also its most common species. There are two kinds of oak trees in the lane — common oak or pedunculate, and sessile or durmast oak. Both these trees are ancient native species. Where the soil is deep and fertile, an oak tree can grow to its full height of around 100 feet (30m). The tallest oak tree in Britain is a 135-feet (41m) high sessile oak in Hereford, and the oak with the biggest girth — a common oak growing in Pontfadog, Wales — is 43½ feet (13m) round its middle. This huge tree could be 800 years old, but the average life-span for an oak tree is 250 years. Oak trees have played an important part in English history, and they are held in great affection by many people. The saying 'hearts of oak', meaning having a strong and loyal character, has become an oft-used metaphor in the English language. Beyond the sap-wood of the oak is the stout core of the dark brown heart-wood, which in its natural state can withstand centuries of hard use. The keel, frame and ribs of every great wooden sailing ship from the early Middle Ages onwards were made of oak. It took the timber from 3,000 mature oak trees to build a man o' war. Oak timber is still used for the hulls of fishing craft built along the east coast of Scotland. Oak has always been used for special places — church pews, pulpits, staircases and panelling in mansions and public buildings, and, because of its enduring strength, for cartwheel spokes, beer barrels and wine casks.

An oak tree teems with life. At various times throughout its long life, the oak may be host to more than 200 different types of organisms, and even in winter a wealth of life is beneath its bark. There are silk button spangle galls covered in tiny, shining hairs; gall wasps making spongy gall; acorn weevils using the acorn nuts as a nursery; oak roller moths eating the leaves. Ivy climbs and winds around the trunk, and myriads of insects use the leaves for cover. Birds are attracted to the insects, and blackbirds often nest in the ivy. The great spotted woodpecker feeds on insect larvae, drilling into the tree to get at wood-boring species of insects, and the wind carries the minute spores of polypody on to the moist tree bark, helping them to grow into mature ferns. Bluebells and primroses bloom around the roots before the summer canopy cuts off the light, and the bright white flowers of ransoms grow in profusion, nourished by the rich leaf-litter.

On the west side of the lane, the fields are planted with oil seed rape. The pale yellow flowering stems rise up in long scented rows, quite tall, from behind the hedge at the left side of the lane and sweep southwards to Brewhouse Farm below. Brewhouse Farm and barn is the ancient red-brick brewhouse which was built in 1575 to provide beer for Hatfield House. For many years it was a thriving farm which had a dairy herd and made cream. Donkeys were in the fields next to the farm, and some geese and ducks, and a few Large White pigs. The pigs were kept in the fields behind the Brewhouse, rooting and snuffling with flat pink noses like the end of vacuum cleaners. The short pink bristles on their faces were blotted with mud.

A path edged with bush vetch, red campion and cow parsley leads off west and then splits into two tracks: one, quite wide, turns sharply northwards and leads to Popes Farm on the site of Pope's Manor House and Popes Pond Holes; the other, Green Street, goes straight on eastwards and is the old Roman road which leads to Woodside Place

facing page   The brewhouse at Brewhouse Farm.

Farm, crosses Woodside just before Pepperpot Lodge and goes south to Millwards Park.

In 1330, William Tooke was the lord of the manor of Essendon, and he and his descendants lived at Popes Manor House. Popes Manor house was a large house with formal gardens, pleasure grounds and ornamental ponds, and later in Jacobean times a temple and a gazebo on a mound, and a summer house. The house burned down in 1745, but subsequently another house was built on the same spot. When Sir Benjamin Trueman lived there in 1790 it was a large Georgian house which had 'fine drawing rooms, four best bed chambers, twenty good windows, handsome servant quarters and excellent stabling for four carriages'. This house was bought by the marquis of Salisbury in 1817 who, it is believed, had the house demolished. Popes Farm stands on the site and Popes Pond Holes are still there.

Now the lane bends sharply north-east, skirts Home Wood, bends north again, passes Harefield Wood and, after a long, downwards stretch, dips into Deeve Wood. Here it is shady and dark as the trees meet overhead. Bluebells are everywhere under the trees — an insubstantial sea of sweet-smelling, curling flowers. In a field on the right is a donkey with long, soft ears, a soft grey nose, its neat tail tucked behind and its dainty hoofs hidden in a cloud of sweet vernal grass. More fields are on the right, rising gently behind the trees, and beyond is a row of poplar trees. On the horizon is the spire of St Mary's Church, Essendon, whose bells were ringing out the way they had done on Sunday mornings for over 500 years.

In the Edwardian era, the bells were used to call people to work in the fields at harvest times. The labourers gathered early. Five o'clock in the morning. They set off, going up or down the lane, carrying scythes for cutting the hay and iron hooks for reaping, making for the fields they were working in that day. They wore jaunty red neckerchiefs around their necks, clean white shirts with no collars, thick corduroy trousers and hefty boots which they treasured. They were tough men with skins browned by the sun and wind, and they worked hard. At 'beaver time' or lunch time, beer was provided by the farmer, but the men brought their own food in plaited baskets — bread and cheese or perhaps salted pork. They worked in the fields until sunset and then it was home, exhausted, and straight to bed. When the harvest was almost gathered in, they had harvest home. This was an important festival, held on the day the last cartload of wheat or barley was brought to the barn — enough to last the winter. The landlord presented his men with new gloves — a traditional gesture, meant to keep their hands safe until the spring — and there was a procession led by a labourer dressed as the harvest lord done up in ribbons and straw. Then came the village band and the villagers, and they sang and danced around the fields and lanes until the moon came up.

This section of the lane rises steeply again and goes past Edwards Wood. High hedges are on the right and a low banking is on the left. More stitchwort, frilling in great splendour, crowning this part of the lane in sumptuous spring glory. The trees echo with the sound of cuckoos. At the top of this rise is the Candlesticks Public House, so called because it used to have candles on the tables instead of oil lamps. On the left, a track hazed with buttercups leads to Flint Farm and Wellington Wood.

West End Lane at this point turns north-east towards Essendon village, and by the turning at the top of the rise was a Tudor house which belonged to Mrs Godfrey and had a perfect English country garden in full spring bloom. Mrs Godfrey took me on a tour: iris, wallflowers, forget-me-nots, ox-slips, Solomon's seal, grape hyacinths, lilies of the valley, tulips, and more. We sat on a garden bench by some blood-red peonies.

'It seems to be a place for writers', she said, discussing Barbara Cartland and Beatrix Potter, 'and film stars too', she added, and went on to tell me how Cicely Courtney and Jack Holbert, the famous 1920s film stars who lived here, had both had their houses burned to the ground within a year of each other. She spoke of the war and the German bombers off-loading their bombs in the fields below when they had missed London and were forced to turn back, short of fuel. We listened awhile to the seven bells of the church resounding over the fields.

'St Mary's Church was badly damaged during 1916 when a bomb dropped from a zeppelin, and during the Second World War the bells used to ring out the all-clear after an air raid to let us know the German bombers had gone and it was safe to go on with our daily lives as much

17 • WEST END LANE

St Mary's Church, Essendon.

as we could. They dropped thirty bombs in one night. Thank goodness they missed the house', she said quietly, looking at the ancient red-brick walls.

Another important house, Bedwell Park, is across the fields at the south-west side of Essendon. In 1406, John Norbury enclosed 800 acres (325ha) to make a park and stocked it with deer. The present house is seventeenth century and was the home of the Courtneys. Gertrude Courtney was married to Henry Courtney, the marquis of Exeter, cousin to Henry VIII and a man of immense wealth. His wife inherited Bedwell Park. She was a staunch Catholic, a lifelong friend to Mary Tudor and godmother to Elizabeth I. Henry VIII appointed Henry Courtney to be commissioner at the trial of Anne Boleyn, but in 1538 he and his wife Gertrude and their son were put in the Tower of London accused of high treason. Henry Courtney was executed. His wife was released after a few years but their son, Edward, was imprisoned for thirteen years and only released when Mary Tudor came to power.

At the side of the house, a lane leads off northwards, going between ploughed fields rising, then dipping down to the River Lea. A little way along this lane is a magnificent oak tree growing in full glory in the middle of a ploughed field, its leaves just emerging from the dark brown bark of the branches. From this point, West End Lane bends north-east, dips, then rises sharply upwards, with curling banks of cow parsley filled with bees at each side, to reach Essendon village and St Mary's Church at the top of the hill.

I sat at a wooden table in the apple orchard at the side of the Woodman pub sipping a long cool drink. It was noon. Everywhere was alive. Blue tits and blackbirds bobbed about in the apple blossom above me. Cuckoos — hundreds of them it seemed — shook the sky with their urgent ringing calls, and collared doves swept down from

ENGLISH COUNTRY LANES • 18

warm cottage roofs, settled in between the thrusting cream candles of the horse-chestnut trees and called throbbing, sexual calls which fragmented the air with a quivering, insistent yearning, impossible to ignore. And opposite was West End Lane, the beginning of it a perfumed grotto brimming with fruit trees stuffed into untidy tumbling orchards and covered in such an outburst of blossom they were a total declaration of splendour. Later, I sat in the buttercups on the edge of the path to Flint Farm watching a buxom figure-of-eight caterpillar twist down to the ground on a slender grey thread — a juicy piece of moving flesh. It dropped on to some early seedheads of stitchwort, scattering the pale green star shapes at my feet. I looked back down the lane, feeling the sun on my face, listening to the sky and thinking that the flowers really 'had appeared on the earth' and the 'time of singing' had surely come.

A siskin sang a sweet, low song in the hedgerow, the plainsong of a robin was somewhere behind me, skylarks tried to outdo the cuckoos, a bright pink bullfinch sat on a wooden post and whistled a single, sultry, in-drawn note, a few blackbirds joined in — some were fluting, some hummed a chorus through closed bills — thrushes and blackcaps began to belt out their high-pitched numbers, garden warblers sang the contralto, a wren added a brilliant solo, and a lapwing sent a knowing, whooping chuckle low over the field tops as it went to join the others. There were lambs bleating, a young colt whinnied, and from below, the muffled sound of a cow and the cockerel still at it. Crickets, bees and wasps made a solid bass line, and the whole of it was truly wondrous.

The Street, Ipsden, Oxfordshire

Jeremy Irons

High spring

'... *there are views on either side which always take my breath away and raise my spirits ...*'

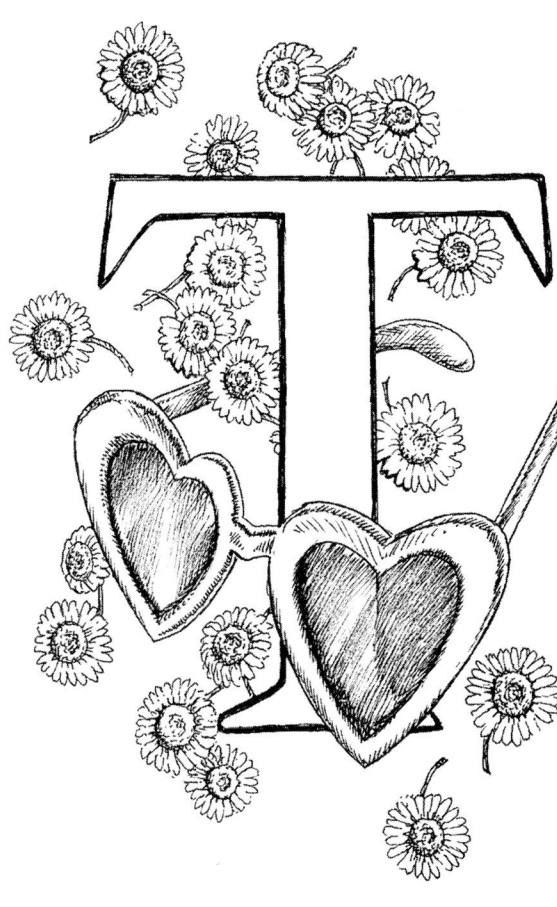

The Street is a quaint, delightful, old-fashioned place — an aged lane — rustic, charming and pastoral. Enfolded in a timeless, rural landscape, it rambles through hushed and muted rolling meadows, passes ancient grassy trackways wreathed in the mists of time, moves beneath high chalk ridges adorned with dark green copses and dense beech groves, then stays, as if sleeping, under spreading sycamore trees before gently winding down through hazy distant horizons to the River Thames below. Cow parsley shines in the warm, moist dawn, spangled with necklaces of fine woven webs; lacewings rest on the stems, resisting the dew. Blackbirds begin the day with their mellow fluting, skylarks lift and soar, wrens, robins and linnets sing in the hedgerows, lapwings tumble and dive, dancing and mating, and starlings with glossy black backs and electric green sheen swoop down to the barley and dig in the shoots. Deer graze warily, lambs bleat in the distance, horses whinny gently and joyfully, foxes and cubs play outside their earth and huge brown hares chase around down sloping, steaming meadows squashing the crops. This is a simple, uncomplicated lane, peaceful and traditional, rooted in continuity, fixed in the rhythms of the seasons and the cycle of life.

Jeremy Irons has often enjoyed walking along the Street, up Berry Hill Lane and along the Icknield Way going between Ipsden and Goring, especially in the spring. 'Nowadays', he writes, 'the lanes here are more like narrow roads but there are views on either side which always take my breath away and raise my spirits. The Street is a particularly lovely place — a lane really —

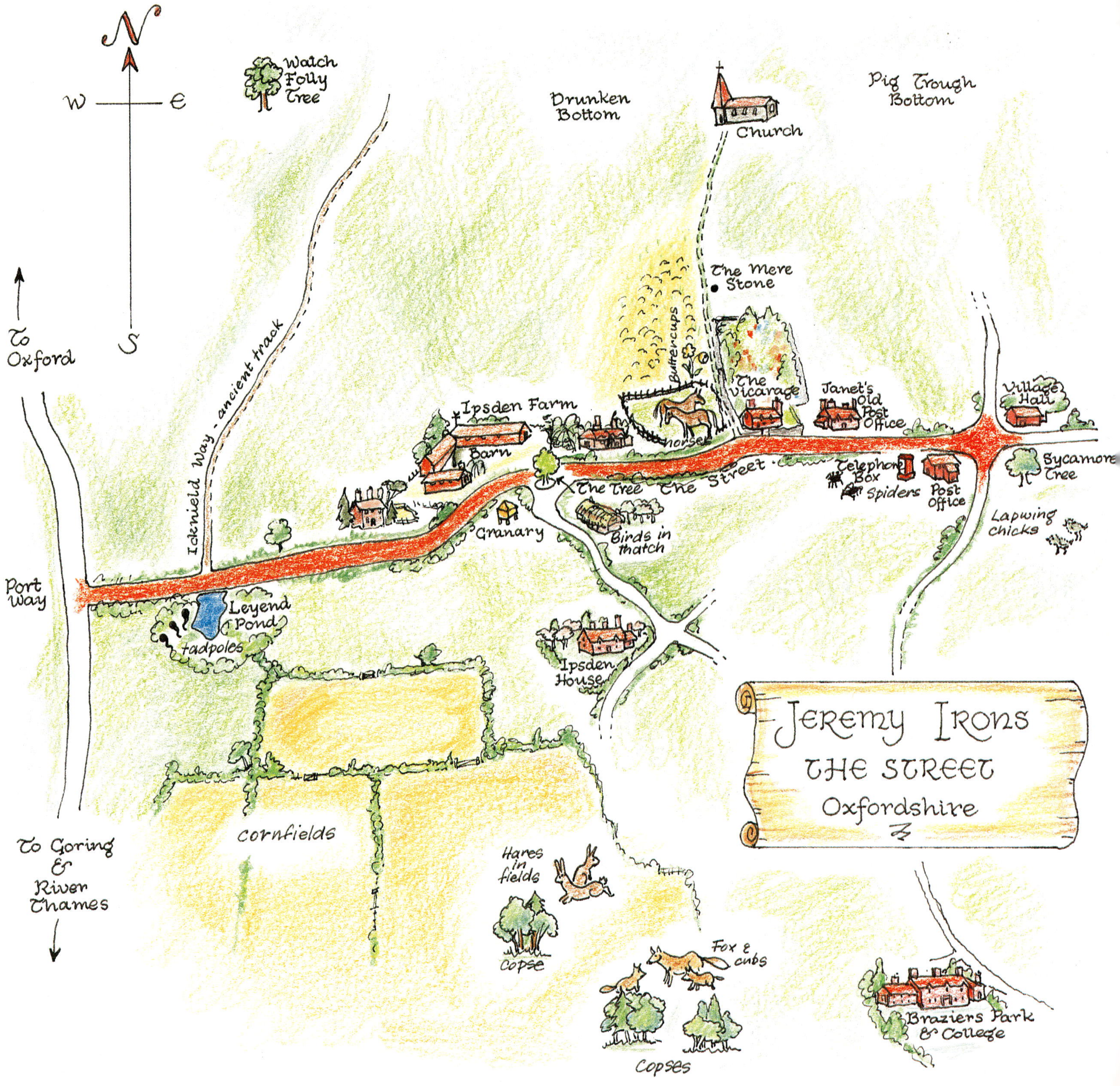

N
W
E
S
Watch Folly Tree
Drunken Bottom
Church
Pig Trough Bottom
To Oxford
Icknield Way - ancient track
The Mere Stone
Buttercups
The Vicarage
Janet's Old Post Office
Village Hall
Ipsden Farm
Barn
horses
Telephone Box
Spiders
Post Office
Sycamore Tree
The Tree
The Street
Granary
Birds in thatch
Lapwing chicks
Port Way
Leyend Pond
tadpoles
Ipsden House
Jeremy Irons
THE STREET
Oxfordshire
To Goring & River Thames
cornfields
Hares in fields
Copse
Fox & cubs
Copses
Braziers Park & College

which is still the main part of the village of Ipsden. I remember the old village post office, the village hall, the cricket matches beneath the spreading sycamore tree; and I can recall the gentle landscape, the perfect hedgerows in spring, the smell of the hay at haymaking time and the song of the birds coming, it seemed, from every tree. This hidden part of Oxfordshire is almost like a forgotten world where one can step back into a seemingly idyllic way of life.'

The Street turns off from the Port Way — the B479 road from Wallingford and Crowmarsh to Woodcote — goes eastwards to Leyend Pond then veers north-eastwards along the only street in the spread-out village of Ipsden. It passes great farm barns, a magnificent Queen Anne vicarage and the Old Post House, turns, climbs southwards into Brownberry Lane, passes Braziers Park, and then winds westwards, going by Icknield Farm and Catsbrain Hill before heading south-west down to Goring. It is a distance of about three miles (5km).

The Street turns off from the Wallingford road into gently undulating fields rising up at either side. At once it is a different world, quaint and unchanged. Cow parsley, meadow cranesbill, common dog violet, charlock, goose grass, shepherd's purse, self heal, speedwell, hedge woundwort and henbit dead-nettle hug the edges of the lane, their fragrance freshening in the undergrowth, their colours muted in the early morning light. A mixed hedge is on the right — hazel, hawthorn, buckthorn, blackthorn, wild privet, crab-apple, pear, cherry and sloe. A little way on, the hedges seem to burst out into the lane, lush grass is underneath with huge patches of creamy white dead-nettle exuding outwards, the pear-shaped flowers set in prickly leaves.

Blackbird nestlings are piping in the branches behind, up already, calling for food. Taller trees — sycamore, hawthorn and elm — are on the right and hidden under these is Leyend Pond, a dwindling pool, once so large that ducks and wild geese swam on it. Now it is deep and glassy, made green with patches of algae. In the pool are developing tadpoles with tiny legs, some just stumps, others longer and sinewy, more with minute webbed feet perfectly formed. They swim to the surface, taking in air through delicate round mouths, then float down to the depths in a dainty, drowsy dance.

By the side of the pool is a memorial stone which reads: 'John Thurlow Reade Esquire, Sehaarunpore November 25, AD 1827. "Alas My Brother".' The stone was erected by Edward Reade, who lived at Ipsden Manor House, which is farther along the lane, in memory of his eldest brother who had died in India. Rather than live the life of a gentleman at home, being heir to the Ipsden Manor Estate, John Reade decided to work for the East India Company so that he could help finance the education of his eleven younger brothers and sisters. One day his mother, Anna Maria Reade, was walking down the lane to the Crowmarsh-Wallingford road to meet the mail and see if there was any post from India, when she saw the ghostly shape of her son by Leyend Pond, seemingly in great distress. She was filled with dread and was convinced that he had died and had not received a Christian burial.

The next day she went to the vicar of Ipsden to arrange a proper burial service in the church. The vicar was amazed. Mrs Reade was a strong Protestant, not superstitious, well educated, highly intelligent and the mother of twelve children. But she was convinced of her

ENGLISH COUNTRY LANES • 24

vision. The vicar held the service as he was asked. The next mail brought the news that her son had died of fever at the very same hour and on the same day as she had seen his shape in the trees by Leyend Pond. He had died in the jungle and his servants had buried him where he lay.

Directly behind Leyend Pond coming from the south is the Icknield Way, a grassy track which continues at the other side of the lane and goes northwards, climbing gradually through the fields past Brockenden Bottom, Cobblers Hill and Drunken Bottom, and crossing Grims Ditch.

The Icknield Way is the famous prehistoric trackway which crosses England from Norfolk to Wiltshire, following the high ground, avoiding forests and moving between enclosed hill villages known as camps. It goes across the East Anglian ridge, the Chiltern Hills, turns southwards on their western edge, passes Ipsden at Leyend Pond, crosses the Thames near Goring, and then goes on to the Berkshire Downs, Stonehenge and Avebury in Wiltshire. This important green track has been in use for thousands of years and it is still in use today. The Icknield Way was a busy place, frequented by drovers, merchants, and travelling priests going across the country, and pilgrims coming from the South Coast to worship at the great cathedrals in the North. Isolated, rough, uneven and often hidden by overhanging trees, even on high ground, the track was a haunt of thieves and robbers who preyed on farms, took sheep and cattle, and robbed travellers.

The slopes of the hill above the lane to the west reach 300 feet (90m) above sea level and an oak tree called the Watch Folly Tree stands gaunt and alone, silhouetted against the skyline. No other tree is nearby and it can be seen for miles around. According to legend, the tree has not grown for many years. The story is that the Ipsden shepherds set a look-out boy on the slopes of the hill near the tree, to watch for robber bands and give them warning. One fatal day, the robbers caught the boy and hanged him from a tree, and ever since then the spot has been called 'Watch Folly'.

Other tracks and lanes lead off from the Icknield Way, going to Pig Trough Bottom, Drunken Bottom, Forest Row, Wicks Wood, Poor Shaw, Hailey and Grims Ditch. Grims Ditch or Dyke is believed to be the northern boundary and line of defence of a Celtic tribal territory belonging to the Ancalite tribe. The dyke is an extensive earth banking and ditch which follows the line of the Ridgeway, another ancient path, from Nuffield Common on a straight course past Morrells Bottom and Nuffield Park to the River Thames.

After the Icknield Way, the lane turns slightly to the north-east. An enormous elm tree is on the left and on the right are wide-open vistas of rolling cornfields filled mostly with the spiky green shoots of barley sticking up through the chalky soil. A few black crows amble up the rows in a slow procession, peering downwards, heads moving from side to side in slow jerky movements, picking off leather-jackets and wire worms and carefully making sure they have not missed a morsel. Starlings follow on behind. Woodland copses are folded into the middle of the fields, the tops of the trees smoking as the mist rises. A cuckoo calls from somewhere inside. Another answers from a distant copse, echoing the first. Then another, farther away — the welcoming sound connecting the copses. Two foxes and some cubs come out from their earth and sit at the top of the field. The vixen stays near the trees, ears erect, sharp eyes glinting, sniffing the air with her long pointed muzzle, watching over the land. The dog fox plays with his cubs, chasing in circles, tumbling and tugging, snuffling and yapping softly. The sound of their play drifts across the quiet fields.

The lane is narrower now, straighter, with grassy banking at either side. Cow parsley mingled with bush vetch, sorrel and clover are along the edges, each leaf bracket covered in the frothing cuckoo spit of the frog-hopper. On the left is a traditional sixteenth-century red brick house with tall red chimneys and a wooden door. This was the bailiff's cottage. A bailiff was the sovereign's representative in a district. Growing around it are lush fir trees and a Scots pine, and by the side is a sandy, chalky damp farmyard with patches of pineapple mayweed, corn camomile and dandelions, pungent and radiant in the warm morning haze. A black and white Sussex hen trots into the lane and looks in the grasses, searching for food. From somewhere behind the bailiff's cottage, a cockerel crows and the hen scoots back into the yard.

To the left of the lane is the famous red-brick traditional barn belonging to Ipsden Farm, said to be the longest in England. The immense tithe barn is 355 feet (108m) long, has wooden perches, ancient beams and a 'rippling red-tiled roof' with old wooden doors. At the corner of the roof is a weather-vane, unmoving in the still air. A traditional barn is a long rectangular building with large doors opposite each other in the central section. A barn is used for storing grain or fodder for the animals. The word *bern* is Old English and means 'barley house'. Barley was, and still is, the main crop in and around Ipsden Vale. A wagon loaded with corn would be brought

The Street.

ENGLISH COUNTRY LANES

Traditional thatched cottages along the Street.

through one of the doors, be unloaded on each side and leave through the other door. The middle section of the barn has a strong wooden floor on which, in winter, the corn stored on either side was threshed by men using a flail. The further parts of the barn were used to store the threshed straw and also hay, root crops and sacks of grain.

Ipsden Farm barn had other uses. Happy village gatherings were held there — christening celebrations, dances and harvest homes. Tables were laid out with great pies, joints of meat, best butter, cream, fresh bread, cakes and pasties, there was beer by the barrel, and music for dancing was provided by fiddlers and local bands. These were happy, friendly times when all the village folk came together and enjoyed themselves. The tradition was carried on for many years by Martyn Skinner, the farmer-poet who lived at Ipsden Farm and wrote *Letters To*

ENGLISH COUNTRY LANES • 28

Malaya, Merlin and *The Return Of Arthur*, books of poetry which made him famous in the 1930s. His poems were often inspired by the eternal rhythms of rural life, the unsophisticated farming ways and the pastoral landscape surrounding his home in Ipsden.

Farming was the only means of employment in this area and everything in the vale of Ipsden revolved around it. Men worked long hours in the fields: women and children as well at haymaking and harvest time. J H Baker and Herbert G Small have both written about Ipsden, and tell of life in and around the village in the early part of this century. Haymaking and harvest time were important times in a village community where everyone worked together to produce enough food to see themselves and their animals through the year.

The work started early. At seven o' clock in the morning. If the workers were late, there would be trouble. So they made sure that they rose at five o' clock in time to eat a breakfast of bread and hot tea and, if they were lucky, some cheese. They had to walk to work and back, sometimes up to nine miles (15km) a day. Going the shortest way through the woods and fields helped to make the many tracks, footpaths and lanes around Ipsden. The men wore heavy boots with 'tipped nails' — metal studs at the toes and heels to stop them wearing out — but even these soon wore down on the rough, flinty lanes. Women and children also wore sturdy working shoes with tips on them.

Men had different jobs according to their skills. There were carters who looked after the horses, bringing them in from the fields early in the morning, or feeding them in the stables according to the time of year. They would return home for their own breakfast, then go back to the stables for half past six to harness the horses and begin the day's work. In the winter, the day finished at half past three when the light began to fail, but in the summertime, especially at haymaking and harvest time, the men worked late. The day men were different. They worked regular hours — seven in the morning until five at night — cutting hedges, cleaning ditches and farmyards and hoeing and thinning the root crops. Special men did the thatching and threshing, planted potatoes and loaded the wagons in the field at hay and harvest time. These men worked longer than anyone else. Other men looked after the animals — sheep and cows mostly — and took the stock to market. Before the stock was sold it was judged in the ring and prizes were given. These prizes were much valued.

Women and children worked in the fields alongside the men. Children were given long summer holidays so that they could help with harvesting and haymaking and one of their main tasks was gathering the hay. From the age of seven, boys would lead the horses from stook to stook or in between the hay rows; eight to nine year olds would

△ *Ipsden Farm.*

lead them from the field to the barn or haystack; and from the age of ten boys would be on the wagons as loaders.

Haymaking was a crucial time in rural communities. The hay had to be cut, turned, dried, and stacked before it rained. It was a race against time. When the hay was cut, it was turned with a horse-drawn side rake, putting it into rows. Early next morning, when the dew was still on the grass, the men would cock the hay to prevent the leaves being knocked off. Cocking the hay involved rolling the hay three turns forward and one turn backward so that it would be easy to lift on to the wagons to go to the haystacks in one movement.

The making of haystacks was a skilled job. Haystacks, or ricks as they are sometimes called, were mostly round. A layer of straw was laid on the ground and the haystack was built on it and a thatch put on the top. If the stack was not constructed properly, it would fall over, the thatch would be difficult to put on and the rain would come in. A badly made haystack was frowned upon.

Harvest time came next. When the corn was ripe, the day men would cut a track around the outside of the field with hooks and scythes in readiness for the horse-drawn binder, which cut the corn and bound it. The other men would 'stook' it — stand it upright, leaning inwards. In earlier times, thirty or more men would cut the corn by hand, using scythes and coming down the field in a long line, while twenty or more women would follow, tying the sheaves of corn together before stooking them. It was left for three weeks, then picked up by the wagons before it rained and taken to the barns to store. When the harvest was gathered in, it was a time for rejoicing and thanksgiving.

Winter work included feeding the animals with hay, mangolds, kale or cow cabbage, and thawing out water troughs and pumps. Spring was also a busy period — in March the fields were cultivated and made ready for planting, meadows were harrowed to remove the dead grass and level the left-over manure, and the thrashing of the previous year's wheat began. It was a hard life, but a satisfying one — all of the villagers worked together to get their own food in and they could see the products of their own labour. When the family came home from the dusty harvest fields in hot weather, the only means of washing was a tin bath filled with water the night before and left in a corner of the yard to get warm. Food was simple. Tea was bread with margarine or dripping. Jam was a treat and a cake made from flour and lard in an enamel pie dish with just a few currants was a luxury.

Horses were important on the farm. They kept going in all weathers and in different depths of snow and they knew their way home — just like cows. At the end of the day, they would come galloping up the lane at full speed, on their own, back to the stable or meadow for their meal. Eighteen to twenty great heavy horses — Clydesdales, Percherons or Shires, the descendants of medieval war horses — nobody looking after them, finding their own way home: a magnificent sight.

These massive animals are gentle creatures. When they were pulling a hoeing rake between rows of crops, they would step over, or stop in front of, a lark's nest on the ground and sometimes, when a cat was curled up asleep in a manger filled with chaff or oats, the horse would gently nibble its way through the food eating around the cat without disturbing it.

Horses wore horse brasses as charms against evil. The favourite designs were representations of the sun, moon and stars. Others included crops such as a wheatsheaf and a bell to make a noise and ward off devilish spirits. When working, the horses did not wear all of these at once because they would have added too much weight to their already heavy burden. Heavy horses can pull up to a ton in weight.

In 1918, there were more than 1,000,000 horses on English farms, but by the 1930s tractors had begun to work on the land and horses mostly went back to their original purposes, for riding or for the pulling of small carts and gypsy caravans. Some farmers still prefer to use horses — they don't break down or get bogged down in muddy fields. In the latter part of the nineteenth century and the early part of the twentieth, picturesque steam traction engines were used in the fields to drive portable threshing machines and for wood-sawing, driving crushing plants, hauling and ploughing. A rapid way of ploughing a field was to put a steam engine at each end, with a plough on an endless wire fixed to the two hauling drums on the traction engines. A man sat on the plough, guiding the mole board and ploughshare from one end of the field to the other. In this way, six furrows could be ploughed at once.

Next to the barn is Ipsden Farm, an eighteenth-century red-brick farmhouse with two hefty stone columns at either side of the front door. The door opens out almost on to the lane, and in the yard by the side of the house is an enormous weeping willow tree with narrow blades of pale-green leaves drooping from a voluminous canopy of branches gracefully touching the ground. A thin Scots pine stands next to it. A blackbird in the topmost branch sings a long, burbling song, its yellow beak bright against the dark needles of the pine. Two more blackbirds potter about in the lane, courting; the male in hot pursuit, intent, oblivious. A young pheasant zooms down from the field on the opposite side — a green and bronze gem lighting up the lane, and a solitary ginger cat strolls languidly along, going to the farm. The blackbirds fly off, but the pheasant stands and stares as the cat passes by.

Across from the farmhouse and barn is the stump of an old elm tree covered in ivy at the entrance to a sloping field, and tucked inside the field is a quaint, old granary, nearly four centuries old with wooden beams showing on the outside. The granary stands on mushroom-shaped saddle stones put there to stop the rats from getting in to the grain. Inside are stone sections where the grain — usually oats — was stored. One section had to last a certain time before going on to the next, so measuring the amount of winter feed.

There is a turning and Farm Hill Lane goes off to the right. A tremendous, spreading sycamore tree stands at the corner and at the meeting of the two lanes is an island and, growing on it, the Tree. Two hundred years old, this aged elm is a landmark in Ipsden. As it grew older, the top became hollow and so it was taken out. The trunk sprouted another tree. Children, up to six at a time, have played inside this marvellous tree over the ages and it has been the village trysting place for many years.

Two farm cottages, immaculately thatched, are nearby the elm tree; swallows' nests are under the eaves. The piping voices of the swallow nestlings mingle with the sound of the fluttering wings of hedge sparrows balancing on wallflowers or flying down to the lawns. One cottage has an orchard and a wilderness area crammed with stinging nettles, brambles, dandelion and dock and gnarled old apple trees. Caterpillars are in the stems: garden tiger moth, mother of pearl moth and the peacock butterfly are hugging the nettles; the green-veined white is feeding on the charlock; and the meadow brown, large skipper and the large yellow underwing moth caterpillar are breakfasting on the grass, cutting out half-moon shapes as they progress up each damp, slender stalk.

A little way up Farm Hill Lane on the right-hand side is Ipsden Manor House, an important building in the area. There are cherry trees in the garden making a faint pink haze behind the house and a sundial leaning, lopsided, at an angle to the ground.

The distinguished Reade family has held the Manor of Ipsden since the sixteenth century and was the principal landowner in this area. The first manor house was built by Thomas Reade in 1540 and was further up Farm Hill Lane, overlooking the fields towards Goring. The present Ipsden Manor House is said to date from the thirteenth century but John Reade had it altered in 1764.

John Reade was a typical farmer squire who loved his land and valued his heritage. He was fond of his house and made it into a real farmer's house, even though he was the lord of the manor. There are spacious sitting rooms, ample downstairs quarters and cellars, a stable yard, lofts, a granary and a brewery. Outside there is a walled garden with yew trees, climbing roses, a dovecote dated 1500 with space for 600 nests and a deep well. There is a donkey wheel in a wheel-house. This was used to pump water from the well into the house. When the donkey was put inside the ten foot (3m) high tread-wheel, he would walk round and round until the water tank in the house was full. The donkey knew when the water tank in the house was full and would stop walking the tread-wheel.

In the late nineteenth century, Ipsden Manor became famous for its hospitality and reflected the grand ideal of family life of the upper and middle classes of English society. There were excellent dinner parties with fine port and Madeira, and on occasions superb curries were cooked by Anna Maria Reade, who had been in India with her father, Major Scott-Waring MP, secretary to the governor general of India. Oxford dons and other intelligentsia were entertained at the house, and Charles Reade, the novelist and playwright, seventh son of John and Anna Maria Reade, would play his violin, at which he was a master, and sing songs accompanied by the piano.

Charles Reade was the most celebrated member of the family. He wrote *The Cloister And The Hearth*, *It Is Never Too Late To Mend* and fourteen other novels. His work criticises the social injustices of his time and shows his humanitarian concern with social conditions.

Reade had an abiding love of the theatre and he wrote and staged over forty plays, many at his own expense. He was a lively, intense man, likeable, sociable and kind hearted. As a young man, he spent much of his time rowing or boating on the River Thames. He had a fondness for nature, and often walked or rode on horseback down the lanes, going through Crowmarsh, Wallingford and Dorchester and on, the full seventeen miles (27km) to Oxford, where he took his degree.

He became a fellow of Magdalen College and was given a post which required hardly any service but provided him with an income on the provision that he must remain celibate. At the age of thirty-five, he resolved to write a book, but first he prepared himself by collating a detailed system of scrapbooks and newspaper cuttings, and took many painstaking notes. He had immense powers of concentration and wrote for many hours with twelve candles set around the table in small candlesticks which he always took everywhere with him'. At Ipsden Manor, when his father was ill and dying, he began to write his first novel, sitting beside his bedside. His mother gave him her private fortune while she was still alive so that he would be free to write, but stipulated that she had enough money to provide for her old age — she lived to be ninety. Soon, however, his literary success made him a wealthy man in his own right.

Other members of the Reade family were notable. William Winwood Reade was an explorer who found the source of the River Niger in Africa and was the first white man to make contact with the cannibal Fan tribe. Edward Anderton Reade was lieutenant governor of the north-west province of India and was distinguished during the Indian mutiny. He saved the life of the maharajah of Benares and, in gratitude, the maharajah had a well built for the people of Ipsden and Stoke Row in 1863. Edward Reade had told him, in conversation, of the difficulty of obtaining water in the chalky uplands of the Chilterns, and of how water from dirty ponds and clay pits was used for cooking and passed on to the next cottage for washing. The maharajah remembered this and had a 368 foot (112m) deep well built, with an ornate cast-iron cupola on top of elegant, tall columns surrounded by railings, and a bucket with winding gear.

He also gave an orchard, a cottage, a pond in the shape of a fish and a bandstand to Stoke Row, which is to the east of the lane, beyond Garsons Lane and the area called the Devil's Churchyard. The grand opening celebrated the return to health of the Prince of Wales in 1872. Every person in the village of Ipsden was given a half-pound of

The Vicarage, Ipsden.

tea, one pound of sugar, two loaves of bread, two pounds of bacon, and a pair of good blankets from the maharajah. There is another deep well with a wrought-iron handle and winding gear sunk outside the Church of St Mary on the north side of the village.

After the Tree and the turning to Farm Hill Lane, the Street keeps on, level and straight in an easterly direction. On the right is another mixed hedge with rowan saplings growing up, covered in bunches of creamy-white blossom. On the left are two traditional cottages close to the edge of the lane. Their front doors have rustic wooden porches tiled in red pantiles to provide shelter from the rain. Wallflowers, tulips, daffodils and pansies surround the cottages, their scent heavy in the still, misty

St Mary's Church, Ipsden.

warmth of the morning. Each flower petal is traced with dew. A man and his daughter were putting a pony into a freshly painted trap. The pony's coat glistened, his hooves shone and his eyes sparkled in anticipation of the outing.

'An early start — going to a show at Ewelme — just up the road', the man said, smiling. They climbed into the trap and set off. The rhythm of the trotting hooves grew fainter as they went along the lane.

Two more cottages are set further back on the same side and at the other side of the lane is a tiny, picturesque barn at least 500 years old. Straggling blackthorn is at both sides and on the left is a glorious pear tree in full flower. A rich, lush grassy banking rises up to a fence. Five brown horses look over the top, watching over the lane and, behind them, acres of buttercups stretch upwards to the trees at the back of the field in seemingly endless seas of shining yellow; brighter now as the veil of mist begins to lift. Meadow brown butterflies are resting on the petals, waiting for the sun. The lane is narrower now, single-track, heading in a broad curve north-eastwards under elm, hornbeam, beech trees and a great horse chestnut on the right.

On the right-hand side is a smallholding. A man and his wife had arrived early. They had already finished hoeing between rows of beans and peas tied to poles put up like the ribs of a tent, and were sitting by their greenhouse at a makeshift table eating buttered teacakes with strawberry jam and drinking hot tea from a flask. The dew was still on the ground and the smell of the soil from the freshly hoed beans seeped into the lane. The fields beyond had wisps of mist lifting as the warmth of the sun's rays began to touch the tops of the beech trees on Garsons Hill. Brown hares were in the field, nibbling at the grass. Heads down, they tore at the grass, rose up on to their hind legs to look around, ears twitching, rested momentarily, washed and scratched, then ran away under the trees.

On the left is a fine flint wall belonging to the vicarage. Hedgerow cranesbill, self heal and white dead-nettle grow under the wall. Blue tits are sitting on the branches of the beech hedge, waiting to pick the caterpillars off the leafy growth. Curving upwards, following the wall, is a smooth grass track. This is the Mere — an elevated bridleway going up to the war memorial, a standing stone and St Mary's Church. It is believed that the Mere was a look-out post for the Roman outpost at Berins Hill which is to the east of the lane. The path is windswept and isolated, the way to the church lonely but picturesque, the views of the vale of Ipsden, the River Thames and the Berkshire Downs set out below.

The tiny Church of St Mary's stands alone on the hill at the end of the track, impressive, serene, with a presence and an aura of profound solitude. The church is twelfth-century Early English, with two bells in the tower. The well-known brasses of Master Thomas Englyshe and his wife Isabell are fixed in the floor here. Man and wife are turned away from each other. The knight is bare-headed and dressed in full plate armour with large spurs. Isabell wears a long kerchief over her head and a long gown reaching to her feet. They died in 1525 and lie here together on this hill where swifts and swallows wheel in the sky and the sun sets over the river.

The vicarage is next to the Mere: a large regal red-brick and flint Queen Anne period house with some seventeenth-century parts intact. There is a pretty garden, and grand wrought-iron gates with a profusion of pink clematis tumbling over them, and thick banks of lavender grow around the front door. Collared doves are on the roof, sitting, watching the morning, then preening and pouting, the male's neck feathers ruffling up as the female coquettishly moves away. A field on the right leads up to a sloping bank and more horses graze beneath tall elm trees.

A little farther on is the Old Post House, over 300 years old; red-brick with tall chimneys at each side and roses with fat green buds, wrapped up tight, growing over the wall. This was the old village post office and the home of Janet Lindsey, a silver-haired Scotswoman who was the sub-postmistress of Ipsden for over fifty years. Janet lived alone at the post office and she was still running it in 1947 when she was eighty years old. The shop was set up in a separate room, and there was an immense fireplace in each room with fires lit in the winter. Stout oak beams hold up the ceilings and the only light came from oil lamps.

Janet was an eccentric woman. Often she would go about the village street in a long, black skirt, carrying an oil lamp with a single wick. She took the oil lamp with her wherever she went, covering the glass with her hand to protect the flame from the wind. If a telegram arrived, she would walk as far as two miles (3km) to deliver it, and then forget the time and go into the woods on the way back and pick flowers or blackberries. At the age of ninety, she continued to walk around Ipsden, the place she loved so well, chatting with the villagers in her 'lovely, young lilting voice'. Janet was loved by everyone, so much so that the new bungalows, shop and post office built at the end of the Street are called Janet's Grove.

After the vicarage, the lane bends gently to the southeast, coming to the post office and the shop at Janet's Grove. A bright, red GPO telephone box stands on the path, tucked under the trees. A swirling sheet of spider's web belonging to the cobweb spider is wrapped around the cables at the back of the box and stretches as far as the trees. Inside are hundreds of newly hatched young. They wriggle and struggle, climbing up the web and out on to the tree branches, unseen and undisturbed, hidden behind the telephone box.

Ipsden village hall is at the end of the lane, under a spreading sycamore tree that almost covers the wooden building. A cricket pitch is at the far side of the hut behind a low hedge of privet, hawthorn and elderberry. Daisies stud the smooth grass in front. The Street ends here, at the junction of two minor roads. A narrow road goes northwards up Wicks Hill to Pig Trough Bottom, Drunken Bottom and Crowmarsh, and another road, Berry Hill Lane, rises upwards quite steeply and is very narrow with overhanging hedgerows at either side — hawthorn, buckthorn, elder and hazel — their strong, flat, rough leaves protruding out into the lane at both sides. Five fat wood-pigeons sit close together dozing on a telegraph wire, their pink and pale grey feathers damp with mist. Some lapwing chicks are in the lane, black and grey, speckled and delicate. They are lost, running all over, panicking, slender legs moving so quickly that they blur into the surface of the lane. Behind the hedge, the mother is calling frantically. The chicks find a hole in the tree roots and disappear.

The lane turns to the west by the entrance to Braziers College, which was once the home of Peter Fleming, the famous explorer, and is now a college. Here there are magnificent views of the Berkshire Downs, and in the meadows below swifts wheel and skim in widening circles, and the song of larks fills the whole sky. After this, the lane crosses the Port Way, rejoins the Icknield Way, passes Icknield Farm, another ancient farm, and then winds down to Goring and the River Thames.

I came here before dawn to catch the morning awakening. Grey mist covered the land. There was no movement, no sound, only the sweet smell of the morning air gathering up around me from the slumbering meadows. The lane was a shadowy path wending its way through the folding vale. Utter stillness, warmth and peace pervaded the air. Somehow I seemed at the centre of things, caught in a perfect moment — sensing the rightness of it all — a coming home to the completeness of this unchanging place.

The sky lightened and the morning began as the dawn came creeping over the beech trees high on the ridges. Birdsong filled the air in ever-widening, resounding circles, rejoicing in the new day, and I stood in the lane and marvelled at the sound of a thousand voices throbbing overhead. When the light became brighter, the grey became green and the dawn was a blue, luminous haze reaching over the trees. Spiders' webs were orbs of light; crystal in the dew. Lacewings were awake watching the aphids, caterpillars languished on the ready-made larder beneath their feet and swallows came and 'twittered on the chimneys' of the cottages or swooped low over the lane. Young birds in the eaves of the barns peeped out over nest edges, yellow beaks open wide in a hungry chorus of cries. Their mothers fed them.

Then I went up high to the top of the lane and watched the mist slowly lifting over the Downs and the singing was still strong up above me. So I joined in, quietly, shyly, overawed by the perfection of all those voices in the sky, humming my favourite hymn as I went along: 'Glad that I live am I. That the sky is blue. Glad for the country lanes, and the fall of dew . . .'

Morning sounds began in the farmyard — hens were clucking loudly, the cockerel still crowed, horses whinnied, a distant tractor engine began, ticking over, muffled and waiting. A voice came through the trees, giving out orders for work for the day. And deep in the far-off copses where the cuckoos were calling, the fox cubs were still playing and the vixen was still watching.

Peddars Way, Thetford, Norfolk

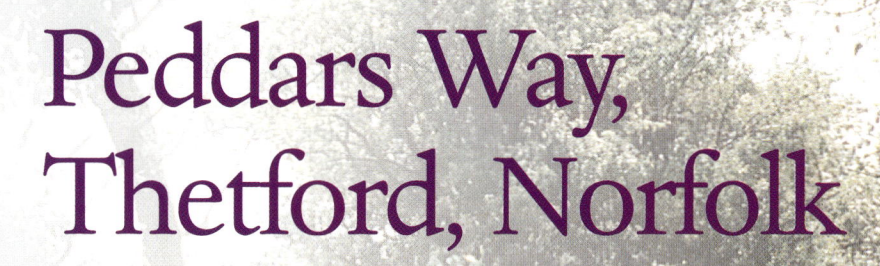

HRH The Duchess of Kent

High spring

'The silence and the isolation along the strange green trackway encourage one to reflect upon the history that has taken place here.'

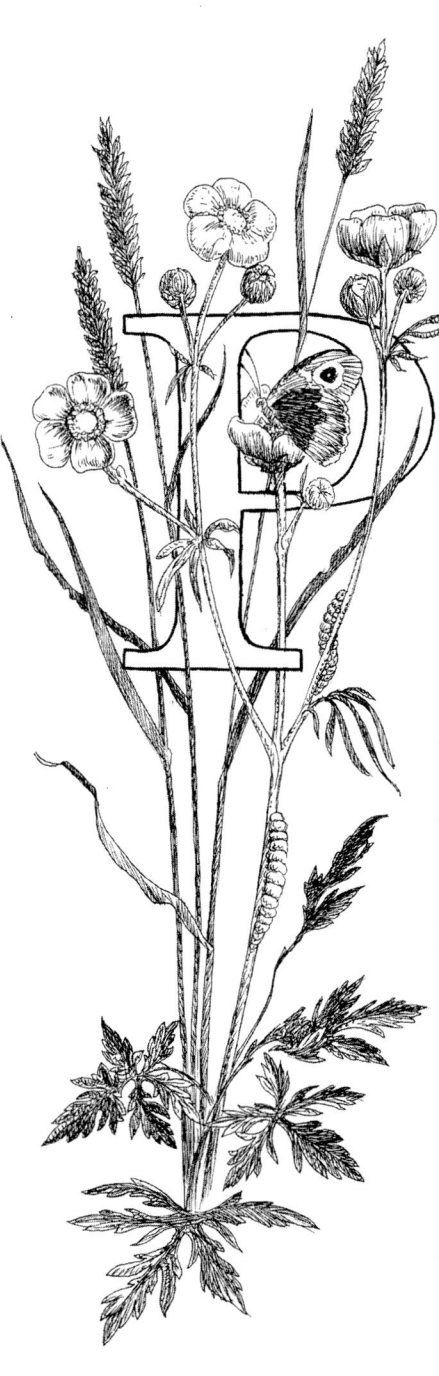

Peddars Way is a fascinating, unfrequented place — defiant, barbaric and disturbing, an ancient green lane which passes over a desolate, windswept landscape, pushes through masses of tangled undergrowth and then continues unchanged for mile after mile on its long, straight track.

This is a wild, prehistoric place — powerful and aggressive yet hauntingly beautiful. Brambles, briars and thorn bushes push themselves forward, taking over, rank upon rank of them, towering and tough. Bindweed and bryony strangle their way through monstrous columns of stinging nettles, sharp thistles thrust themselves through banks of tattered willow-herb and bracken sends up sinister fists like the knobbed and waiting fingers of some incredible green foetus struggling for breath in the rasping undergrowth. Ants hurry, spiders lurk, slugs hide and fungus — pale as death — invades each splitting wound on finished trees. Here is a place of silence and solitude, of presence and importance, and all around is the echoing sadness of a million lost footsteps and a thousand lost dreams.

When Her Royal Highness the Duchess of Kent does not have official duties to carry out, she spends her weekends with her husband, the Duke of Kent, at their country house in Norfolk somewhere near Peddars Way.

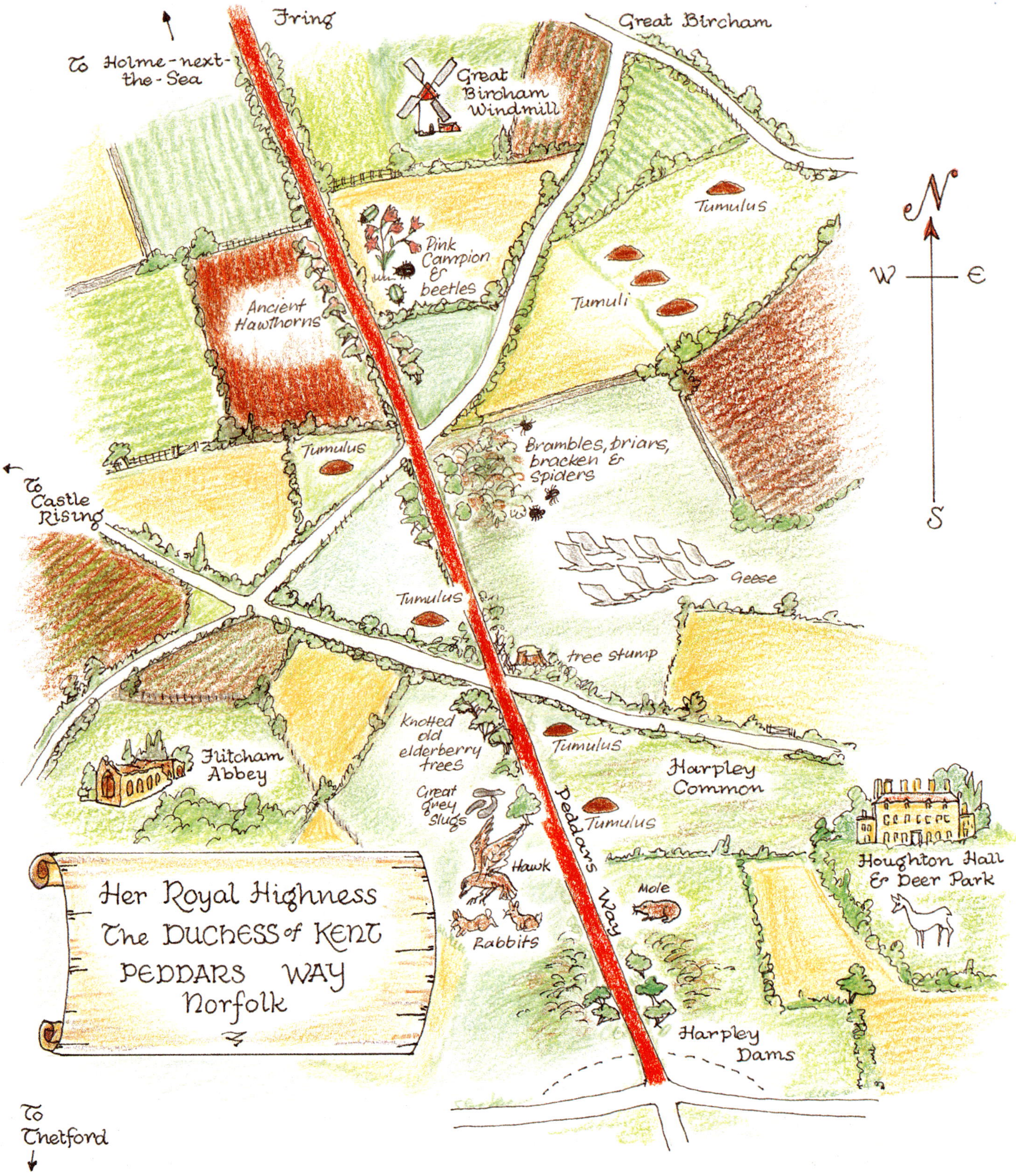

Fring
To Holme-next-the-Sea
Great Bircham
Great Bircham Windmill
Tumulus
N
W
E
S
Pink Campion & beetles
Ancient Hawthorns
Tumuli
Tumulus
Brambles, briars, bracken & spiders
To Castle Rising
Geese
Tumulus
tree stump
Knotted old elderberry trees
Tumulus
Flitcham Abbey
Harpley Common
Great Grey Slugs
Tumulus
Houghton Hall & Deer Park
Hawk
Peddars Way
Mole
Her Royal Highness
The DUCHESS of KENT
PEDDARS WAY
Norfolk
Rabbits
Harpley Dams
To Thetford

'Norfolk has been my home now for many years', the duchess writes, 'and I have grown to love the gentle countryside, the wide-open skies and the coastline fringed with salt-marshes and reed beds and alive with sea birds. The landscape here is very different from my native Yorkshire with its limestone walls, its moors and its fells echoing with the bubbling song of curlews. There, as a child, I used to explore the surrounding lanes and hedgerows and sometimes picnicked with my family in the heather high on the moor tops under skies filled with the sound of skylarks.

Here in Norfolk I find the same kind of peace, especially when I walk the lovely, lonely stretches of Peddars Way. After a hectic but enjoyable period of work in London or other cities, I gain much pleasure from watching the secluded private lives of the animals and birds in Peddars Way. The way is an unusual place — a lane most unlike the lanes of my childhood — sometimes a pretty place, particularly in late May when the hawthorn is in full flower. Then the way is blossom-flanked and incredibly beautiful and the fields at each side are lush and full of crops and the windmills dotted here and there are busy still, grinding corn. At other times, it can be an aggressive place — an untamed wilderness, powerful in its intensity — the hedgerows full of thorns and brambles and briars rising up like fortresses, symbolic somehow of its turbulent history. The silence and the isolation along the strange green trackway encourage one to reflect upon the history that has taken place there.'

Peddars Way begins at Holme-next-the-Sea on the north Norfolk coast and runs in a straight line southwards to join with the Icknield Way, a distance of about fifty-five miles (90km).

Peddars Way starts as a wide green track — shaggy, rough, unkempt, the wilderness fenced in. Straight away there are thorn trees and bushes: blackthorn, buckthorn, hawthorn, spiny crab-apple, brambles, briars, wild currant and raspberry. They grow six feet (2m) deep at either side. Great banks of bracken stretch as far as the eye can see and at one side is a grassy patch — a sort of car park with space for two cars. Around its edges are the spikes of field penny-cress, a few weak buttercups, some bugloss, speedwell, clover, white campion, daisies and mint and a few clumps of common horsetail standing together in tight, impregnable groups. A little way along on the east side is a gap in the bushes and through it a vision of high, wide skies and flat, sandy fields filled with corn and barley and carrots. Overhead a flock of white-fronted geese flies in formation through the silent sky and close behind some swifts shoot past like black arrowheads against the blue.

A mile (1.5km) across the fields towards the south-east is Houghton Hall and deer park, and the village of Houghton which Oliver Goldsmith (1728-1724) immortalised in his poem *The Deserted Village*. Houghton Hall is the palatial home of the marquis of Cholmondely. It was built in 1721 by Sir Robert Walpole, England's first prime minister. The largest and finest mansion house in Norfolk, it stands amongst the trees, the delicate Yorkshire stone shading from pale yellow to light green and soft pink. There are stables for a hundred horses, a herd of white fallow deer in the park, peacocks on the lawns and elegant formal gardens which surround the house.

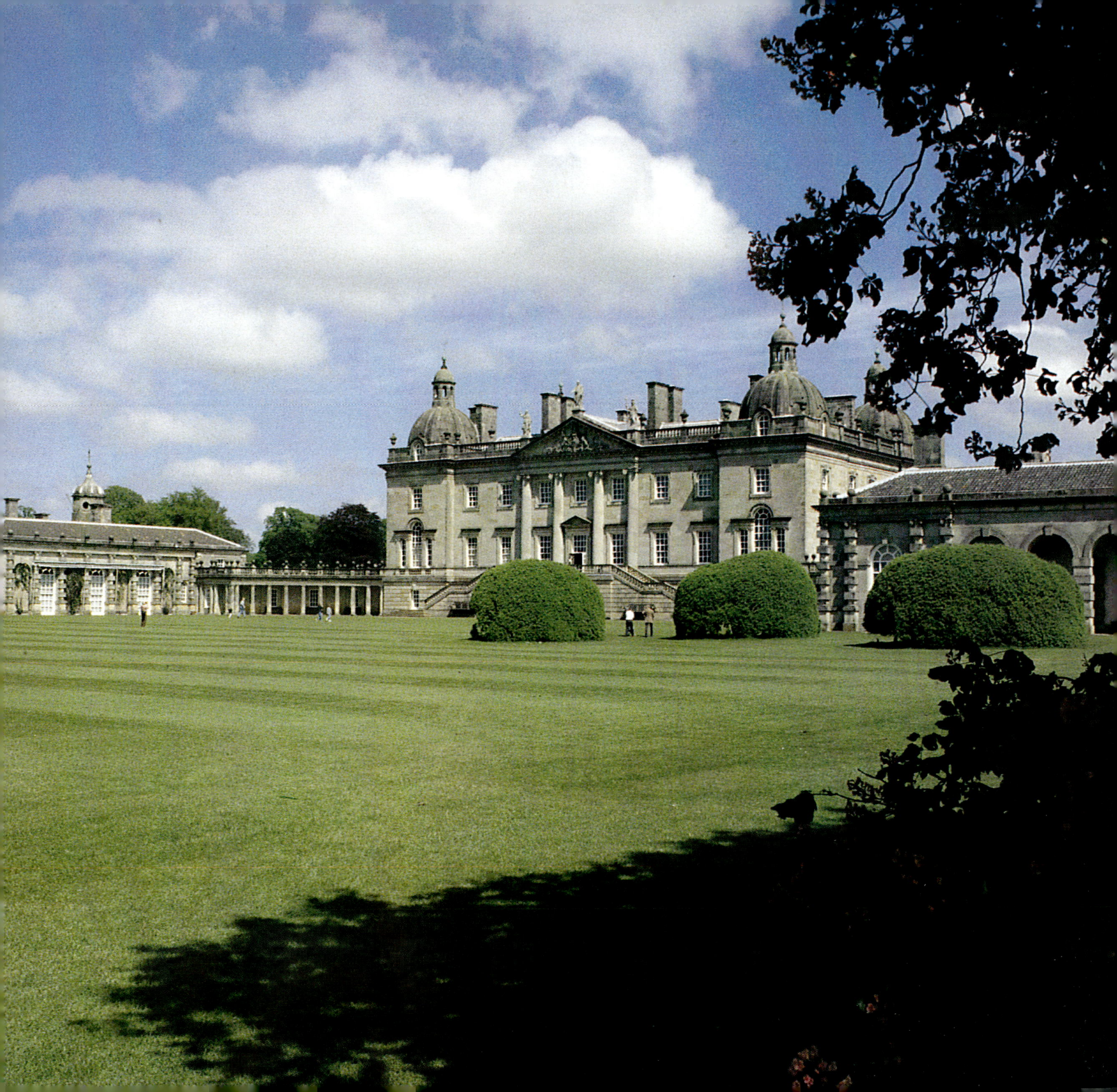

Sir Robert Walpole (1676-1745) was the first earl of Orford — an English Whig statesman who sought the supremacy of Parliament and came to office soon after the Hanoverian succession to the throne of King George I in 1714. He is considered to have been the first true British prime minister. He was the first lord of the treasury and chancellor of the exchequer and he was in power for twenty-three years. He was a good finance minister, a peace minister and a member of Parliament. He managed Parliament, encouraged trade through his pacificist foreign policy and received an earldom in 1742. Lord Hervey said of his visits to Houghton in 1731:

'We used to sit down to dinner, a little snug party of about thirty odd, up to the chin in beef, venison, goose, turkey and generally over the chin in claret, strong beer and punch... in public we drank loyal healths and talked of the times; in private we drew plans and cultivated the country.'

One of Sir Robert's successors, George, the 'mad' third earl of Orford, lived at Houghton Hall in 1777. He was a gambler and got himself into so much debt that he had to sell his fine collection of paintings for the then large sum of £40,555 to Empress Catherine the Great of Russia. They are now in the Hermitage Museum in St Petersburg.

Barbed wire fronts the gap in the bushes and nearby is a rotting stump of beech covered in dead men's fingers. They stand out on the tree stump, their dingy fungus shapes like the withering palms of some petrified creature inside the wood. In the tangled roots other fungi erupt: Jew's ear on the elder, tinder and razor strop on the birch, stinkhorn and shaggy ink-cap in the undergrowth, St George's mushroom at the front, and on the path a single morel fungus sticks up like a sickly brown finger full of gathering skin.

The path continues in a straight line through seas of ferns with thistles, brambles and rose-bay willow-herb at the back. Ancient hawthorns, some probably dating from Saxon times, drip heavy, white blossoms on the ferns below. On the left is an isolated group of knotted old elderberry trees, their trunks twisted and gnarled, their branches reaching out towards the path, beckoning and evil.

For many years, the elder has been considered an unlucky tree. The Celts and the druids believed that the tree was the abode of the Elder Mother and, unless her permission was asked before breaking so much as a twig of elder, doom and disaster would be sure to follow. Judas Iscariot, it is said, hanged himself from an elder tree. Hedgers will not take the elder wood home to burn for their fire, for 'to burn it brings the devil into the house' and their wives will not have the pretty, white elderflowers indoors. Witches, it is said, sometimes changed themselves into elder trees and, if by accident an elder tree was felled on Midsummer's Eve, black blood ran from the wound.

Beneath the elderberries an enormous bramble bush pushes out almost into the middle of the path. It is seething with spiders: hunting spiders, wolf spiders, cross spiders, zebra spiders and jumping spiders. Some wait under the leaves: others, like the spindly, long-legged harvestmen pick their way across the prickly stems, avoiding the webs strung up inside. There are hammock-shaped webs, orb-shaped webs, bell-shaped, tubular and triangular-shaped, haphazard mazes and gossamer clouds. They blanket the thorns with a deadly softness, and carefully concealed in the folded leaves are the spiders' cocoons. Under the path a mole moves and punctures the surface with a moist brown hill. Realising its mistake, it carries on burrowing, heading east, holding its tail high to see if its body will fit the tunnel and, next to some thistles, a soldier ant captures an earwig, splits its thorax and pumps its body full of poison. There are more ants: meadow ants, wood ants, red ants, slave-making ants and the black mound-building ant which goes about collecting aphids, grazing them on the best bits of dew, fattening them up for the winter, thinking ahead. Only the great grey slug seems at the centre of things: a pair of them climb a tree, circle, lick and taste each other then, turning and twisting, they slide to the ground down on a long string of love-juice lost in the mutual labour of lust.

By the side of the path are the ferns, pale green and very dense, their delicate tips tightly curled. They go on quite far. Next to them are clover, buttercups and speedwell and here and there are more bramble bushes covered in pale pink flowers. Wood-pigeons are in the trees. Beyond the bushes on the left is another gap in the trees leading to a wide expanse of wilderness crammed full of thistles and briars and gorse, and behind the wilderness in the middle of a field is a Bronze Age tumulus or round barrow dating from 2200 BC. Farther south by Anmer Minque, Bunkers Hill and Harpley Common are more, some of the largest tumuli in Norfolk. There are eight altogether, clustering very close to the way. Some are overgrown but all are upright and about three metres high.

Heroes of immense standing were placed in graves such as these. Their bodies were put in the exact centre of the barrow; their weapons, the horns and antlers of their game, and the bodies of their servants lay at their side. At their feet were the bodies of their favourite dogs. The most noble men were laid out full length; children and others were bent into the foetal position and bound by cord ready for rebirth in the next world. A dog's head was placed in the grave of a child in the belief that the dog would show the child the way into the after-life. Oxen, pigs, goats and sacred geese were left in graves as food along with beakers and vessels and bronze awls. Bronze knives and daggers were usually interred with women while bronze razors were left with the men, but red ochre powder, other colouring materials, baskets, ropes, stakes and cords were left in most graves.

Protection against evil was gained by leaving objects which are still believed to have special powers — white quartz pebble trinkets and amber shale. Flint and iron pyrites were made especially for the burial. They helped the dead to keep warm and warded off evil spirits. Jewellery was also left in their graves to adorn them in the after-life: jet and amber beads, earrings, pendants, amulets, studs for ears and lips, clasps, buttons, pins and other tiny pieces — star shapes, quoits, oblong, spherical, cylindrical and spiral shapes made from fine-grained rocks.

After the ceremony, the bodies were buried in shallow graves, and earth was carefully piled over and around the bodies, or in some cases around the cremated ashes, which were in a ten foot (3m) high collared urn, and then the earth was shaped into a mound. The barrows were left where the warrior in his 'eternal sleep' was not

47 • PEDDARS WAY – HRH THE DUCHESS OF KENT

'choked in a minster charnal house amid green damp and droning monks but out under the full sky with his weapons around him, his horse, his dogs and the antlers of his game'.

For over 2,000 years, the tumuli or round barrows were regarded as special places for burials. They usually contained a single burial, but sometimes there were collective burials and often, over the years, bodies were added to the graves. The barrows near Peddars Way are bell barrows: that is, the earth was heaped up in a simple mound without any ditches or fences around them. The Iron Age Celts mingled with the early Bronze Age people in some areas and they also had the same strong belief in the after-life and buried their dead in round barrows.

The Celtic tribes settled in the 'frosty, marshy country' of East Anglia in 1000 BC and this large peninsula became a separate kingdom. The Iceni tribe was in west Norfolk and the Trinovantes were in the south, towards Suffolk. These were non-Belgeic tribes. The Belgeic tribes came from France, Belgium and West Germany and, of these, the powerful Catuvellauni tribe came to the south-east near Cambridge.

The Celtic people were sturdy and strong and as tall as present-day average men. They had moustaches and long hair. The women let their hair grow very long, dressed it carefully, and sometimes held it up with an assortment of pretty combs. They painted their fingernails, dyed their eyebrows black with berry juice and used a kind of rouge called ruam on their cheeks. Celtic women bathed quite often using some sort of soap and afterwards scented their bodies with oils and herbs. When they had finished their toilet, they checked the effect in exquisitely carved mirrors of highly polished brass.

The Celts were known for their unusual and colourful clothes. They introduced trousers to Europe and both men and women wore them, but they were more popular with men. Trousers were made from linen or wool in bright colours, often in bold patterns such as big black and diamond checks. They wore magnificent jewellery — brooches to hold cloaks at their necks, gold and silver ornaments with detailed designs on their tunics, both at the shoulder and at waist level. The women wove beads on to the end of the plaits in their hair and gold threads into the silk of their tunics. They had solid, carved gold rings on their fingers, bracelets of gold and bronze on their arms, and torques of figured gold on their heads and around their necks.

Because there was no stone in Norfolk, they built houses and huts of the simplest design. They farmed corn, wheat, broadwheat, barley, oats and beans and traded grain, cattle, gold, silver, iron, hides, slaves and hunting dogs for imported ivory, amber, glass, pottery, wire, oil and continental wine.

Nature was very important to the Celts. They worshipped mysterious Mother Earth. Gods inhabited rocks and mountains, they illuminated rivers and were in the darkness of lakes, and the gods belonged to special trees — the ash, the oak and the yew. Prayers were said among oak trees on a grassy hill next to a pool or small stream and they revered animals — the raven, the swan, the bull, the stag, the boar, the horse and especially the goose.

They were a dark, brooding people; mystical, emotional men rather than logical ones, whose fine sensibilities and profound artistic skills contrasted strangely with the other side of their nature — that of the frenzied barbaric warriors who painted their naked bodies blue with woad, and brawled and screamed before hurling themselves into battle.

The Celts prized their weapons above all else — they believed them to be hand-in-hand with the gods and regarded them as relatives. Great skill was lavished on their decoration: the profound symbols of interlocking limbs of human and animal were tooled into spears, shields and daggers with precise mathematical formulae. The images of stags, boars, wolves, eagles, fishes, birds and the sacred goose were set in spiralling, curving knotwork amidst interweaving organic patterns — their symbol for eternity. To take away an ancient Briton's weapons was to take away his manhood.

The Romans came in AD 43, conquered the tribes, disarmed them, ate their sacred geese and, according to some sources, forced the Iceni and the other tribes to labour at re-organising Peddars Way. They widened it and cleared it, added flint, chalk or quarried stone in layers. After that, they rammed everything down and made ditches at either side and the agger or mound in the middle formed by these layers became the 'highway'. Other sources say that the road was a military road put down in the policing years immediately after the Celtic uprising in AD 61.

Peddars Way is as straight as if the Romans had laid a ruler on the land. It was one of their chief vicinal ways — a direct route for the rapid movement of the legions from London via Colchester to Brancaster (Brandinium), their headquarters on the northern shore of East Anglia which later became a large Roman shore fort built to ward off the menace of Saxon pirates. Red and white helmets flashed colour on the barren landscape as the legionaries of the Roman imperial army marched along Peddars Way in meticulous order. Most of the Roman soldiers were on foot. Only the aristocratic commanders-in-chief or the Barbarians — who were hired mercenaries and brilliant horsemen — rode small horses. Centurions headed a century of men. Six centuries in each cohort, ten cohorts in each legion, ten legions going to Brandinium — up to 60,000 men marching on Peddars Way.

It was hard going. They wore full armour: an iron coat of mail and a bronze helmet, carried a metal shield, a pilum or heavy seven foot long javelin, a dagger and a double-edged sword. Slung over their shoulders was a Y-shaped pole on which they hung a big animal-skin bag containing a pickaxe, a shovel, entrenching tools, turf cutters, mess pots, rations for fifteen days, a cloak, underwear, shaving gear, first aid equipment and some leather straps. All of it weighed ninety pounds (40kg). After having marched eighteen miles (29km) or more in a day — even if they had been fighting — the legionaries had to build a camp consisting of a command area and officers' quarters, dig a five foot (1.5m) ditch and earth ramparts for defence, put up their own leather tents and prepare their own meals. Sometimes there was an extra duty to do. Mutiny against these conditions was dealt with swiftly and harshly — flogging or death for every tenth man in the ranks. Legionaries signed on voluntarily for twenty years. To be in the Roman army, a man had to be a Roman citizen, at least five feet eight inches (1.7m) tall and very tough.

Mules, hundreds of them, would come along behind the soldiers carrying tents, extra armour and siege weapons, and after them came the camp followers: shady merchants and delicacy traders, soothsayers and travelling tavern keepers. They sold food, wine, new boots, bags of nails, raw materials — wood, leather, iron, tin, gold — anything that the men might need. The Roman settlers came last. Poor travellers went on foot, rich ones on horseback. Some had a small two-wheeled cart called a *cisium*; others rode in *raedae* or large four-wheeled carts;

Tumulus near Peddars Way.

the luckier ones travelled in *curri*, which were big carriages used for sleeping. All the wheels were iron-rimmed. Behind each conveyance, a mule or two carried all the belongings.

Eventually, relay or posting stations were built all along Peddars Way, six to sixteen miles (10-26km) apart. These were where the soldiers slept and the ostlers kept fresh horses for the imperial couriers, who rode across country at very fast speeds with letters and documents. The commanders stayed at inns or villas reserved for officers but there were other inns along the way for civilian travellers — farmers, postmen, pedlars, muleteers, drovers and wandering minstrels.

The Romans were superstitious, arrogant and greedy, and they frequently insulted the ancient Britons, laughed at their beliefs and took what they wanted without payment. They also thought that no one would dare to challenge them — that is, until they came into contact with a fiery, hot-tempered widow with bright red hair hanging down to her waist: Boudicca (Boadicea), queen of the Iceni, one of the greatest threats to the Roman Empire.

Boadicea was an impatient, sharp-witted, highly intelligent woman who had married Prasutagus, the only king of the Iceni, and they had two daughters. When Prasutagus died, the Romans put great pressure on the Celts by levying taxes of every kind. They took natives for soldiers and slaves, and forced the farmers to give food and livestock to feed them. Many people had to borrow money from Roman money-lenders and in AD 50, Seneca, the philosopher, tutor and advisor to Nero, loaned 40,000,000 sesterces to the Britons. It was a lot of money. Suddenly he wanted it back. Groups of soldiers and slaves were sent around the country collecting it by force. A posse of them reached Boadicea's palace at Caistor St Edmund. It was morning. Boadicea was taking breakfast with her daughters. The soldiers pushed their way in. One of them insulted her and she rose up in a fury. She was seized and flogged; her daughters were raped in front of her. News of this appalling outrage swept through East Anglia.

This was the signal for revolt.

The tribes gathered and moved in their thousands, many going south along Peddars Way to join up with Boadicea. She made a daunting sight as she stood on her wicker chariot waiting for them — tall and terrifying, her hair loosened on to the thick mantle and brooch which she wore over her tunic of many colours. The thick golden torque which she always wore twisted around her neck glittered as she moved. Behind her were 250,000 furious Celts — men, women and children, filled with hatred, sick of repression and servitude. Her eyes were fierce, her voice harsh as she urged them on with violent speeches in which she told them that they outnumbered the Romans, and that they should remember their ancestors and come back again and again until victory was won. Then she released a hare to propitiate the gods and her army cheered and roared and clapped and blew hunting horns as they moved off to meet the Romans.

They took Colchester, a colonia of 20,000 Roman settlers, and slaughtered them all. They went to London and butchered, burnt, skewered and crucified. They were making for St Albans when Suetonius Paulinus, the Roman general, caught up with Boadicea. He drew her into a narrow valley in hilly country and attacked. Boadicea turned to fight but she was downhill, her tribes were disorganised and tired, and she was soon defeated. She returned, it is believed, to the fields somewhere near Peddars Way to put an end to her life with poison.

Later, the way was used by Saxon colonists; Norsemen from the coast; medieval pilgrims going to Flitcham Abbey, which is south-west of the way; and Norman barons going with their servants to Earl Wareness's

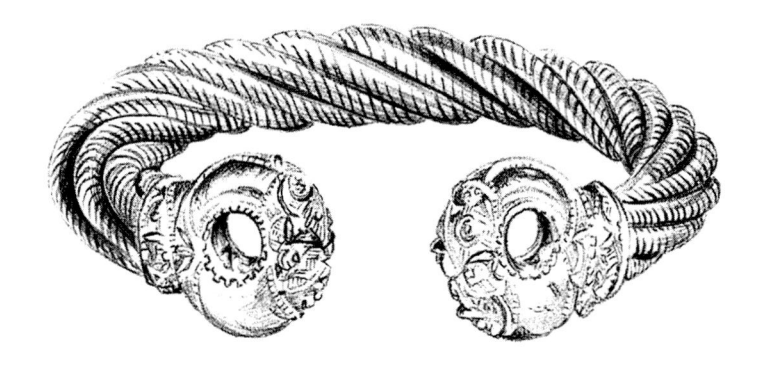

Beyond the wilderness are more elderberries and some tall willow trees. Branches are torn off. They lie on the ground. A strange smell of animal decay drifts over the path and a rabbit hidden in the bushes thumps out a soft but singular warning on the sandy soil. At each side of the path are more stinging nettles spiking up through the lower branches of the trees. Their stems are thickened with the wriggling black caterpillars of peacock butterflies, their spiny growths waving defiance from the swathes of cream cocoons. On the right, a patch of pale pink campion, white yarrow and hedge woundwort mix together and soften the harsh edges of the undergrowth. Leaf beetles, lacewings and green shield-bugs crawl across the flowers like iridescent lamps. Opposite are slender yellow cat's ear, startling and delicate in the primeval green.

The way narrows slightly; an oak tree branch hangs over on the right-hand side. On the left is a very large ash and some dead trees and on the path are more fungi. Here the trees are cut back and another bank of pink campion goes up to the edge of the field on the east side. Beetles move around the base of the plants — soldier beetles, sexton beetles, tiger beetles, scavenger beetles, bombardier beetles and devil's coach-horse beetles. Assassin bugs hide in the shade, hunting spiders are static by their lairs, and scorpion flies, muslin moths and snout flies patrol the dandelion and the dock.

Outside the confines of the way, fields of corn, carrots and kale stretch across rich farmlands to distant horizons marked out by trees. Shernborne, Snettisham and Sandringham are in the west, Fring and Great Bircham are in the north and north-east. Harpley and Houghton are in the east, Great Massingham and Little Massingham are in

stronghold at Castle Acre or the great castle of the d'Albinis at Castle Rising. Later still came packhorses, gypsies, sheep, shepherds and drovers, and in the 1800s the famous Norwich School of painters worked here led by John Sell Cotman (1782-1842). Now there is only the occasional tractor, farmhand or rambler.

ENGLISH COUNTRY LANES • 54

the south, and Hillington and Flitcham, with the remains of its abbey and its flax, are in the south-west. All the farming here is arable: barley, wheat, oats, rye, carrots, kale, oil-seed rape, turnips, potatoes and beans growing in the chalk escarpment left when the ice retreated. There are wide skies, a continental climate, low rainfall and many thunderstorms. Bracing breezes come from the sea in spring and in winter the sea-fog hangs over the fields.

Sir Henry Rider Haggard (1856-1925), the Victorian writer and Norfolk farmer, lived at Ditchingham and sometimes visited Peddars Way. He was fascinated by burial mounds, ancient civilisations, death, spiritualism and immortality. He liked to come here during thunderstorms or when the fog lay thick over the path and place his open hands on to the burial mounds, trying to contact the spirits of the dead Celts. Perhaps the ancient track, the landscape and its associations, the isolation, the burial mounds and the connection with feelings of otherworldliness helped him to create his mesmerising stories about immortal women, immortal love, lost kingdoms, and ancient civilisations in books such as *She*, *King Solomon's Mines*, *Ayesha*, *Allan Quatermain*, *People of the Mist* and many more — seventy books in all, fiction and non-fiction.

Rider Haggard's characters were vivid and strong, his pages filled with fantastic landscapes, and his favourite themes the eternal ones — love, hatred, loyalty, curiosity and fidelity. He liked sombre, weird and grand landscapes where 'every valley became a mysterious deep, and every hill and stone and tree shone with that cold, pale lustre that the moon alone can throw. Silence reigns, the silence of the dead.'

He was a brilliant, energetic man who had many talents and ambitions: a traveller and adventurer, a social reformer and an agricultural revolutionary whose ideas on rural England were in advance of their day. He wrote many books on agriculture, and was the first man to investigate and expose the evils of depopulation of the countryside. He believed in stopping the rural migration to the cities and he was sure that one of the worst fates which could befall England was that her land should become a plaything or a waste. He was sent all over the world on royal commissions considering such subjects as coastal erosion and afforestation, but he was most famous as a writer of romantic fiction. Another writer, Charles Kingsley, visited the area around Peddars Way and set his Saxon tale of *Hereward the Wake* in the fields nearby.

Now the surface of the lane becomes uneven, rutted and eroded. The hawthorn trees end and a farm track goes off to the left. Corn chamomile, rayless mayweed and a few small poppies struggle through the dark soil. Rabbit burrows are under the clipped hedge on the right and flat cornfields fall away gently at either side of the way. A solitary pheasant and some pigeons flee from a hawk and a brown hare sits up on the path, stares at the sky and then slips silently away.

Across the fields half a mile (0.8km) away to the east and marking the end of this part of the way is a tall, grey

ENGLISH COUNTRY LANES • 56

windmill with four white sails. It towers above the countryside like an aged and peaceful sentinel: dignified, striking to look at, unmoving in the afternoon sun. Great Bircham windmill is a tower windmill which was built in 1846. It has complete shutters, four wooden sails and a six-bladed fan winding the ogee or curved cap. There is a fine stone flour gallery on the first floor and the mill still works, but is kept as a museum for visitors.

Windmills date from the twelfth century and they were used to grind corn into flour. When there was corn to grind, the local farmers sent for the miller's cart or wagon, loaded it with empty sacks and sent them to the mill. Occasionally the farmers sent their own wagons pulled by magnificent carthorses — Clydesdales, Percherons or small sturdy cobs.

When the corn arrived, it was hauled up in the sack hoist to the top of the mill where it was put in the grain bin. A chute took the grain to the hopper above the millstones. Grain trickled from the bottom of the hopper on to the feed shoe which was agitated now and then by a shaker on the crutch pole or by a rotating damsel. As the upper runner stone revolved, a few grains at a time were fed into the eye of the stone and were ground before coming out as meal around the edges of the circular stones. The meal fell into the meal spout and lastly in to the bin on the floor below. Only the top stone or runner revolved and it did not touch the bedstone. A minute space was left between them. The more controlled the space, the better the corn.

The miller was a busy man. He could work only when the wind blew and, as long as there was wind, he worked night and day. He often caught up with a few hours' sleep in the mill so that he could keep on working, but if he worked on Sundays, he was punished by the religious authorities. He was alert at all other times as he had to keep the gap between the stones just the right size — even if the wind blew in gusts. The faster the wind blew, the quicker the corn was ground. In the early days, before the invention of the centrifugal governer, he had to do this by hand. The miller had to know the power of the wind, to be able to judge how much sail cloth to spread out, to be able to stop the mill under sail, and either take in or let out the cloth — at that time, there were no patent sails. Before the days of the fantail, he had to watch the direction of the wind as well as keep the wind sails square to the eye of the wind. He had to dress his stones and do all the running repairs. He dreaded storms and long calms but, it seems, always made plenty of money.

From this point, Peddars Way goes past the hamlet of Fring with its medieval church and wall paintings, the remains of a Romano-British villa on the east side, on to

ENGLISH COUNTRY LANES • 58

Sedgeford and Ringstead to Holme-next-the-Sea with its wild shoreline of reed beds and sedges.

Here was the strange experience of walking alone in the wilderness for hours and hours, of seeing no human habitation and meeting no other living soul; of my setting off on a hot spring day and into a long, green corridor of ancient trees — the sun glaring down, lighting every leaf, expanding every flower in that white-scented silent path with the hawthorns musked and heady, stilled and breathing, and the pollen hanging in the simmering, yellow air tipping the tall nettles, transfixing them and tracing them with gold. The birds sat motionless in the thorns, suffocating in the heat. And by the side of me were the tumuli — mystic, looming and harmonious, standing undiminished in the fields. The isolation was intense, the world far away.

And as I reached this part of Peddars Way, a soft breeze began, there was no sound, the sun was still hot in the sky and I heard a crunching in the undergrowth. Another strange smell — then nothing until a neurotic pheasant exploded from the bushes, flashed an iridescent head, crossed the path then disappeared, scattering the white flowers as it went. The breeze suddenly stilled and a mist came over — heavy as steel. The trees seemed eerie, the flowers went waxen — they turned themselves inwards, hiding their crimson stamens, and in the sky a hawk dropped low and hovered 'steady as an hallucination'. Four grey pigeons hid in the thorns. I quickened my pace, agitated, seeing the tumuli in the fields, and I stopped — sensing them, standing for a moment out of time, reckoning their significance and thinking of the warrior, buried and crumbling, laid where 'he might come up on a moonlit night and scent the rushing breeze'.

And I wandered on to Fring, feeling somehow connected with it all — perhaps it was putting my feet down, knowing that I trod the same piece of ground as others before me. Later the mist lifted, the stars appeared and some bats flew about, silently and softly going into the dark night.

△ *Great Bircham windmill.*

Marly Lane, Hoath, Kent

David Jacobs CBE

Late spring

'... here I was, a child, seemingly in paradise.'

Marly Lane lies in a serene, saffron landscape — a gentle, tranquil, sensuous place made sweet with warm crop smells and sea smells, fields of barley, scarlet poppies, and the sound of morning bells from the distant misty skylines which mingle into the soft moist land.

This is a fertile, open lane, simple yet solid as it moves through the flat landscape, drifts by ponds and pools, curves past ancient houses then disappears into far-off lost horizons. Lapwings hush and ruffle the warming air, swallows and swifts cut deep into the haze, black crows with husky voices spread out across the lemon-blue skies, and the larks hover and soar and sing. Ponds fringed with reeds seethe with life —mallards doze, frogs croak, water beetles sit tight in air-bright bubbles, moorhens dance over the lilies on spindly legs and a hundred midges dither close to the surface, dicing with death. And all around, the fields swell with an inexplicable secret and sufficient growth.

During the Second World War, David Jacobs was evacuated from London to Hoath, Kent, and he stayed at Rosary Farm which is on the north-east side of Marly Lane.

'I can remember quite vividly the day that I arrived. It was September. The sun was shining; the countryside and its colours and sounds thrust themselves upon me and I was totally unprepared for the effect it had on me. I had

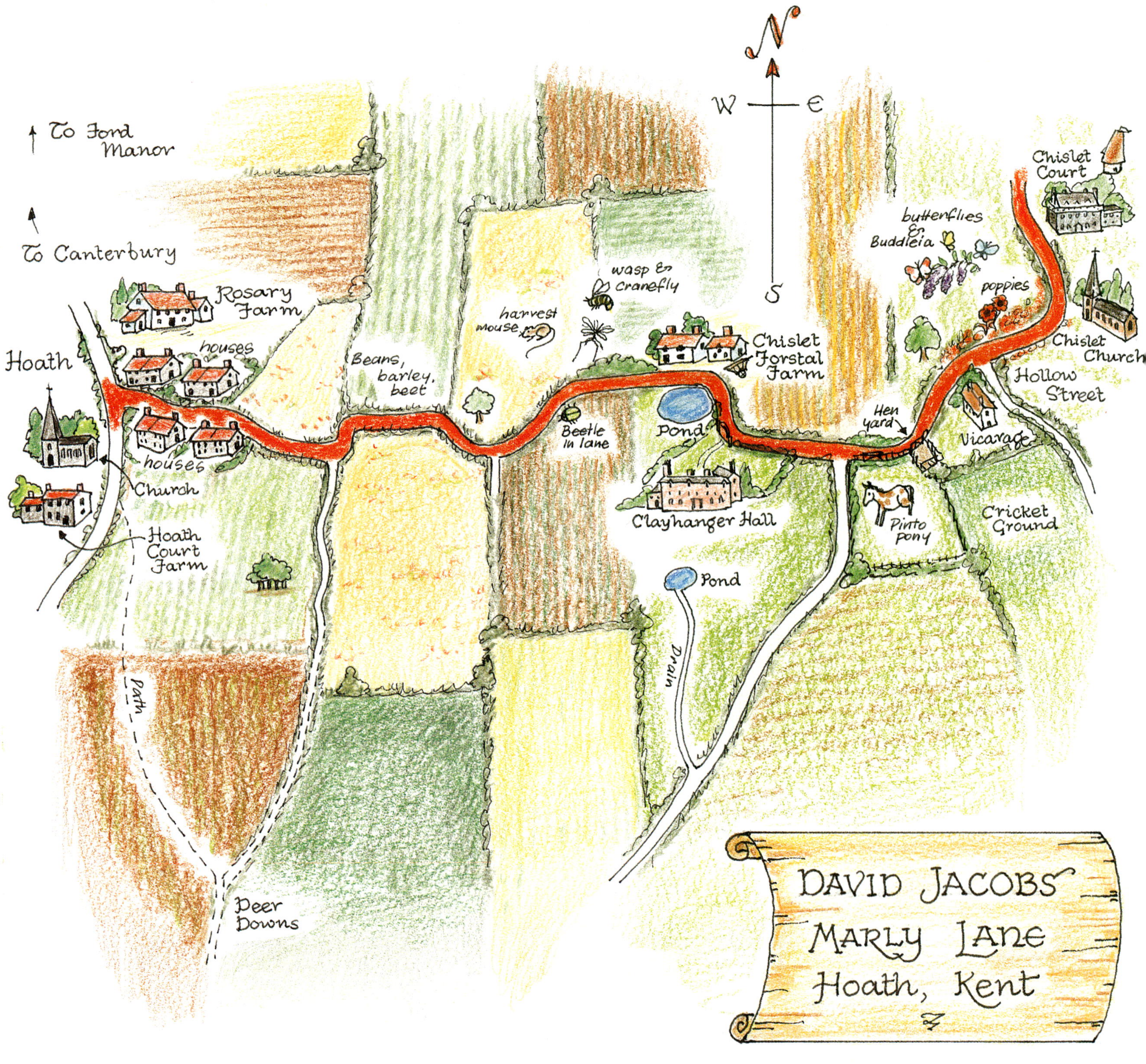
N
W
E
S
To Ford Manor
To Canterbury
Rosary Farm
houses
Hoath
houses
Church
Hoath Court Farm
Beans, barley, beet
harvest mouse
wasp & cranefly
Beetle in lane
Pond
Chislet Forstal Farm
Clayhanger Hall
Pond
Drain
butterflies & Buddleia
poppies
Chislet Court
Chislet Church
Hollow Street
Hen yard
Vicarage
Pinto pony
Cricket Ground
Path
Deer Downs
DAVID JACOBS
MARLY LANE
Hoath, Kent

left London with its huge square buildings, its smoke and fog, its noise and busy streets, and here I was, a child, seemingly in paradise! There were trees, fields, flowers and hedgerows dripping with ripening berries — the sky was bursting with the singing of birds, the air was fresh and sweet with the warm smell of the corn stubble left in the fields and the salt smell of the sea from the coast three miles (5km) away. The impact was indescribable.

And then came the joy of discovery. I was allowed to wander the lanes and I hunted for birds' nests, learned the names of the wild flowers and followed the hens and cockerels which wandered freely all over the place. I spent hours by the pond halfway along Marly Lane, watching the newts and frogs, the ducks and all the busy goings-on under the water. Sometimes I would spend all day there, sitting, fishing with a long, thick twig and some string. I can't recall catching anything, though! They were perfect days — the unconcerned time of childhood. Of course, I worried about the war and being separated from my parents, but I was well cared for at Rosary Farm. There was always enough to eat — fruit, bread, cheese, meat and milk and always, I can remember, flowers on the table and vases overflowing with them on every available window ledge and surface. Ever since, I have had my houses filled with flowers — sometimes gathered from the Surrey hedgerows — enormous bouquets of natural beauty.

Other memories are still strong in my mind — often returned to and savoured. Going along Marly Lane and the surrounding lanes to Chitting Puddledock, Nethergong, Deer Downs, Heart-in-Hand, Plucksgutter and other such fascinating places in a pony and trap, the sun beating down, the hedgerows at either side heaped with shining berries and the sound of the pony's feet clip-clopping along the surface of the lane and the metal on the wheel rims making a continuous hiss behind. We took vegetables and other things piled up in the cart and sometimes there was a trip to the seaside! When I think back to that time, I can still feel that wonderful sense of freedom — my legs in short pants being browned by the wind and my feet in sandals with no socks on and my sitting behind that pony in utter contentment. On most days there were no aeroplanes, no cars, no engines of any sort — only the sound of the birds. My life and my career is concerned with sound: the human voice, music and the transmission of, I hope, happiness and pleasure through the medium of sound. For me, as a child used to the noises of London, to be in Kent, under those skies resounding with song, was a profound experience. In some strange way that terrible war brought unexpected gifts and Marly Lane was one of mine!'

Marly Lane starts at the hamlet of Hoath near Canterbury, goes eastwards to a dog-leg curve, enters the parish of Chislet at Chislet Forstal Farm and the Tudor House, passes the cricket ground, then ends at the crossroad going to Chislet church, Chislet and Upstreet — a distance of about two miles (3km).

A post office in a shop and some semi-detached houses are at the beginning of Marly Lane, and across the road next to Hoath Church is the medieval Hoath Court Farm. After the houses are the fields. They come right up to the very edges of the lane, with just a narrow margin of soil and a thin strip of grass between, and they rise gently, one behind the other, stretching across to the distant horizons, each large field only a few metres above sea level and filled with barley. To the north and north-west are the

ENGLISH COUNTRY LANES • 64

hamlets of Old Tree, Shelvingford, Under-the-Wood, Marshside and Chislet Marshes. The hamlet of Chislet is at the far end of the lane, and to the west are Maypole and Ford.

The lane is almost flat and spreads out in front like a sandy-coloured stony strip laid on top of the fields. The barley is almost ripe; the stalks are green, the heads are brown — they bend over with the weight of the seeds. In the margins are a few stray field beans left loose from last year's crops, and beneath the barley in various patches are bright red poppies, corn chamomile, gallant soldiers, sneezewort, clusters of white-blossomed yarrow, more stray field beans, nettles and the odd, vigorous potato plant in full flower. A single blue speedwell struggles to grow in the shadow of the immense plants above. Birds come from different directions over the fields, their feathers lit by the sun. Swifts and swallows fly in wide circles, skylarks drop and fuss in the barley, greenfinches and chaffinches chase the sparrows at the seeds, and a huge, black jackdaw lands on the lane, gives a chipped, subdued, repetitive 'tchack' and searches in the stalks for food.

Four elm trees, bare and dying, the last of many, mark the edges of the field and a little farther along is another tree, part of a small copse. A tractor stood next to it, the engine switched off. Dick Fuller, the farmer who owned all of this land, stood beside it, smoking his pipe, looking over his fields, his Jack Russell terrier sat at his feet, panting, tongue hanging out, ears pricked up, eyes alert, waiting for some orders. We talked about the weather.

'A mild climate here', he said. 'Not much snow, although cold winds do come from the sea — straight from Russia, they say — but the land is good for growing. Some of the finest farmland in Britain.'

He shaded his pale-blue eyes with a strong brown hand, gave a small, satisfied sigh and pointed towards the far end of the lane with the stem of his pipe.

'This land was reclaimed from the sea', he went on. 'Man and nature worked on it together for about 1,800 years. Natural silting from the River Stour made it into boggy heath and marshland, and by Roman times it had become salt-pits and -pans and underwater meadows with a few pastures. By the twelfth century, the art of draining and embankment had become a sophisticated craft. Highly skilled men made walls, droves — narrow routes which animals are driven along — drains, pits and ditches — they are all over my fields — some just a little farther along from here after the turning to Chislet Park. They empty into the sea at Reculver.'

Dick Fuller knew a lot about his land.

'It's all arable now', he continued, 'but field beans and broad beans along with a little corn have grown in these fields since medieval times. In those days, most of the land was pasture with vineyards for the abbot at Chislet Court.' Once again, he used the stem of his pipe to point down the lane towards the church spire at Chislet. 'A busy place then — houses and cottages on every corner, tenants of the abbot, who worked the land. Then in the 1800s, it was all hops — grown to add to beer to help it keep. There were many acres of hops in Chislet and Hoath, and workers would come from the East End of London in September to gather the harvest and earn some extra money for their holidays. They came to Kent in their thousands, men, women and children in the early days of the late nineteenth century. They slept in barns, stables or tents but later they had brick huts.

It was hard work. Twelve hours a day and sometimes cold. At night, they built enormous fires and sat around them singing, telling jokes, playing mouth organs and accordions with the young ones flirting. When the hops were picked, they had to go to the oast-houses to be dried — there's one still at Chislet Court — then by hoy, a large sail-boat, around the coast and up the Thames Estuary to London to the breweries. Fine times and busy times they had, my grandfather used to say. A few large hop gardens are left at Marshside and Chislet Marshes but most of them were grubbed up in the war.' He climbed on to his tractor, lit his pipe, leaned over and smiled: 'A fine life is farming ... I'd want no other.' The dog jumped up on to the tractor and they drove off down the lane.

There is a gentle curve southwards, the lane straightens out for a while, then turns south again. The fields here are planted with broad beans. They are covered in pale cream flowers and bright red poppies are everywhere — streaming down both sides of the lane or mingling among the crops. Bindweed curls around the beanstalks, climbing quite far in a flowering, white, woven fence and the air is filled with the sweetness of the corn farther on. Telegraph poles stand out at different angles, the cable between them heavy with house martins sitting in long, blue rows. There is another small copse of oak trees in the fields to the south, some hawthorns, a few wild rose bushes and then a narrow track which leads off to the right and goes to Deer Downs and Chislet Park.

Chislet Park and Deer Downs were the hunting grounds and mansion house belonging to the see of Canterbury. The park, along with much of the land here including the Blean Forest to the west of Hoath, was run for over 1,000 years by successive monks and abbots from Chislet Court, the ancient monastery and manor house founded by King Ethelbert in AD 605, which stands at the end of the lane in Chislet. From the reign of King Edward I in 1275 until Henry VIII's rule in 1509, the land belonged to the Crown but was granted to the Church by royal charter. The land was farmed by monks, and they had hay and corn, sheep and pigs, and salt from the salt-pans along the receding Watsum Channel and shore two miles (3km) away. Grapes were grown in extensive vineyards at Chislet.

By the thirteenth century, most of the work on the land was done by the tenants of the abbot at Chislet Court. They had many duties to perform for him as part of their tenancy and if they refused, the abbot, who had much power, sent them away. The farming year was rigorous and the tools were simple. The tenants had to plough, sow and harrow certain areas of the Chislet Court fields as well as their own. They cut hay and carried it, grazed the sheep and the cows, caught fish and birds, made salt on the Chislet salt hills, took it to the herring house at Sturry for salting the herrings for the monastery, carried corn to the mill and took the flour back to Chislet. When the king was in Canterbury, they each had to take one truss of strewing straw to the court there. For this duty, they received a dole of bread and ale which they had to eat and drink in front of the abbot.

In late February or early March, work began on the land — their own as well as the abbot's. They dug and scattered manure, collected bundles of wood for the abbot's vines to climb up and, in March and April, planted the seeds. At Easter they brought Easter eggs to the court — one for each acre (0.4ha) of land that they held. The month of May meant a rest from court services and at that time they caught up with the work on their own land. June was haymaking time and everyone worked from dawn to dusk, swinging their scythes and wearing straw hats as protection against the sun. When the hay was cut, it was turned over daily so that it would dry out in the sun and then carried away to be stacked in the barns. August and September were the busiest times — vital times in medieval days when the corn was cut and the harvest taken in.

After the fields had been cleared, they took up the leftover corn straws from the fields for thatching, and they threshed in the great barn at Chislet or helped with the grape harvest in the vineyards. October meant grape treading in the large vat at the court, and November was ploughing and harrowing. Before Christmas, the pigs were taken to Blean Forest for fattening and, when they were judged to be ready, the tenants would drive their pigs along the lanes to Canterbury for the abbot at St Augustine's.

Christmas Feast was the time of rest, and on Christmas Day everyone would go from their hovels to the church at Chislet, glad to see the candles and the stained glass, hear the chanting of the mass and share in the church ales. For most of January they stayed indoors by 'a goodly fire' and then in February began digging over the land once more.

During the Dissolution of the Monasteries in 1538, Henry VIII gave Chislet Park to Thomas Cranmer, the archbishop of Canterbury. Two years later, in the manipulation which went on between the Church and the king, he gave him Chislet Court and all the land. The archbishop was fond of Hoath, Chislet Park and Chislet Court, and he spent much of his time there. His summer residence was the great brick palace at Ford, the remains of which are just north-west of the lane on the Roman road to Reculver. In 1544, King Henry VIII came to stay with Cranmer at Ford and together they rode along the lanes to hunt at Chislet Park.

Henry was a flamboyant and ostentatious king who came to the throne when he was not quite eighteen. He was a magnificent athlete and six feet two inches (1.9m) tall. Handsome and talented, he loved to dress in fine clothes and jewels, and spoke French, Latin, Italian and Spanish. He wrote poetry, played several instruments and composed music. He loved the sea and built up the navy, but he was ruthless and obstinate and grew up to be cool and calculating. When he came to power in 1509, he soon spent his father's money in a glut of tournaments, feasting and dancing.

He married Catherine of Aragon, the Spanish princess, but the eighteen-year marriage produced no male heir and he fell in love with Anne Boleyn, a beautiful lady of the court. He wanted the pope to declare his marriage to Catherine unlawful so that he would be free to re-marry. The pope refused to dissolve his marriage, so Henry was enraged and decided to break with the Roman Catholic Church. He ordered the pope's name to be erased from every book and prayer book, and in 1534 he set himself up as the supreme head of the Church. He believed himself to be next to God. Eventually, he closed all the monasteries in England, and took over all their lands and money.

Chislet Court.

ENGLISH COUNTRY LANES • 68

At this time, Thomas Cranmer, the archbishop of Canterbury, arranged for Henry and Anne Boleyn to be secretly married, said that the marriage was valid and crowned Anne Boleyn queen. She gave birth to a daughter, Elizabeth I. Soon Henry tired of his new wife and made up stories about her infidelities. She could not defend herself adequately and she was beheaded. Henry's conduct aroused severe disapproval from Sir Thomas More, the lord chancellor, and other leading churchmen and politicians. Thomas More was beheaded because he would not accept the king as supreme head of the Church. Henry had become a cruel and suspicious despot.

Henry then married Jane Seymour in 1536. She gave him a son, Edward VI, but died soon after childbirth. Henry's fourth wife was Anne of Cleves, but he did not like her. She was ugly, he said, and he should not have listened to Thomas Cromwell who had suggested the marriage, so he had Cromwell beheaded and divorced her. Catherine Howard was his fifth wife. Young and flirtatious, she was recklessly in love with her cousin, Thomas Culpepper, and did not want to marry Henry. But, as Henry was the king, she had to do as he ordered. Henry's jealous suspicions were soon aroused. Once again, he was enraged and so she too was beheaded. Finally he married Catharine Parr, who was a widow from the north of England. She nursed him, cared for him and outlived him.

Throughout his early life, Henry VIII visited Chislet Park. He found it peaceful and would stroll under the trees with Cranmer and Nicholas Ridley discussing the articles of Protestant faith.

In 1538, Ridley was the vicar of Herne, a small town on the coast three miles (5km) away. Ridley had helped Henry by getting Cambridge University to condemn the pope's spiritual power. At first Ridley had not fully committed himself to the Reformation, but by 1536 he had read deeply on the fundamental beliefs of Protestant faith, and discussed the root questions with Cranmer and the king. When the king was at Ford with Cranmer and Ridley, they would ride together to hunt in Chislet Park and they would return to Ford Manor to wine and dine and consolidate their decisions about their beliefs. In 1541, Ridley became chaplain to Henry VIII and then, in 1555, bishop of London.

Henry was fond of Archbishop Cranmer and when the king died in 1547, he was clutching Cranmer's hand and repenting his sins. Cranmer and Ridley revised the forty-two articles of Protestant faith at Ford, Thomas Matthew's version of the Bible was studied there, and Cranmer was at Ford when he was arrested by Queen Mary I and taken to Oxford to answer accusations of heresy. Queen Mary had re-established the Roman Catholic Church and she made sure that Cranmer never saw his beloved Ford or Chislet again.

ENGLISH COUNTRY LANES • 70

Ridley had taken an active part in the Reformation and the Catholic Bishop Gardiner set a case against him, accusing him of doubting the value of confession and decreeing that the mass — the *Te Deum* — should be sung in English. Ridley had helped Cranmer to compile the Protestant prayer books and signed letters acknowledging the title to the throne of Lady Jane Grey. He was offered a bribe of a rich Durham bishopric to keep quiet about his Protestant beliefs but he refused. So in 1555, he was taken to Oxford, along with Hugh Latimer, the bishop of Worcester, a leading Protestant reformer, for examination by important churchmen. They were declared heretics and asked to recant. Both Ridley and Latimer refused. Ridley was asked to write out his beliefs and they were considered to be so blasphemous that he was at once excommunicated, and he and Latimer were condemned to death.

Latimer and Ridley went to the stake set up in front of Balliol College in Oxford with a bag of gunpowder tied round their necks to hasten their end. As the fires were lit Latimer shouted to Ridley:

'Be of good comfort Master Ridley, and play the man. We shall this day light such a candle by God's Grace in England, as (I trust) shall never be put out.'

Hugh Latimer was overcome by smoke and soon died, but Nicholas Ridley suffered atrocious torments before he died.

Thomas Cranmer was a gentle, kindly old man who was loyal to King Henry when he denied Rome. Along with Nicholas Ridley, he was one of the most important theologians of the Reformation. It was Cranmer who insisted that people should understand that Christ exists in faith, not in material symbols. When he published, along with Ridley, the *New English Bible* and the *Common Prayer Book*, it set the Church against him. When he was taken away to Oxford, he was so distraught that he signed a confession denying the Protestant faith. Even so, the fate of this broken, aged man was to be burned at the stake on the very same spot where Ridley and Latimer had died a short time before.

On the 21st March 1556 — the morning of his execution — he was led out of his room at Oxford to repeat his confession in front of the crowd of people who had come to watch the spectacle. The frail, old man was stripped to his long white undershirt and bound by the waist to the stake. One hundred and fifty faggots of furze and 100 faggots of wood were stacked, waiting to be set on fire. As he knelt in prayer, the crowd, expecting to hear Thomas Cranmer, archbishop of Canterbury, repeat his confession, were shocked and overawed when he stood up, head erect and made the most defiant statement of his faith. He denounced the pope and the Roman Catholic Church. As the fire began to engulf him, he thrust his writing hand into the flames so that it burned in front of everyone and cried to God: 'This hand has offended Thee'.

After the track to Chislet Park, the lane bends sharply north again. Two drains, twenty yards (20m) apart, go off to the south, and there is another sweep northwards and then a long, straight stretch which goes to Chislet Forstal Farm. The crops here are potatoes, spiky yellow rape and more barley and by the side of the lane there are coltsfoot, creeping jenny, buttercups, a few nettles and some parsley. Just before the farmhouse wall is a hawthorn hedge with the top clipped off. A wren inside it bursts into song. Then a kestrel comes over, pauses and hovers and stares

△ *Chislet Farm.*

down at the bare twigs. The wren stops singing and a grey partridge suddenly breaks from the barley and scuttles behind the roots of the hedge.

Chislet Farmhouse is painted white and backs on to the lane. Roses are across it, angling up as far as the eaves and on each large blood-red petal the dew has gathered into a single perfumed sphere. On the ground beneath the roses, a wasp is stinging a crane-fly to death, ferociously tearing off its wings and hissing and droning like a beast possessed. After the farmhouse is a farmyard. Tractors and other farm machinery stand silent and coils of silage are stacked up waiting to be moved.

Behind the yard in a field of corn is a solitary standing stone. Many early people were in this area: the Beaker Folk, the Belgae, Romans, Angles, Saxons and Jutes. They sailed through the Watsum Channel to anchor in the creeks and gulleys, and settle in the headlands. The Romans left roads and villas in Chislet, there is a Roman burial ground in the churchyard, and the church itself was built on the site if a Roman temple. Beyond the stone is the path to Old Tree, where some German bombers crashed during the Second World War.

The lane continues in front of the farmyard, takes a dog-leg curve to the south, leaves Hoath and enters the parish of Chislet. In the crook of the bend on the right is a small pond about ten yards (8m) across. It is rich and dark and deceptively still, like a startling green emerald set in a yellow and amber landscape Round the edges are rushes and reeds: spike rushes, bulrushes, bur-reeds, reed poas, and sedges. Tall flowers bush up in between — water parsnips, woody nightshade, purple loosestrife, kingcups, yellow flag iris and billowing banks of meadowsweet, their creamy, white flowers warm and fuzzing. Their fragrance mingles with the smell of the corn. White water lilies float in the middle like small crisp islands and weeds — duckweed, Canadian pondweed, arrowhead, frogbit and pale water starwort with its strange, spoon-shaped leaves — grow in dense patches all around.

In the water are sticklebacks, water scorpions, water spiders, water stick insects, water bears, water beetles, drone flies, pot worms, pea mussels and pond snails, and fat, green frogs hide in the leaves. On the surface are whirligig beetles, water boatmen, and water skaters and a swarm of midges hangs low over the surface taunting the frogs. A coot goes over the lily pads on spindly legs, a mallard duck and her ducklings quack across to the other side, and the drake dozes unheeding in a warm hollow on a fallen willow, his glossy green head on his folded wing. And smooth newts with rosy bellies sleep, deep in the silent rushes.

Twenty yards (18m) along from the pond is a high yew hedge with a wide gate and drive belonging to Chislet Forstal House, now called Clayhanger Hall, a fine Tudor medieval hall house built in red brick with nine tall red-brick chimneys. Set back in a field on its own, it has stood almost unchanged for 400 years. There is a large, rough-hewn oak door and a bay window with tiny slatted leaded window lights. Most of the house dates from 1440.

▽ *Clayhanger Hall.*

73 • MARLY LANE – DAVID JACOBS CBE

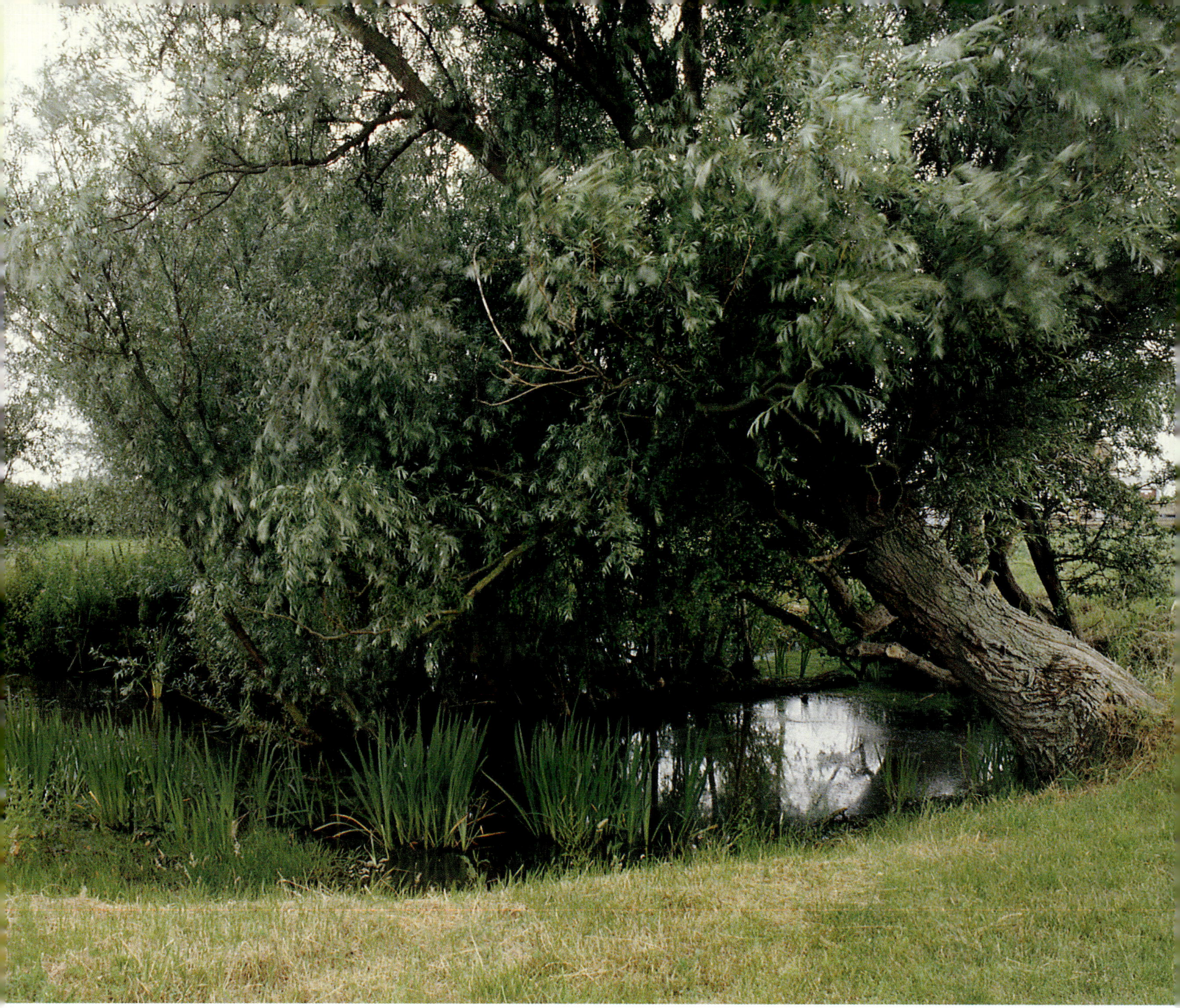

Behind the house is a dying elm. A great spotted woodpecker sits on a branch. In the distance a sedge warbler whistles, a dove settles in the elderberry trees on the side of the lane and a pinto pony in the next field closes his eyes against the sun. His long blonde lashes fringe his cheek.

The lane bends right again, a path leads off on the right to another large drain, and the lane keeps on, past more fields of beans and sugar beet until it dips down between high hedges of hazel, birch and beech. Patches of meadow cranesbill begin to stir in the slight breeze which has come from the sea, the tall stems of rose-bay willow-herb bend a little, the slender-stemmed poppies shiver slightly and some hoverflies work at adjusting their speed. A musk beetle crosses the lane quite unconcernedly. The hedges become lower and another small path to one side of a field leads south to Nethergong Penn, a large drainage cutting, and the tiny village of Upstreet.

In 1275, this land was the holding of William de Beaveise, one of the four French knights who served the king on behalf of the abbot at Chislet. Nicholas-de-Hopland held land at Hopland, just south of Chislet Park and Heresden, Tenementum domini-William de Grey held the Grays on the north side of Chislet Marshes, and a knight from the Hopland Soldark family held another part of Hopland. The abbot and monks at Chislet Court were not allowed to fight for their king and so, when in the thirteenth century Edward I called for soldiers to serve him in the Crusades, these men went off to war in place of the abbot and monks. In return, they were given the freehold of good farmland and the men to work it.

This was at the time of the later Crusades in the Holy Land. In the Middle Ages, people thought that life was a battle between God and the Devil, and the best way to save their souls was to go on a pilgrimage to Palestine to pray in the Holy City. But the Arab chieftains who held the city, and their Islamic laws, prevented them from doing so, and so the Crusaders vowed to rescue the Holy City from the infidels and return it to the true believers in Christ.

The four French knights, along with men from the land, went off to join other companies of knights and their armies of foot soldiers, grooms, servants, armourers, priests and pilgrims. They took with them heavy wagons specially made for the knights' tents, spare suits of mail, the lances, shields, swords, maces, battle-axes, barrels of arrows, bowstrings, spades, ropes, cooking pots, the extra-thick trappings of cloth for the knights' precious horses and all the rest of the equipment that they needed for the long journey to Palestine. Before they went, they came along the lane on their magnificent heavy horses in full

Clayhanger Hall.

heraldic colours to receive the abbot's blessing and gather the rest of the company together.

They came early. Probably at dawn. In full armour — their curcoats blazing with their own coats of arms. Their chain-mail shirts or hauberks and their chausses — metal leggings — shone in the early morning light. Underneath they wore long garments of padded fabric or leather and some had fur trimmings. The steel helmets with their stiff nose-pieces on top of their skullcaps and coifs hid the knights' grim faces and, as they sat on their impatient horses, they held their shields at the ready in a ceremonial position waiting for the abbot to say the blessing. When everything was ready, the trumpets blared, banners were raised and the knights turned their great horses towards the coast to sail for France and the Holy Land, not knowing if they would ever return.

    Farther along on the right, the lane rises a little and turns north-east. There is another drain, a path to a cricket ground and a fair-sized hen yard made from wooden poles and bits of makeshift fencing. The gate is wide open and a vigorous Ancona cockerel with bottle-green tail feathers and a forceful voice struts out into the lane, its bony yellow legs and feet pushing into the ground, its body arched with pride. Other cockerels follow, larger, more virile and decidedly aloof, and the hens come out afterwards, clucking and teasing and turning their tails. Two fat sparrows bathe in a sandy hollow and there are more inside the hen yard,

Chislet Church.

ecstatically picking at the bare patches of earth made by the hens.

Crowding round the fencing are red-hot pokers, hollyhocks, pinks, goldenrod, honesty, sow thistles, dandelions, pineapple may-weed, rough comfrey, shepherd's purse and more poppies, all mixed up together and spilling out in a riot of colour on to the sides of the lane. Goose-grass filled with cuckoo spit grows in front and blackberry bushes, hawthorns and deep purple Buddleia is at the back of the fence. Butterflies are all over the flowers, trembling in profusion: yellow brimstone, orange-tip, small tortoiseshell, green-veined whites, large whites, silver studded blues, black-tipped Essex skippers and a cloud of red admirals float round the Buddleia, shimmering in the heat.

After the hen yard the lane goes to Hollow Street and the vicarage at the end of the lane. The last bank of bright poppies grows in the grass by the house gates. From here, a road turns right to Upstreet and left through gently sloping fields to Chislet Court and Chislet church.

There was a quiet morning's walk in this gentlest of places — myself in a soft, yellow landscape soaking up the subtle beauty. The air simmered, the blue came through the haze and the skylarks were up already, singing and rejoicing and anticipating a sizzling summer's day. Church bells rang for morning prayer and the sound throbbed through the sky. Then all was still and a significant silence quickened the fields. Beans with thick, green stems and pale white flowers smudged with velvet black stood in long, muscular rows. Butterflies danced on them. Corn chamomile dipped and bent with some unseen vibration, and the silken petals of the poppies moved to a secret music. Everything here was vital and familiar and yet the source of it was unknown.

The heat haze stayed still on the tops of the barley as I strolled along in this peaceful place — myself in a quiet, golden land, enjoying the simple beauty of the fertile fields, listening to the skylarks still up high, watching the swallows working, hearing the crows grumbling and my mind filled with the words of George Herbert's poem:

'Can there be any other day but this,
Though many suns to shine endeavour?
We count three hundred but we miss:
There is but one, and that one ever.'

And then there was my midday lunch by the pond and afternoon hours gazing, belly down, at the water, watching the busy beetles carrying the air-bright bubbles down to the murky depths and the coots still on the lilies. The bells on the faraway skylines began to ring and a harvest mouse stirred in the barley, shook the stalks, climbed to the top and looked out across the lane. The sun pierced the haze and touched its chestnut coat with fire. Its whiskers were lit like rainbows and its black eyes were dark as jet. And deep in the thick forest of crops the humming of hidden creatures began, each one busy in the fresh new day.

Crummack Lane, Austwick, North Yorkshire

Clare Francis MBE

Early summer

'… a sense of wonder at the wide, empty, vast and ancient landscape, and a feeling of freedom and solitude.'

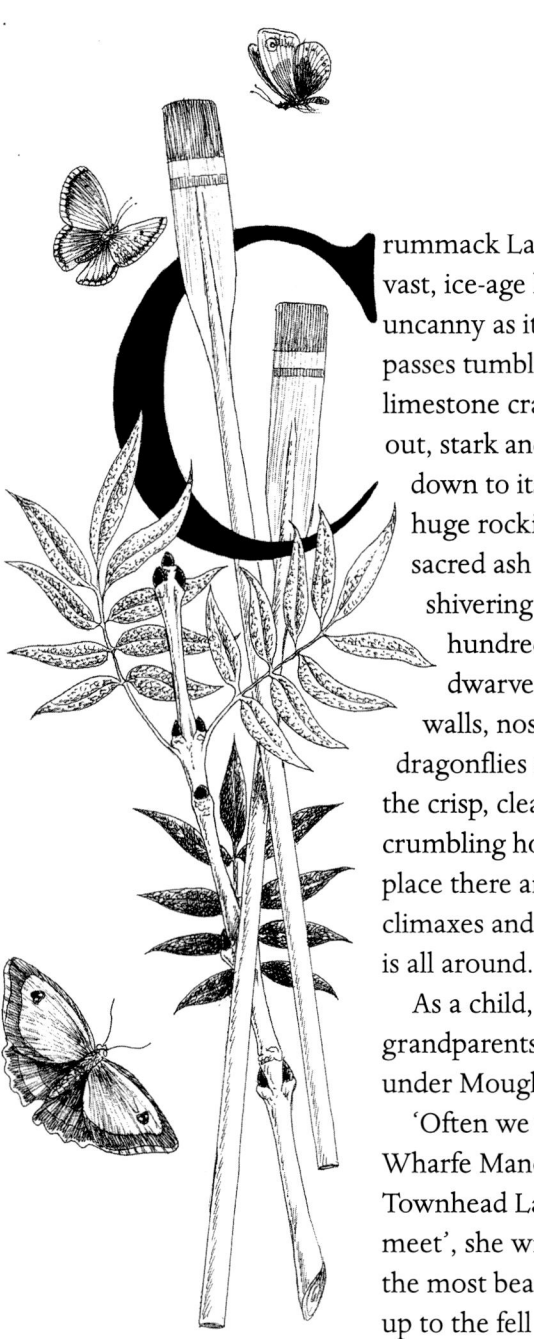

Crummack Lane is a harsh, wild and empty lane set in a vast, ice-age landscape. It is intimidating, primeval and uncanny as it snakes its way between gritstone walls, passes tumbling stony becks, stretches up through strange limestone crags, carries on, unrelenting, then opens itself out, stark and naked on to the immense fells which come down to its very edges. There are weird white cliffs, huge rocking stones, hills with grey exposed faces, sacred ash trees, mystic rowans, ancient junipers, shivering banks of blue harebells, self-heal by the hundreds and hawthorns high up like stunted dwarves wizened by the wind. Sheep lie under walls, nose to nose or rump to rump, weasels patrol, dragonflies zip up and down, curlews twist and thrill in the crisp, clear skies, and huge brown hares sit on the crumbling horizon and stare at the silent hills. In this place there are unexpected additions, unimaginable climaxes and the incredible, salutary force of the Earth is all around.

As a child, Clare Francis spent her holidays at her grandparents' house, the White House, Wharfe, nestling under Moughton Fell near Austwick.

'Often we would wander up Whitestones Lane, passing Wharfe Manor and climb up to the crossroads where Townhead Lane, Thwaite Lane and Crummack Lane all meet', she writes. 'We turned northwards, surrounded by the most beautiful countryside, and walked the packways up to the fell tops, watching the birds and noting the

to Viking Longhut
To Sulber Thieves Moss & Beggars Stile
Crummackdale
to Penyghent
Moughton Scars
Crummack Farm
Ingleborough
Ingleborough Caves
sheep
Gaping Gill Pot
Norber
North & South Craven Fault
curlews
Austwick Beck
Moughton Fell
cows
Whitestones Lane
ravens
curlews
juniper trees
ferns
Rocking Stones
Robin Proctors Scar
Clapper Bridge
N
To Wharfe Manor
Norberbrow
Harebells
W
E
Crummack Lane
Pumping Station
weasel
Norber Sike
Scout Camp
Slipstream
Dear Bought
To Clapham & Ingleborough
Thwaite Lane
S
To Caves
seat
To Wharfe
Stile
Austwick Hall
Gamecock Inn
Schoolhouse
to Austwick
CLARE FRANCIS
CRUMMACK LANE
Austwick
Craven, Yorkshire

different flowers appear as the seasons changed. There were joyous moments of discovery as we watched the insects, mammals, the sheep and the cows, and the shimmering patterns of sunlight through the ash trees. On reaching the high fells there would be a sense of wonder at the wide, empty, vast and ancient landscape, and a feeling of freedom and solitude. The ceaseless wind would touch our faces and we could almost smell the pure sea air as it came from the Irish Sea.'

Crummack Lane is a continuation of Townhead Lane which begins just behind the village school at the north-east end of Austwick in the Craven area of the Yorkshire Dales National Park. It ends at 1,000 feet (300m) next to Crummack Farm, high up in Crummackdale, a distance of about two miles (3km).

At the bottom of the lane are clusters of grey cottages with thick, stone walls and small windows to keep out the winter cold and the summer heat. Wood smoke fills the air, curling up in spirals from out of tall, grey chimneys. Ash — a soothing, ancient smell, pungent and ripe, mixed with the scent of early summer flowers in cottage gardens. Rowan trees, planted to ward off witches, are by the garden walls.

The lane rises and there is a sense of peaceful calm, a continuation. On the left, set back under the trees, is Austwick Hall, a squat, grey ancient hall, almost hiding under tall, dark trees. It has been a dwelling place for over 600 years. The Ingilby family lived here in the 1570s, when it was a small fortified manor, and during the Civil War they were Royalists. At that time, the hall had a pele tower. Part of the pele tower is still to be seen in the massive wall at the side of the house. Plundering Scots were still a threat in the Craven area and houses were built so that they could be defended. Sir Winston Churchill later spent some time at Austwick Hall painting the landscape.

The lane bends to the north, and there is a steep, sharp rise. Tall stone walls built on high banking tower up at each side; it is gloomy and grey, the light shut out. On the left, a wooden stile goes over the wall into a field and a footpath goes westwards towards Clapham. The grey stone cottages at the bottom of the lane are already hidden. The smoke from their chimneys comes up from below. Small sycamores, rowan saplings and a very old ash tree with deep ridges in the bark grow on the banking — the roots loop into the soil like long, sinuous fingers then disappear under the surface of the lane. Higher up, where the light comes through the shimmering leaves, slender flowers are hidden in soft, round-headed grasses. Cocksfoot, smoothsow thistle, dog's mercury and ivy, yellow milk vetch, great plantain, ribwort, red clover, hawk's-beard, ragwort, lady's-mantle, self-heal and yarrow and the sage-green leaves of monk's rhubarb fan out from the foot of the wall.

The stone walls which go all the way up the lane are made from Austwick Grit. Darker than limestone, it is sharper and more angular — almost flint-like. One and three-quarter tons of stone go into each yard of wall, and a man and his lad can lift seven yards (6.5m) a day: twelve tons of stone lifted to a height of two yards (1.8m) each day. The stones in Crummack Lane are five feet three inches to six feet (1.6-1.8m) high.

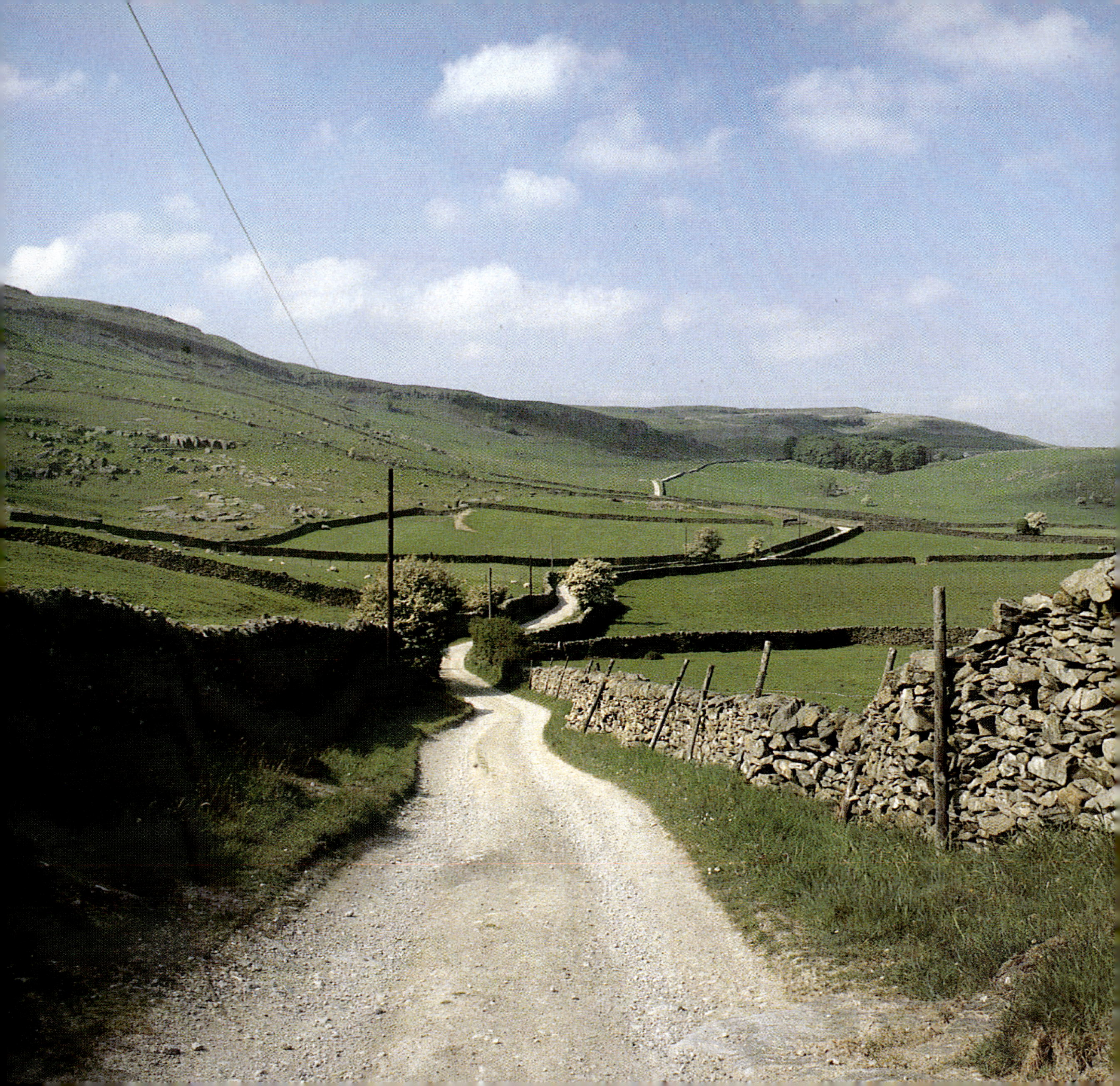

A strong tradition lingers here among stonewallers. On arriving at the wall at the start of the day, the heaviest hammer is thrown up the field or fell side, and where it lands is the spot to wall to that day. Stonewalling is mostly winter work: finger-numbing, breath-blowing, hard physical work. Stonewallers keep a brazier burning nearby to bring the blood back to frozen hands.

During the early 1800s, squads of stonemasons would move to the area to be walled, settle themselves in barns or outbuildings, have makeshift bunks for sleeping and little fires for cooking. Their diet was oatcakes and porridge, and their life was rough and ready: outspoken, down-to-earth, blunt Yorkshiremen who lived with the weather, the birds, the beasts and the glorious ancient hills. Their whole lives were spent surrounded by spectacular scenery and powerful fells, and human problems were put into perspective. They had no patience with the fascination for the trivialities of life.

Stone walls are really two walls built close together, leaning inwards and filled with smaller, sharper stones or 'heartings'. No cement or binder is used to hold them. Only well-balanced stones, cleverly chosen by the wallers, rest against each other. At regular intervals are 'throughs' — large stones which go from one side of the wall to the other, sometimes left sticking out like steps to bind the wall together and stop the sheep climbing over. These large stones are 'carted' from other places but the stones in the walls are gathered from the surrounding fields. Some wall tops have 'buck and doe' capstones, or topstones — high and low stones going along the tops of the walls. Other walls have regular capstones, taller and thinner, leaning against each other. Every so often a hole is left at the base of the wall. These are 'cripple' holes to let the sheep through to other pastures, but not the cattle. A length of wall is ended at the openings by a 'head' — big stones levelled off ready for post 'creaks', or wrought-iron hooks for the gate.

Each stone is different in the way it is shaped and placed, the dips in it and the types of lichen on it — small, circular bronze lichen, upright stem green lichen, black patchy lichen, orange cracked and crusty lichen — and spiders' webs are strung across the crevices at cunning angles, connecting them and covering them with a shadowy, silken smock. Some stones are as smooth as marble, rubbed by the sheep. Inside are ants, snails, beetles, bugs, frogs, wheatears, pied wagtails, yellow wagtails and weasels.

The walls go as far as the horizon, criss-crossing the landscape like a crazy, historical jigsaw. The maze of crooked walls close to the villages and homesteads dates from the sixteenth century or earlier; those surrounding the villages and more rectangular in shape are from the eighteenth century, and the square fields further out are the nineteenth-century enclosures. The fields in Crummack were enclosed in 1811. Thousands of hours of patient work by skilled men are here in Crummackdale. A well-built wall, well settled, will last for hundreds of years or more.

Many narrow tracks and drovers' packways edged with stone walls weave about the dale, zigzagging to Oxenber Fell and Feizor south-west of the lane. The walls are so close together that two horses would have trouble passing. The walls give shelter and heat for the vegetation; the narrow banking undisturbed for years. Plants grow shoulder-high, thrusting their presence on the twisting packways and the passer-by: tall foxgloves, ferns, nettles, dandelions, ivy, vetch, sheep sorrel, plantain, lady's-mantle and broad-leaved dock.

Pack-horses and ponies were the main form of transport in the Dales for over five centuries. A pack-horse train had from four or five to forty horses and ponies, depending on the status of the carrier. Each pony train had a driver, and one or two attendants or 'drovers', and the ponies in this area were imported from Germany and known as Jaeger or 'hunter' ponies. The pony at the front of a pack train had iron or brass bells fixed to a harness whose tinkling sound kept the ponies following on and warned other drovers of their approach, especially at sunken, muddy, awkward corners.

The ponies carried panniers or a wooden pack-saddle. They took loads of two and a half hundredweight (130kg) and carried coal, charcoal, peat, iron ore, lead in small pieces, silver, salt, hides, ribbons, jewellery, spices, comfits, pottery, and wool for combing and spinning to remote farmhouses all over the Pennines. The cloth was then carried to markets, and to dyers and finishers. Packways were busy routes. Monks going to outlying granges or distant abbeys, colliers, charcoal burners, shepherds, salters and other pack-men would follow the pack-horse train for company and safety.

The banking here becomes level with the lane surface; the walls are lower. It is 600 feet (180m) above sea level. Over the wall tops are magnificent views of the woods, lanes and walls, and of Oxenber — the Viking 'Ox Hill' — and Feizor, with its tight, twisting lanes which were a meeting place for other packways and lanes. To the north-east is the hamlet of Wharfe under Moughton Fell, and directly south, the Wenning Valley and the River Wenning stretches across to the Forest of Bowland, the Trough of Bowland, Morecambe Bay and the Irish Sea.

On the east side of the lane, just before the crossroad, is a field filled with thistles and sheep. Tall, prickly-winged marsh thistles with purple-red heads stand in dense patches by the bogs and left-over ponds; creeping thistles grow by the walls, and spear thistles mix with melancholy thistles and make jagged, erratic islands around the mounds of sitting sheep. At the corner of the field is a stone-walled sheep pen with a sycamore tree above for shading the sheep. Next to it, Thwaite Lane, an ancient bridleway, cuts across Townhead Lane going west toThwaite Tunnels, Clapham and Ingleborough Cave, eastwards past a homestead called Slaindale and down to the road which leads to Wharfe Mill Bridge. At this point, Townhead Lane finishes and Crummack Lane begins.

A few yards on, on the south side of Thwaite Lane, is a wooden seat set back off the path and facing north up Crummackdale. Two geologists were sat on the seat, eating sandwiches and looking at the magnificent view. They had spent the day, they told me, in the bright sun, surrounded by mammoth crags, the limestone pavements, the clints and grikes, and lunar plateaus high on top of the dale.

'We found the ancient green Austwick pebbles, coral fossils, and the wave-cut platforms of the old seabed', said the small, sweet lady with the wind-browned skin.

'And rocks which have been exposed for many millions of years', added her husband excitedly. 'Enormous earth fractures occurred at the close of the Carboniferous Age, separating the flat rocks of the Dales from the crumpled rocks of the Craven Lowlands. This is the North and South Craven Fault, and Crummack Lane lies on top of it.

ENGLISH COUNTRY LANES • 86

87 • CRUMMACK LANE– CLARE FRANCIS MBE

Crummackdale itself was carved out by a glacier 1,100 million years ago and this area has the finest examples of clint exposures in the whole of Great Britain. Limestone pavements on the top of Moughton, Norber and on towards Ingleborough are called karsts — limestone crisscrossed with deep fissures called clints and grikes. Over the centuries, the rain wears them down and they become swallow holes, pot-holes and caves. There are 800 pot-holes and caves with cracks and fissures which go deep into the earth, and some of the oldest stone in the country lies behind Wharfe Manor House.' He pointed to a house by the foot of Moughton Fell.

'Of course', his wife continued, 'Gaping Gill, the most famous pot-hole in the country, lies just two miles,

ENGLISH COUNTRY LANES • 88

or three kilometres, to the north-west of Crummack in the foothills of Ingleborough. There is a gigantic opening in the earth with a drop of 360 feet — that's over 100 metres — to the floor of the chamber.'

'York Minster can fit inside it', he said passionately. 'At one time, visitors were let down into the cave by a rope but now, at certain times of the year, there is a winch with a bosun's chair driven by a small motor — a fantastic experience, especially in wet weather!' He stood up and pointed west along Thwaite Lane. 'A bit further on Thwaite Lane is Ingleborough Cave and it's quite easy to walk into. You can get a guide from Clapham if you need one. The cave's dry and has lots of stalagmites and stalactites — there are pinnacles, columns and clusters and small waterfalls with the Pool of Reflections and an underground lake', he went on enthusiastically. 'They're lit up and really beautiful — almost eerie. Then there's the Giant's Hall — hard to get to', he said, shaking his head, 'unless you're a good caver. But watch out for the fairies, ghosts and hobgoblins who are supposed to haunt the caves! Never seen any myself, though', he said laughingly.

'Seriously though', he went on, 'this is a place of the dead.' He looked up at the steep, limestone crags surrounding Crummack Lane. 'Difficult to believe that the crags and terraces surrounding this lane were made from the broken and powdered skeletons of primitive organisms — billions and billions, there must have been. All that life, crushed into this landscape.'

'And the fossils', his wife broke in, 'trilobites, crinoids, graptolites — buckets-full of them, all embedded in the white limestone and easy to see.' She swept the view with her plump arms in an enthusiastic embrace and declared: 'It's a geologists' paradise.'

A few fields away, on the east side of the crossroad between Thwaite Lane and Crummack Lane and directly opposite the seat, rising to 1,300 feet (396m), is Moughton, the old Norse 'sheep hill', its corrugated head full of ravens, rare, exotic ferns and ice-age junipers. Moughton rises out of the huge expanse of Great Scar limestone with clints and grikes in the limestone pavements on top, and the ancient bed of Silurian rock at its base. Penyghent, one of the renowned Three Peaks of the Yorkshire Dales, lies a few miles behind Moughton to the north-east, its domed head rising to 2,273 feet (694m). Whernside, another peak, is 2,414 feet (736m) high and is north-east of Crummack; and Ingleborough, the most famous peak, is 2,373 feet (723m) high and peeps down over Crummack, easily visible from the top of the lane.

Ingleborough is really many hills together — Simon Fell, Park Fell, Southerscales fell and Little Ingleborough. The top of Ingleborough rises up from the foothills of Little Ingleborough, bare and treeless, with fifteen acres (6ha) of soft grasses covering the millstone grit. The Ingleborough massif is a mixture of Silurian slate, limestone, shale and sandstone, the slopes covered in coarse grass and bog cotton in the dips. This immense hill has not changed for over a thousand years. In the past, beacons have been lit on the flat, angular top to celebrate events and communicate across distances, horse races have been run here and a tower was once built to shelter shepherds. Even today bonfires are lit on Ingleborough to mark important events.

Norber, the Viking 'hill to the north', rises to 1,050 feet (320m) and lies north-west of Crummack Lane and Thwaite Lane, across the first field on the left. It is a sombre, grey hill with a startling, unexpected face, half exposed, half fallen away, formidable to see; staring down over the lane. The world-famous Norber 'erratics' — huge blocks of Silurian slate —are on the top, some as big as houses perched on slender limestone pedestals. They move at the slightest touch. At the end of the Ice Age, 12,000 years ago, melting glaciers crept down the landscape, carving out new valleys and fells, and shifting boulders from their original locations. The Crummack Glacier lifted the Norber erratics 400 feet (120m) and left them to rest on the Great Scar limestone — strangers to the place where they lay. The boulders are a hundred million years older than the limestone on which they rest. Over thousands of years, rain washed the limestone away but the stone beneath the erratics was sheltered, and so the rocks have been left balancing on slender limestone pedestals about two feet (60cm) high.

At the edge of Norber cliff face, slightly to the east from the Norber boulders, is Robin Proctor's Scar. One dark and stormy night in the early nineteenth century, so it is said, Robin Proctor, a local man, left the Game Cock Inn in Austwick, having had too much to drink. By mistake, he sent his horse up Crummack, lost his way on the tops, came to the Nappa Scars, headed for the Old Limekiln area, reached Norber, and he and his horse fell over the edge. Both were killed. Robin Proctor's head was severed from his body, and the ghost of his face is said to hang about the cliffs.

After the crossroad, the lane slopes down gradually, going northwards. The stone wall facing the west is covered in thick green moss, each stone encrusted and creped with it, vibrant in the clean air of Crummack.

Whitestones Lane leading off Crummack Lane going to Wharfe.

ENGLISH COUNTRY LANES • 90

A few gooseberry bushes, 'wildings' from the gardens, are growing in the shade by the side of the wall. The pale green, prickly globes of the developing fruit glow like lanterns against the moss, half hidden in the spiky leaves.

On the right-hand side is Dear Bought Plantation, a shadowy copse of ash and birch, the grass beneath it carpet-smooth. Here the lichen on the stones in the walls is thicker, heavier, more brilliant in the dark. A man was offered this plantation for nothing if he could scythe a meadow by hand in a day. He began at dawn and finished at dusk. And then he fell down dead. So the plantation was 'dear bought'.

On the opposite side of the lane to Dear Bought Plantation is an unobtrusive water-pumping station. Norber Sike tumbles down from Nappa Scars and Norber boulders, crashes on to rocks and stones, hits the hollow banking, widens, narrows, dashes under the lane and into the fields below going to Slaindale and Austwick Beck. The bubbling water echoes in the quietness. Harebells grow in blue profusion on the banks of the sike, their delicate stems bending in the breeze. Buttercups and hawkweed speckle the grass and beneath the surface a dipper walks upstream, head down, wings flapping, looking for a fish. Above, some gnats dither on a fascinating spot and from further up a blue emperor dragonfly, prehistoric and carnivorous, zooms in and hangs suspended like 'a blue thread loosened from the sky', then shoots away, sparkling, electric, a living sapphire in the sun.

Snails are glued to the stones: amber snails, ram's horn snails, round-mouthed snails and nerite snails. Two of them come up out of the foam at the edge of the sike, press together and rock to and fro, dancing a love dance and sending love darts into each other's cold bodies. A rare crystal snail, discovered here in Austwick, shifts its bulging blue body into the rushes, the clear shell glinting in the bright light.

Clouds of creamy meadowsweet mark out a slipstream coming from the sike — their sweet, lush smell catches at the wind and fills the lane with perfume. Water avens, rich patches of orange, red and green, grow along the slipstream edges, and goose grass with its twin seed spheres and million fine hooks meshes in and out of the meadowsweet. The crumpling dark leaves of water-mint are stacked behind. A weasel came to the water to drink. It stared and sniffed and, startled, it lifted its head and furiously held my eye. The bright, black eyes burned, the chestnut fur bristled, the white belly tightened and the whole of it shook with rage. It hissed and spat, then silently went into the wall.

After the sike the lane rises steeply, climbing to 800 feet (250m). Lawkland, Eldroth and the Wenning Valley are spread out below, and in the distance, mist-covered and looming over the horizon, is Pendle Hill, home of the Witches of Pendle who were burned at the stake for their religious beliefs. Black and white cows are in the fields, lying down full-length, fast asleep, fat stomachs rising into the air. Only the flick of a tail swatching the flies shows that they are alive.

On the left-hand side the banking is quite high, dotted with yellow hawk's-beard, pink clover, vetch, and purple self-heal. Sheep are in the fields behind. Hawthorn trees are on the banking, a small rowan tree shakes its berries in the breeze, and some ash saplings struggle towards the light.

The ash tree was the sacred tree of the Vikings. They worshipped it for they believed that it held up their whole universe. The first man was called Askr — Ash — after the gods had breathed a human soul into an ash tree. Axe handles and arrow shafts were made from the wood, and the fire and lightning they believed was in the tree gave them courage and strength.

They came in their wooden longboats, sailing from the north, dragon prows pointing to the western coast of England, single, square sails facing into the wind and rows of oars rhythmically slicing into the Irish Sea. The Vikings — raging conquerors, blonde-haired, bright-cheeked, blue-eyed. Tall, powerful men clad in leather and bronze with horned helmets on their heads, swords quenched in blood thrust down their belts, and double-edged axes in their hands, honed in urine, fine enough to split a hair.

They walked the Trough of Bowland, went through the forest, crossed the Wenning Valley, the river, the marshlands of Lawkland and Eldroth, skirted Feizor Woods, found Crummackdale, the ash trees, the ravens — a bird of magic power for the Vikings — the limestone terraces and the bleak high fells which reminded them of home. So, after pillaging the countryside around for many years, they eventually settled here in Crummack and farmed sheep.

In summer they played games to keep their raiding skills in trim: hunting, falconry, archery and sword play. And in the winter, when the fells funnelled the north wind down to the sea, they stayed in their long houses by great wooden fires with their women, their cattle

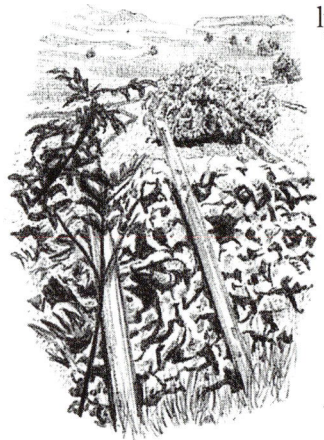

ENGLISH COUNTRY LANES • 92

Whitestones Lane going on to Crummack Lane.

CRUMMACK LANE– CLARE FRANCIS MBE

and their dogs, feasting on mutton, bread, barley, beans and eggs, listening to famous stories of heroes and dragon slayers and of 'monsters, moorlands, misting fells, warm wounds and bubbling, blood-filled tarns'. Eventually many of these long heroic tales were written down, and thrilling narrative poems such as *Beowulf* can be read by us today.

The Vikings wore simple clothes. The men had long woollen shirts with long socks attached. The socks were bound with leather thonging and they had soft leather shoes. Both men and women wore make-up: lip colour, eye shadow and eye liner. And jewellery — rings, brooches, bracelets and necklaces made of silver and gold in the shape of animals, leaves or flowers.

Viking art, at this time, was an abstract and involved form — sophisticated art, the craftsmanship of high creative genius. Animals were the main elements in their designs and were abstracted, twisted and contorted until only a few parts could be seen — an eye or a snout, a leg or arm, usually set in gilt bronze. There was a need for art in daily life — even the humblest brooch would be covered with ornament.

They lived in long-houses, forty to 100 feet (12-30m) in length and about eighteen feet (5.5m) wide. The foundations were deep and most of the house was below ground level to protect it from the cold. Walls were made from logs; wattle and daub was added. There were no windows — only holes in the turf roof to let out the smoke from the fires which went the whole length of the room. The Vikings loved and cherished their dogs, and the dogs slept in long lines in front of the fires. Sweet-smelling flowers such as meadowsweet were strewn on the floor and tapestries were hung to keep out the draughts. The weapons, shields and standards bearing the Viking emblem of a raven were placed around the room for decoration.

There is the remains of a long house high up in Crummackdale and more at Clapdale, Braida Garth and Penyghent Gill. Neolithic man was here and Iron Age, half-buried walls and the ruins of round huts are found near Beggars Stile and Thieves Moss. The Celts left a bronze cauldron in Crummack, the Romans came and traded with the Brigantes, and in 1455 the Wars of the Roses made this area into a place of violence and confusion.

The lane rises to 800 feet (245m) above sea level here and turns sharply northwards on Norber Brow. A farm track going to Sowerthwaite Farm is on the right, and on the left are fields filled with bracken, dotted with sheep and strewn with more Silurian slate boulders left from the Crummack Glacier.

There is a long straight stretch of uneven surface and hawthorn trees, some in groups, some on their own, are at each side. Taller than the walls, they bend backwards at their tops, showing the way that the prevailing wind blows and underneath are rows of foxgloves and more self-heal and harebells are sprinkled in the short grass — soft ribbons of palest purple and blue.

There is a steep dip down and on the right a tremendous horizontal rock face heaves out of the ground, the sandstone smooth and curving, bowing and folding under the backdrop of Moughton's vertical clints and grikes, and crumbling top. Sheep, cows and some young bulls sit in the sun on ledges of the curving sandstone, surveying the scene below. Above them, a brown hare sits in the field and stares at the silent fells.

95 • CRUMMACK LANE— CLARE FRANCIS MBE

Black crows soar about and some lapwings hush and throb their way through the sky.

The lane rises again, with high walls on the left, and Whitestone Lane leads eastwards to Wharfe and Wharfe Manor. Along Whitestone Lane is a stone sheepfold and a clapper bridge over rushing Austwick Beck and great slabs of Silurian stone are underfoot. Stone walls climb vertically up the side of Moughton and a hawthorn tree clings to the fellside, echoing the shape of the rock face. A wooden stile goes over the wall and footpaths lead up to Beggars Stile, Thieves Moss, Sulber, Selside, Simon Fell and on into Ribblesdale.

Wharfe Manor was an outlying grange belonging to the Cistercian monks of Furness Abbey, members of a Roman Catholic monastic order founded near Dijon in Burgundy in 1098. The monks came to Yorkshire in 1132 to follow the austere life they had chosen: solitude and hard manual labour — to work was to pray. Cistercian monks slept, ate and worked in perpetual silence. They were vegetarians and much of their diet was pease, grain and pulses and maslin — a mixture of wheat, oats, barley and rye flour. At Wharfe a few monks would look after the lay brethren and abbey tenants and make sure the church services were kept up.

An early rule of the Cistercian order said: 'Let no women enter the court or their granges save by order of the prior, nor let any man speak alone with a woman. But let the women milk our sheep in the fields and not in walled houses and let young and pretty ones be avoided as far as possible.'

The monks would walk the ancient packways to their other distant granges, coming from Fountains Abbey into Wharfedale, across to Kilnsey, along Mastiles Lane, over

ENGLISH COUNTRY LANES • 96

Malham Moor and through Ribblesdale, going to their great monastic granges in the Lake District. When they were at Wharfe, they would walk up Whitestone Lane, Crummack Lane and Thwaite Lane — tracks before they were enclosed — in their pure white robes collecting monk's rhubarb and other herbs from the fields, or tending to their sheep. Cistercian monks were called 'White Monks' because they always wore a white habit.

Each sheep belonging to the monks was cared for all its life, called by name and usually died of old age. Old sheep, past lambing and not having good wool, were collected into special pastures near the grange and cared for as a sort of retirement pension for giving milk and wool for all of their lives. Ewes were milked, and cheese and butter sent to the priory to be sold in various quantities, up to as much as nine stones (57kg) at a time. There were about 200 sheep in a flock. At shearing time, the lanes and packways would have been noisy, busy places. The sheep in Crummack are the hardy Swaledale breed, emblem of the Yorkshire Dales National Park, and Mashams — half-bred lambs crossed from Swaledales and Wensleydales — a breed not so hardy and kept on lower pasture.

In 1539, a man called William Anderson came to Kilnsey to give 'evidence about the management of the sheep' for the records of the area. He was eighty-five and knew the land for many miles around. He had served with the monks as 'heardman and shepeheard' and he had been given a lamb in his 'firste yere'. So well had his flocks produced that his one lamb had become 'three score and thirteen good ewes'. There is still a widespread custom on Dales farms of giving the young boys of the family a lamb to start off their own flocks.

At the top of the lane is Crummack Farm, nestling on the fellside 1,000 feet (300m) high. Here they made the best butter in all the Dales. Two sheepdogs, Bob and Bill, were tied to their kennels and a terrier dog stood by the door. Next to the wall is a sheep pen and a neat concrete sheep dip, three feet (1m) deep. In the 1800s, in the middle of June, all the farmers around Austwick gathered their flocks from their 'stints' on the high fells and came with their sheep and their sheepdogs for dipping, clipping and foot trimming. Sheep are kept on the same pasturage or 'stints' year after year, even though the owners of the flocks may change, and this helps the flocks to know their own area. When all the flocks were gathered, the men started work. They began at dawn. A man stood in the 'dub' — a dam they had made from the sike coming from Long Scar. The sheep were shoved into the water and the long, laborious task of cleaning the 'sheddings' — one-inch (2.5cm) partings of the fleece — of sand and grit and

thick tar salve began. It was a busy time; the men working and gossiping, the women preparing the food at Crummack Farm for the evening meal that they shared when the work was done.

From the farm, a footpath goes upwards and northwards to Beggars Stile and Clapham Lane, on to Long Scar and south-west to Clapham Bottoms, Gaping Gill and Ingleborough. To the south, the white surface of the lane winds down Crummackdale with a backdrop of fells and fields set out below in breathtaking splendour.

The sky was splintering blue as I went up this Viking path one early summer's evening. Woodsmoke curled from grey cottage chimneys — a ripe, ancestral smell, one I had always known. Rowans grew by each door, ash leaves shimmered in the slight cool breeze and the sheep dozed in the fields. Nothing had changed. Spiders' webs were strung from stone to stone, dragonfly wings sliced up the light, the warm brown weasel hunted in the walls and the haunting melancholy cry of the curlew tore into the air as it circled the thermals in the echoing amphitheatre, waiting above. And crowding in, overpowering and waiting, were the timeless shapes of the magnificent fells.

At the end of this lane, I felt exhausted, drained. The power in the hills was overwhelming, the forces incomprehensible. I was small, insignificant, a speck in the all-encompassing rightness of the plan. Here, somehow, was the measure of the earth.

When I had finished looking at the fells, there was a welcome at the farmhouse: tea, oatcakes, a crackling fire, terriers round my feet, the farmer's soft voice, and tales of farm life past and present. Then the walk down a moon-bright lane, feeling the chill in the air, watching the sheep begin to huddle, the silhouettes start to stand out, and me alone, exhilarated, surrounded by the spectacular, the silence broken only by an owl's quick call.

Castle Lane, Fotheringhay, Northamptonshire

Dudley Moore OBE

Middle summer

'Lanes — dearest treasures of the English countryside to be cherished in my memory and placed forever in my heart.'

Castle Lane leading to the Nene Way is a soft, shimmering lane set in a forgotten Arcadian landscape. An important, enigmatic yet subtle lane that stretches out under golden skies; meanders by gleaming mill ponds, shining tumbling weirs and silver streams; wends its way through ripening cornfields turned crimson by the setting sun; lingers by the gentle, rippling river and the castle mound crowned with purple thistles; then rests, as if adrift, among rows of ancient cottages, each one complete with a thick, warm thatch.

Here is an overwhelming, venerable place — a place of glowing fields, smudged horizons, slanting sunbeams and vermilion skies. Cattle sit under the trees lowing gently, chewing the cud, sweet cow breath scenting the evening air. Horses lie down or stand and hang their heads, dozing, eyes closed, velvet muzzles moving, tails softly swishing, brushing the dusk. Glow-worms light the air, snails leave silver trails, bats flit, moths dance, wild geese criss-cross the river, hedgehogs clamber along the edges of the corn and barn owls quarter the still, silent fields or sit like ghosts on wires or posts and watch for the coming moon. This is a memorable, distinguished lane — a place of pilgrimage and destiny, of greatness, ambition and resolve, surrounded by sadness and stillness, the shadows of longing and the finality of lost hopes.

'My career has taken me far away from England and its countryside', Dudley Moore told me, 'and so, for me, the words, 'English country lanes' conjures up the mood of

---

101   •   CASTLE LANE — DUDLEY MOORE OBE

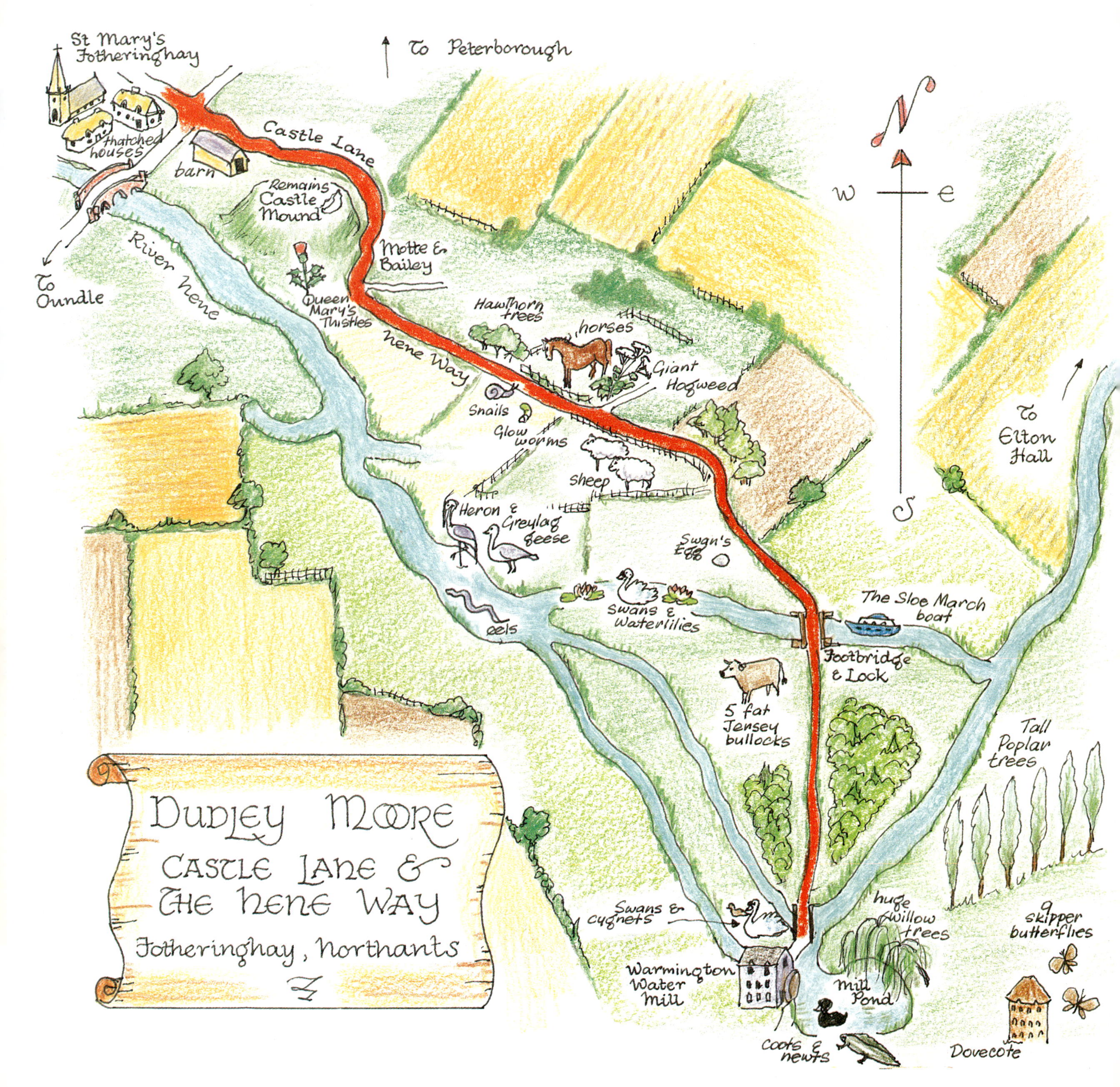
St Mary's Fotheringhay
To Peterborough
thatched houses
barn
Castle Lane
Remains Castle Mound
Motte & Bailey
To Oundle
River Nene
Queen Mary's Thistles
Nene Way
Hawthorn trees
horses
Giant Hogweed
Snails
Glow worms
Sheep
Heron & Greylag geese
Swan's Egg
swans & waterlilies
eels
The Sloe March boat
Footbridge & Lock
5 fat Jersey bullocks
To Elton Hall
Tall Poplar trees
W
E
N
S
DUDLEY MOORE
CASTLE LANE & THE NENE WAY
Fotheringhay, Northants
Swans & cygnets
huge willow trees
skipper butterflies
Warmington Water Mill
Mill Pond
Coots & newts
Dovecote

that wonderful song *We'll Walk Together Down An English Lane*. It is one of my very favourite songs and reduces me to tears if I allow myself the exquisite pleasure of playing it. Whenever I hear that music, the lane springs up, ideal and sweet-smelling in my brain, and so that romantic, tranquil and rather idealised lane is probably the only one I "know" really well. But the historical events which have taken place in and around so many English lanes have always fascinated me — those such as Castle Lane in Fotheringhay, now a quiet place in an almost forgotten corner of England running alongside the River Nene, which at one time was the most well-known place in England after London. So many historically important people have lived here or have been born here — among them, Richard III, the ruthless Plantagenet and Mary Queen of Scots was imprisoned and executed here. It is a place of intrigue, corruption and desperate power struggles, the machinations of the court and the focus for the beliefs of a country. The course of English history has been changed here.

English country lanes are hidden treasures which were embedded in my childhood consciousness. When I was young, I can remember thinking that a country lane was one of the few places where one can savour one's isolation and yet not feel alone. England has so many winding, truly lovely lanes — even the secret "lost" lanes in the cities. Here, the unexpected vision of elderberry trees in full bloom growing in the sparsest soil along narrow edges, softening the hard shapes of the buildings, stuns the senses; or the sight of yellow fringes of coltsfoot struggling out of cracks between cobblestones or even thrusting up through strips of cement, and the lyrical song of a blackbird somewhere above, lightens the heart.

▷ Warmington Dovecote.

CASTLE LANE – DUDLEY MOORE OBE

ENGLISH COUNTRY LANES • 104

And in the countryside, the lanes going by waving cornfields or wending their way by full, flowing rivers — lanes teeming with wildlife, with flowers in abundance, insects, birds, sounds and scents — each one astounds in its glorious beauty. Lanes — dearest treasures of the English countryside to be cherished in my memory and placed forever in my heart.'

This section of the Nene Way leading to Castle Lane begins by Warmington Dovecote and Warmington Water Mill, goes by the mill pond, across fields, over footbridges, by weirs, along a small track between cornfields, and then changes to Castle Lane, passes the river, the remains of Fotheringhay Castle mound and moat, runs past an ancient long barn, along a farm track and ends by the thatched cottages in the village of Fotheringhay. It is a distance of just under two miles (3km).

An eighteenth-century farmhouse and working farm is at the beginning of this part of the Nene Way. The way goes downhill, passing a warm, grassy banking which rises into a mound. There are flowers mixed in the grasses and behind the banking are voluminous blackberry bushes in full flower. A host of brown skipper butterflies hovers among the pale pink petals or floats effortlessly across to the grasses. A hawthorn tree farther on has pale green berries forming and, peering out from between its branches, are two inquisitive goats, brown and white, their sleek ears sticking up, almost poking through the leaves, listening and standing up on their hind legs, front legs resting on fencing, trying to push as close as they can to the path. Here the A605 road, hidden by tall trees, cuts across the way and Warmington Dovecote stands in the corner of the field called Chair Field, left, isolated, somehow out of time.

The dovecote is 300 years old. A circular stone building with a wooden roof, it housed 800 pigeons. The Romans introduced dovecotes into England and their use was later revived by the Normans in the eleventh century. Pigeons were bred for their meat. The birds entered the dovecote through a covered opening at the top of the roof called the lantern or glover. Nest boxes were usually made of stone but those in this dovecote are made from wood covered with mortar. Inside, there is a rotating ladder called a potence used for collecting pigeons and their eggs. The doorway is small so that a person had to bend down to enter and the pigeons were not frightened. A pair of pigeons produces two offspring, called squabs, eight to ten times a year. The eggs hatch in seventeen days. In the seventeenth and eighteenth centuries, eating pigeon meat was believed to prevent plague and other diseases and pigeon milk is similar in taste to mammals' milk. Pigeon droppings were used to make potions and treat baldness, gout and tumours. They were also a source of the saltpetre used in making gunpowder. Pigeons' feathers were collected for stuffing pillows and beds. At one time, only important landowners could own dovecotes but eventually the right to have them was extended to other people.

After the grassy banking, the way goes under the road tunnel and arrives at a large mill pool next to Warmington Water Mill and the River Nene. The mill pool is deep and round; the surface dark, green and still. Poplar trees and crack willow are at the far side. Their pale leaves flutter and shimmer in the warm evening breeze. Great reed mace, rushes, sedges, purple loosestrife, yellow flag iris, kingcups and codlins and cream are crushed together, striving for the best position to reach the sun. Water lilies are static in the centre of the pool like yellow islands.

◁ *Warmington Water Mill.*

---

105 • CASTLE LANE – DUDLEY MOORE OBE

White butterflies are on the lilies. In the reeds are reed warblers, frogs, toads, newts, great crested newts and water shrews, moving around in the rushes and reeds, restless after a hot drowsy day. Some house martins swoop low over the pool, picking off the midges for their evening meal. Farther away from the pool where the grass is smoother are banks of clover and daisies and a thick sward of great hairy willow herb is besieged by banded damselflies.

Warmington Mill is a three-storey, partly restored stone-built water mill belonging to the Probys, descendants of Sir Peter Proby and Sir Thomas Proby who lived at Elton Hall in 1666. The mill is not working now but until the 1860s it was a busy place. The mill was called a double mill because there were two stones made from millstone grit for grinding corn — a rough stone for coarse flour and a smooth stone for finer flour. The miller was usually a peasant who had to work in the fields as well as run the mill. Two water-wheels made from sturdy 'wet' oak were on the inside of the mill and the beams in the roof were made from the same wood. The water flowed from the river into two millraces beneath two tunnels going under the mill. The tunnels channelled water to the wheels.

A mill has stood on this spot since 1086 when it was recorded in the *Domesday Book*, but the present mill dates from the early nineteenth century. At the front of the mill are sluice gates and locks with a cast-iron winding handle and gear wheels, carefully oiled, dating from the late eighteenth century. Carts would come rumbling along the uneven, rocky lanes to the mill, pulled by heavy horses. They would stop underneath the projecting crane house, waiting to unload the grain or collect the flour.

Sometimes they had to cross the river at the ford to go to Woodnewton and Kingscliffe in the north-west, Nassington in the north and Elton and Water Newton to the north-east. Tatterstock and Tansor were to the south.

Attached to the back of the mill is an eel trap — a section of fast-flowing water passing through a grille. Eels were a staple part of the diet in the Middle Ages and a valuable source of income. At that time, Warmington Mill was valued at forty shillings and the rent could be paid in eels. The abbot of Ramsey paid the abbot of Peterborough, which is eight miles (13km) away, a fee of 4,000 eels for the right to quarry stone.

In summer, the river is thronged with eels. They come from the Sargasso Sea, thousands of miles away across the Atlantic. They travel as transparent, leaf-like larvae and are carried to the coastal waters of this country. Here they are transformed into three-inch (7.5cm) elvers and they find their way into most British rivers and still waters. Eels can live out of water and can move overland for short distances in autumn when the ground is wet, breathing aerated water carried in their gills. Female eels grow up to sixty inches (150cm) in length and males up to twenty inches (50cm). Silver-grey and greeny-brown, they writhe through the water in great numbers. At the end of summer, the mature eels set off back across the Atlantic to spawn and die.

After the mill and mill pool, the Nene Way footpath bears north-east, crossing a slightly undulating grassy meadow by the edge of mixed woodland. Glistening grasses shimmer and bend in the warm breeze, their silky heads lit up like luminous glowing haloes: timothy, rye, meadow foxtail, meadow fescue, couch grass, false oat grass and more. Brown skipper butterflies flutter around

▷ Fotheringhay Bridge

ENGLISH COUNTRY LANES • 106

107 • CASTLE LANE — DUDLEY MOORE OBE

wild iris at the side of a wooden bridge spanning boggy ground. A short distance along the path is another footbridge which crosses a wide stream coming from the mill and main body of the river, then goes by a dried-up stream with a few isolated hawthorn bushes, bramble bushes in full flower, and magnificent clumps of soft-headed spear thistle. Peacock butterflies surround the purple thistles. A large blue swan's egg is on the ground, one side of it smashed in, bite-size; yolk dripping out, the culprit disturbed. Overhead, a grey heron goes by on a straight course; serene and regal, it flies on, legs neatly tucked under its body, neck folded, head facing forward, intent on its destination.

The way approaches Warmington Lock and Weir. A bridge is incorporated in the iron structure. Five fat Jersey bullocks are sitting down next to the iron railings, close together in a pale brown heap. Their eyes are closed, shutting out the slanting rays of the sun. A blue-painted boat with the name *Sloe March* painted on the stern is approaching the lock. It has a shiny brass Samson post and brass-ringed portholes, and a new white painter attached to the bow. A petite lady with short, grey hair and an engaging smile hops off on to the lock side, throws a stern line around the bollard and begins to wind the handle which opens the lock gates.

'Hard work, this', she said smiling, 'especially alone. But I am determined to do it.' She continued winding the iron handle. 'I want to prove I can still sail my boat single-handed on the river. I've been away from it for a while and I've missed her so much.' She carried on winding and the first set of lock gates began to open. 'Slowly at first', she said, 'so that the water pressure can equalise. This is a guillotine lock', she explained, 'because the high iron pulley looks like the guillotine. There are quite a few locks on this stretch of the river but I enjoy them. It gives me a chance to stretch my legs'.

ENGLISH COUNTRY LANES • 108

The water levelled off and she pulled the boat into the lock with the painter attached to the bow. Keeping hold of the painter with her left hand, she wrapped the stern line around her shoulder and with her other hand continued guiding her boat through the lock.

'A tricky manoeuvre, this', she smiled disarmingly. 'There is absolutely nothing boring about this river. It's my favourite. The name "Nene" is an old English word meaning brilliant — and it most certainly is. This part of the river splits into three wide, meandering loops and farther on is the beginning of an ox-bow lake, caused by natural erosion and silting. It's a fine river — clear, clean and tranquil — the slowest-running river in the country, so they say, and stuffed with fish: tench, gudgeon, bream, carp, roach, minnows, sticklebacks and plenty of eels. The river spans thirty-two miles [51km] in this district, from Rushden in the south to Yarwell in the north-east. My moorings are at March in Cambridgeshire, twenty miles [32km] away downstream. I'm having a few days' holiday and going where my fancy takes me — messing about in boats. That's me.'

She began to open the second set of lock gates, still holding on to the lines.

'The river has always been navigable from way back. Romans, Saxons, Danes and Normans used it to bring cattle here and this made it an important agricultural area.'

Reluctant to let go of the line attached to the stern she held in her right hand, she juggled the painter at the bow to make sure that the boat went through the lock.

'Later it was a means of access to and from the tanning and leather industries for which Northamptonshire is famous. Way before all that, this whole area was marsh-land or fen with rich vegetation — reeds and sedges. Now there are lush alluvial meadows growing corn. Someone in the sixteenth century — a man called Leland, I think — described this land as "mervelus faire corne ground and pasture". He was right. I love to sail the *Sloe March* along the River Nene, passing through the meadows. An utterly peaceful occupation.'

Here the Nene Way skirts the riverbank. There are reeds, flowering rush, wood club rush, toad rush, water-mint, water parsnips, great burnet and yellow iris in enormous knotted bunches. A mother swan and her cygnet cruise into a backwater thickened with white and yellow water lilies. Together, they dip their heads into the water, bending their slender necks, the cygnet mimicking the mother's every move. The long rays of the sun light up the shape of their heads, silhouetting them against the orange sky. Behind them a full moon, low in the sky, is reflected on the river surface.

On the banking, a large mixed flock of Canada and greylag geese watch anxiously as a multitude of goslings move up and down the river, breaking ranks. The parents follow, waddling on the banking, first upstream, then downstream, the greylags hooting crossly as they are ignored. A couple of dedicated parents take to the air to get a better view, then settle on the water in front of the goslings, pushing them off-course, showing them who is in control.

After Warmington Lock and Weir, the way crosses a field, reaches another stile and becomes a farm track going north-west through cultivated fields and over a disused railway line. Barley, oats and wheat are massed at either side — waving yellow crops as far as the eye can see. Skeletons of giant hogweed stand sentinel along the track, their heads embossed with ripe, brown seeds. Underneath are poppies, nettles and golden grasses with hairy tops. There is utter silence until a clumsy pheasant crash-lands in the barley and sets up a squawking, irritable, chattering cry.

A field further on has been harvested. Stubble sticks up in bare rows, the long stalks already picked up for straw. Some of the straw is used for bedding, some for thatching. Wheat straw is often used for thatching, along with reed, heather, gorse and broom. The thatching in Fotheringhay, Elton and the surrounding districts is reed thatching.

The craft of thatching has hardly altered since the Middle Ages. Bundles of reeds, or yealms, are secured to the roof beams with iron hooks; more yealms are added in horizontal layers and fastened to timbers with spar hooks and hazel sways. Sways are often used to decorate the thatch with the thatcher's own style. The thatcher uses a leggat — a square, flat pad with serrated edges to get the thatch into the shape he desires. When he has the shape he wants, the roof ridge is strengthened by rows of hazel pegs. A good thatch can last up to sixty years. The cottages at the end of Castle Lane in Fotheringhay have picturesque, honey-coloured thatch, and there are more beautifully thatched cottages, houses and public houses in Elton and all over this area.

Across the wide meadows to the south-west is Cotterstock Hall with its fine avenue of elms reaching down to the River Nene. Cotterstock Hall was built in 1658 and is an elegant country house made from wrought stone with mullioned windows. John Dryden (1631-1700), the greatest English poet, dramatist and literary critic of the late seventeenth century, lived here with his cousin.

Dryden was born at Aldwinkle, Northamptonshire, the son of a country gentleman. He was such a great influence on the literary scene of his day that it was known as the Age of Dryden. He wrote heroic, public poetry with scientific ideas reflecting the new Age of Enlightenment, and celebrated events such as the victory of the English fleet over the Dutch and the Londoners' survival of the Great Fire of 1666. He was made poet laureate in 1668. His early work as a dramatist thrilled audiences who loved to be entertained by 'drums, trumpets, rants and extravagances, stage battles and exotic scenes' but later he became famous as a brilliant, sophisticated satirist.

A mile (1.5km) away eastwards across the fields is Elton Hall, the romantic, Gothic house that has been the family home of the Probys for over 300 years. The land and property was granted to Sir Peter Proby, lord mayor of London and comptrollor of the royal household, by Elizabeth I. In 1666, Sir Thomas Proby completed the building of the house. Every room contains famous works of art: old masters by Constable, Reynolds, and Gainsborough, and pre-Raphaelite works by Millais and Alma Tedema. Henry VIII's prayer book, which contains notes written by himself and two of his wives, is in the library. Elton Hall stands in unspoilt landscaped parkland and the Victorian garden has 1,000 old-fashioned roses. On a warm July afternoon, their fragrance is a memorable experience.

Now the way becomes a narrow track between the fields, continuing north-westward. Wheat, barley, maize and oat grass grow in mixed profusion at both sides of the path, spilled out of the fields from previous plantings. The soft hairs on the seed heads are incandescent in the amber light. Dipping down through meadow cranesbill, common mallow, cornflowers, woundwort and more thistles, the way passes twisted hawthorn trees with winding pink convulvulus beneath.

A large burdock stands in isolation at the corner of the path with four-spot ladybirds on its strong, thick stem. Border Leicester sheep sit down in the field near the river, settled for the night. At this point, the Nene Way becomes part of Castle Lane with the lantern tower of St Mary's Church, Fotheringhay, looking down. A black corrugated farm building is on the left with black bags of silage stacked up nearby. The sweet smell of the grass inside them seeps out into the lane.

A little farther along is a gate on the left-hand side which leads to Fotheringhay Castle mound and the moat. The grassy mound is riddled with rabbit holes, twisted hawthorns grow all over it, and on the top are tall and stately Scotch thistles — purple-headed milk thistles with pale green prickles growing in great splendour. Fat bees, wasps, hoverflies and burnet moths are in their heads. It is said that Mary Queen of Scots planted the original thistles when she was imprisoned in the castle to remind her of home and that they have survived and multiplied since that time. The village people call them 'Mary's thistles'. By the side of the river, in a square iron enclosure, is one large piece of stone — all that is left of the majestic castle which once stood here.

Fotheringhay was, at one time, the most famous place in England next to the capital. The castle was built by Simon de Liz, first earl of Huntingdon, in 1100, as a Norman stronghold against raids from the English in the Fens. It had a motte and bailey, a strong tower of stone and cement with crenellated walls on top, a deep ditch, two chapels, a great hall, two chambers, a kitchen with a stone oven, and a gate-house with a chamber above and a drawbridge underneath. Outside the castle were two gates, a moat around the north and west sides, and a river on the south side, and the castle had a strong keep. There was an outer moat on the right-hand side of the lane and behind this, a lake. The outer moat went around to Fotheringhay Bridge over the river.

From 1461, Fotheringhay was the principle seat of the Plantagenets and a favourite residence of King Edward IV. He had a great affection for the castle, and it was said that 'the love he bare to Foderingey' never diminished. Yet for others, the castle was cursed. Many tragic events took place there. The castle was the home of Mary of Valence, countess of Pembroke, whose husband was killed in a tournament on their wedding day. Edward, second duke of York, rode out from the castle to gain glory in the French wars but was killed at Agincourt in 1415. His body is buried in the collegiate chuch of Fotheringhay. His nephew, Richard, duke of York, lived at the castle and became the father of two kings: Edward IV and Richard III. During the Wars of the Roses, 1455-1485, Duke Richard and his third son, Edmund, earl of Rutland, were killed at the Battle of Wakefield in 1460. After a temporary burial at Pontefract, their bodies were brought back to Fotheringhay in July 1466 in great pomp, escorted by the future King Richard III. Their coffins were carried along the lane in a chariot, 'covered in black velvet, richly wrapped in cloths of gold and Royal habit'. They were to be buried at the Church of St Mary — the magnificent, Perpendicular church which towers over the landscape at the end of the lane.

Richard III was an enigmatic and controversial king who was born in the castle and spent the first six years of his life at Fotheringhay. Henry Tudor, Richard's rival during the War of the Roses, engaged him at the Battle of Bosworth Field in 1485. Richard's forces were more numerous than Henry's, but several of the king's most powerful nobles changed sides at a crucial moment in the battle and Richard was killed. Richard was the last Yorkist king of England and the last English monarch to die in battle. His life was haunted by tragedy and political treachery, and his reputation is that of a 'sinister, monstrous villain', who took the twelve-year-old

▷ *Fotheringhay Castle mound.*

ENGLISH COUNTRY LANES • 112

Edward V and his nine-year-old brother into custody and put them in the Tower of London for safe-keeping. In August 1483, they disappeared. Their uncle, Richard III it is said, had them murdered so that he could proclaim himself the rightful king. His reign lasted only two years, but during that time he became known as an astute statesman and a good general, and was brave, charming and loyal to his subjects. A quiet, sincere man, slightly puritanical, he did not approve of the frivolities of the court. During his rule, he tried to free poorer people from oppression. He created a court for poor men's pleas, founded councils in the North to provide justice and harmony, and instituted financial reforms throughout the country.

In 1509, Henry VIII gave Fotheringhay Castle to his betrothed wife, Catherine of Aragon and then later, wanted to imprison her there. Knowing the reputation of the castle, she refused to go unless 'bound with ropes and carried thither'; and in 1587, the most tragic event of all took place when Mary Queen of Scots was beheaded in the great hall.

Mary Queen of Scots first came to Fotheringhay on the 25th September 1586, by way of Perio Lane to the east of the village, passing the great Church of St Mary and the college, and going along the wide village street and down Castle Lane to her internment in the castle. As she approached, she had a great sense of foreboding that she would never leave this place. She was kept prisoner here until her execution.

Queen Mary Stuart — Mary Queen of Scots — was born in 1542 in Scotland and was sent to France to be educated as a child. She was cosseted in the French court, and as a young woman she was surrounded by luxury and splendour as she stayed in French palaces and chateaux. Her everyday existence was filled with lavish entertainments — riding, dancing, music. She had fine jewels and exquisite clothes, and she had a great love of animals — birds of all kinds, falcons especially. She had four big dogs and twenty-two lap dogs, but her great passion was music. She was highly educated and spoke Greek and Spanish, with French her first language. Mary was an amazing beauty. Tall, at five foot eleven inches (1.8m), with a slender figure, red-gold hair and amber-coloured eyes. She married a young prince — the Dauphin — and was a widow at eighteen. She grew into a French woman rather than a Scot.

Mary had Tudor blood, inherited through her grandmother, Henry VIII's sister, and because of this she was next in line to the English throne. When she returned to Scotland in 1561, she was totally unprepared for life in the small, sparse castles set in bleak highland countryside surrounded by uncouth Scottish nobles who spent their

ENGLISH COUNTRY LANES • 114

time in petty feuding and whose way of speaking she could not understand. This was a great shock to a sensitive, romantic, impressionable young woman.

She felt that she could not rule the country unaided, and fell in love and married Henry Stuart Darnley — a handsome, weak, reckless and vicious man who was an ambitious womaniser. He was also jealous and hated her cultured, intellectual and sophisticated private secretary, David Riccia — Rizzio — with whom the queen spoke French, played cards and made music, and whom she relied upon for advice. One evening while they were playing cards at Holyrood Palace, Darnley burst in with a group of nobles, dragged Rizzio from the room and stabbed him to death in front of the queen's own eyes. After this, she never trusted her husband again, believing him to be after her own life.

Soon Mary became totally fascinated by James Hepburn, earl of Bothwell, who was a good-looking, virile man. After a grave illness in 1566, not long after the birth of her son James — who later became James I of England — she decided to divorce Darnley. An attempt was made to blow him up in a house in Kirk o' Field in Edinburgh. He escaped, but was caught and strangled. Bothwell was the chief suspect and Mary was implicated. Three months after her husband's murder, she allowed herself to be married to Bothwell. She believed that his strength of personality would help her to rule Scotland. The Scottish people were furious and lost faith in her. They wanted the infant James to be king, so they locked Mary up in Loch Leven Castle. During a brief interlude of freedom, she tried unsuccessfully to regain her throne and, defeated, she fled to England to seek the protection of her cousin, Elizabeth I.

Elizabeth was a Protestant and Mary was Catholic, dangerous to Elizabeth because she represented Catholic hopes in England. Knowing that Mary posed a threat to her position, Elizabeth kept her under house arrest in various castles around the country for nineteen years.

In 1586, Anthony Babington hatched a plot to assassinate Elizabeth I and replace her with Queen Mary. When this was discovered, Mary was said to be the instigator. At her trial, she was faced with many lawyers, but was not allowed one lawyer to represent her, and she was condemned and brought to Fotheringhay Castle, where she endured the 'dark, dense winter fogs' of the Nene Valley, homesickness and loneliness. Eventually, against her will, for she did not want to be responsible for Mary's death, Elizabeth signed her death warrant.

They came in the evening. At eight o' clock. February 1587 — to tell her that this was to be her last night on this earth. When she heard the news, her reply was dignified:

'I thank you for such welcome news. You will do me great good in withdrawing me from this world out of which I am very glad to go.'

'Well, Jane Kennedy, did I not tell you this would happen', she said to her attendant. 'I knew they would never allow me to live. I was too great an obstacle to their religion.' She was forty-four years old.

She had little time to prepare herself. After a frugal supper, she carefully went through all her possessions: money, clothes, jewels, personal mementos, silver boxes, miniatures and enamelled tablets, and divided them up for her servants and royal relations abroad. She made her will to provide for the welfare of her servants. Then she said farewell to her chaplain for she was to be denied all spiritual comfort in her last hours. Finally, she wrote to her brother-in-law, King Henry of France, relating the circumstances of her death. All this took until two o' clock in the morning. Then she lay down on her bed to rest, and rose at six to pray and prepare herself. Just before eight, she looked out of the window for one last time at the skeleton shapes of her Scottish thistles standing on the castle mound, the nearby River Nene and the peaceful fields.

At eight o' clock she was sent for and came to the great hall in silence. She was to die alone. Her servants were to be held back. Only when Sir William Fitzwilliam, who had been extremely courteous to her during her imprisonment, had the servants' word that they would not cry out, were six of them allowed in. Three hundred spectators gathered to watch the famous queen beheaded.

Queen Mary had taken care to dress elegantly and regally for her execution in a black satin dress embroidered with black velvet and set with black acorn buttons of jet trimmed with pearl, the sleeves slashed with royal purple. She wore Spanish leather shoes in black edged with silver. Her garters were green silk and her petticoat crimson, and on her head she wore a black mantle and white veil with white lace next to her pale face. Mary's cool and dignified approach to her death, her absolute faith in her innocence, and the knowledge that the court that had condemned her was illegal and that she had died a martyr to her faith, contrasted with the 'panic-stricken' behaviour of the English after the axe had fallen and the queen was dead.

They were frantic in their attempts to get rid of all the blood-stained relics. They washed and re-washed Mary's pet dog which had hidden under her petticoats and accompanied her to the execution block, for it was covered in its mistress's blood. After the execution, no one was allowed out of the castle except Lord Talbot, who set off at full gallop along Castle Lane, going to London to tell Elizabeth that the deed was done. In July of the same year, they took Mary's coffin to Peterborough Cathedral in the dead of night in a torchlight procession which went first along the lane, then by Elton and Orton. Later her son, by now James I, had her body buried in Westminster Abbey. Queen Mary's tempestuous life, her lost loves, her doomed marriages, the betrayal by her son, her many years of imprisonment, her execution and the dignity with which she faced all this have made her into a legend.

After the gate, the lane turns to the right. Pied wagtails bob about on the sandy surface and some dapple-grey horses are in the field at the side of the lane. Collared doves call out from tall pine trees and finches are roosting. On the opposite side is a very ancient, extremely long barn, the aged pantiles on the roof thickened with dark, green moss and white stonecrop. Valerian grows out of the walls. The lane bends to the right once more and a row of thatched cottages comes into view. Castle Farm guesthouse is on the left at the end of the lane and the New Inn, now a private house and the place where Queen Mary's executioner spent the night in secret, is on the right, with its large Gothic arch decorated with roses and quatrefoils — the arms of the House of York.

A little way along from the inn, opposite more pretty thatched cottages, to the south-west is Fotheringhay Bridge, restored by order of Queen Elizabeth I in 1573 because she could not cross the river other than by a deep ford.

The lane ends in the Main Street, Fotheringhay, a quiet, wide street, its width showing the importance of its position in Norman times. Farther along the street there are more picturesque cottages, perfectly thatched, and at either side and behind them are giant chestnut trees and the gateway to St Mary's Church. From here, the road goes to Model Cottages and Walcott Lodge, with a section turning southwards to Perio Mill along Perio Lane to Cotterstock.

I spent the evening wandering down the river path, mesmerised by the

◁ *Thatched cottages in Fotheringhay village.*

ENGLISH COUNTRY LANES • 118

reflection of the sun's rays on the surface of the water, the low light on the leaves of the willow trees by the mill pool, the rainbow colours in the weir and the prisms in the bubbles rising up from below. The sky was blood-red; the strong sunbeams struck the scarlet fields and the tops of the thatch on the cottages in the village. Everything was peaceful and perfect and still. Pink and orange and gold clouds gathered above the church tower as the sun was setting, the tower splitting the rays, radiating them outwards, illuminating the landscape, warming the castle mound.

I sat on the banking by Fotheringhay Bridge, listening to the songs of two young men, playing guitars, resting by their tents as they camped on the mound. A narrow-boat was moored by the last piece of castle stone, the owners dining outside, a table set on the grass, a lamp and a bottle of wine shining in the late evening light.

I waited until the moon was high, then walked into the lane thinking about the woman imprisoned in the castle and longing to be free. Knowing she had seen the same sun, the same tranquil river, the same skies and the same full moon, I puzzled at the strength of human vows, our deep and desperate beliefs, our minds and the longing in our souls. I stayed until the moon rose higher and watched the sheep still playing in the thistles, the rabbits sitting under the twisted trees, the geese and swans sleeping by the river, and the bats beginning to be busy in the clear night sky.

Then I stood in the silence, watching the shadows of the moonlit grasses on the surface of the lane, the silver trails of the snails and the glow-worms under the trees, savouring the sweet smell of the crops in the fields, the presence of cow breath on the soft night air and the sound of the bullocks still snoozing on the same warm spot.

◁ *St Mary's Church, Fotheringhay.*

Chiddenbrook Lane, Crediton, Devon

Dame Margot Fonteyn

High summer

*'I loved the deep Devon lanes sunk into the red earth
all set about with blossom-filled hedges …'*

Chiddenbrook Lane adorns the landscape like a softly blossoming frill as it dips and rises and curls across slumbering, hump-backed fields rich in their counterpane colours.

Here is a picture-book lane, perfect and complete, which folds into small, warm valleys, languishes under hedgerows matted with honeysuckle and wild white roses, dawdles by glistening streams, then dreams on through breathtaking grass verges which go on and on. A million flowers grow in the sun. Snails — whole armies of them — climb succulent slender stems, ladybirds like dappled lockets creep through miniature green thickets, grasshoppers sit on the leaves and send out their signature tunes, and shining black bugs sleep on huge platesful of creamy elderberry flowers crowding round hidden cob cottages set deep in the red earth. Black and white cows graze on multicoloured coombes, bright yellow tractors drone around their distant hay-making, and feather-bed clouds float on in idyllic nursery skies. This is a place of childhood — of memories and warmth and sweetly drawn dreams.

Margot Fonteyn used to go to Devon with her mother and her brother for their summer holidays when she was a teenager.

'We thought it marvellous to bring tents and camp out in the rolling fields. We would wake up on a fine summer morning and feel ourselves in perfect harmony with the earth and the sky, and we would set off and wander barefoot across the sand dunes, and once we found an abandoned church half-buried in the wild grass — this was

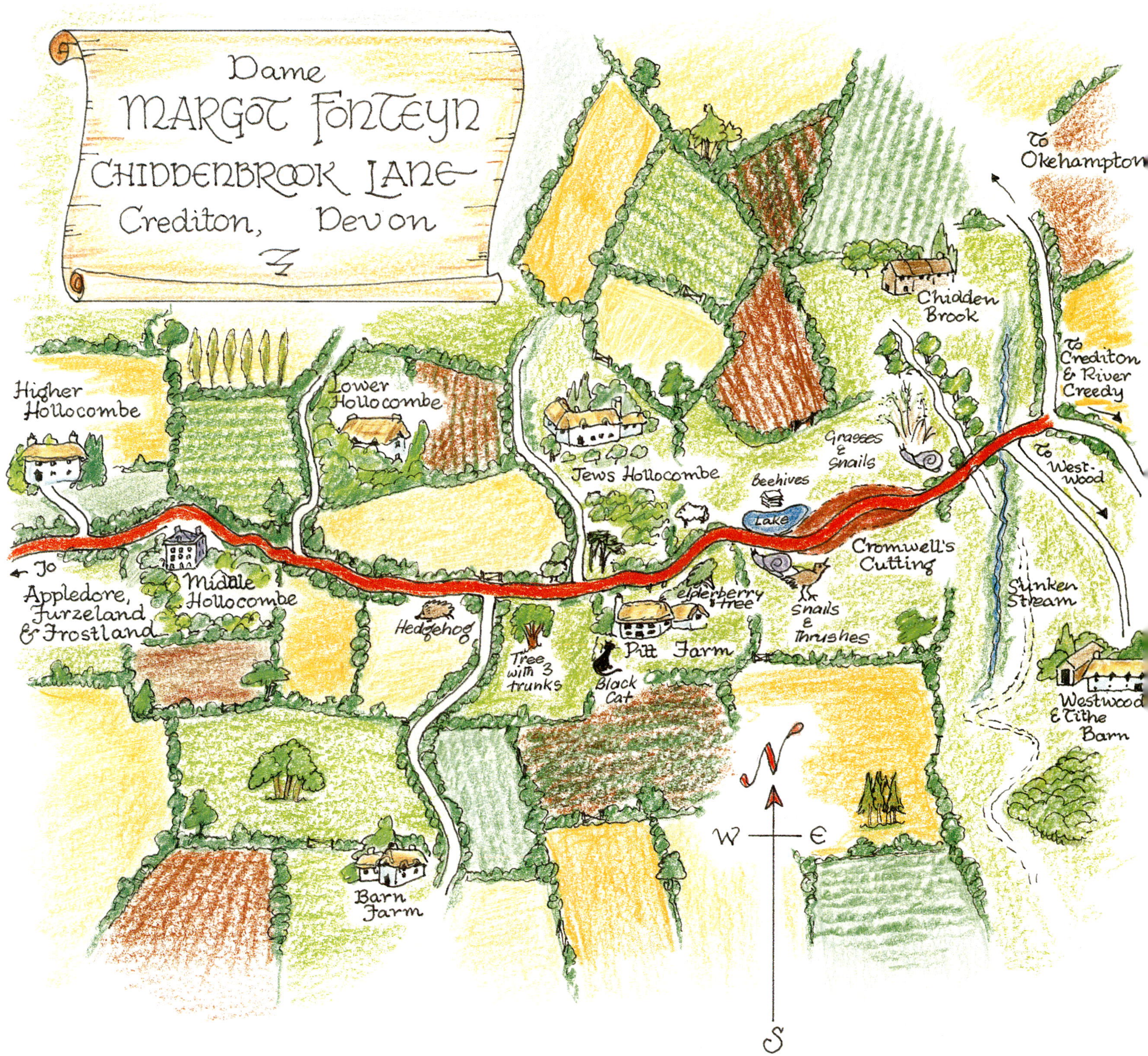

Dame
Margot Fonteyn
Chiddenbrook Lane
Crediton, Devon
To Okehampton
Chidden Brook
To Crediton & River Creedy
Higher Hollocombe
Lower Hollocombe
Jews Hollocombe
Grasses & Snails
To West-wood
Beehives
Lake
Cromwell's Cutting
To Appledore, Furzeland & Frostland
Middle Hollocombe
Hedgehog
elderberry tree
Snails & Thrushes
Sunken Stream
Pitt Farm
Tree with 3 trunks
Black Cat
Westwood & Tithe Barn
N
W
E
S
Barn Farm

the epitome of romantic feeling for innocent teenagers. And then we would explore the country lanes, feeling the history in them and sensing the people who had used them. I loved the deep Devon lanes sunk into the dark red earth all set about with blossom-filled hedges, festooned with flowers and soft grasses — their fragrance filled the air and I can still recall it. Ever since I was quite young, certain combinations of landscape have aroused a curious sensation in my soul. It is somehow a sensual desire — to unite with the sun-dappled countryside and at the same time an overwhelming nostalgia as though I once inhabited those very places in centuries long past. Occasionally I have felt those brief flashes of understanding that Wordsworth described as "the intimations of immortality". These elusive experiences are always associated for me with the sun, which has an extraordinary importance in my life — and in Devon as a child, the sun always seemed to shine.'

Chiddenbrook Lane is at the east end of Crediton along the road which goes to Yeoford. It begins by a signpost which says 'Hollocombe Hamlets' and goes up Pitt Hill, past Pitt Farm and the turning to Jews Hollocombe, and ends at Hollocombe Cross. A distance of about two miles (3km).

At the start of this lane is a narrow wooden bridge which goes over a thin, sunken stream. The stream crosses under a bridge at right angles and continues in a straight line through the fields at either side. Stinging nettles, bog-bean, creeping buttercup, skullcap, watermint and tall clumps of meadowsweet go on quite far without a break, marking its course. Beyond the bridge, the lane climbs up at once, with hedges of birch, hazel, hawthorn and willows growing on high banking. The wide verges underneath are bursting with life — the grasses growing in earnest: wild oat, timothy, couch, cocksfoot meadow fescue, marram, tall brome, tor grass, tufted hair grass, black grass and sweet vernal grass. They are all along the edges, jumbled together in a brown haze baking in the sun and, mixed in the grasses, their colours blazing, are the flowers: cat's ear, field mouse-ear, mouse-tail, spiny rest-harrow, eyebright, speedwell, meadow vetchling, bristly ox-tongue, bindweed, agrimony, willow-herb, ragwort, goats-beard and more, and the hedge parsley, wild carrot and hogweed billowing up behind is piquant and heavy, and their heads stretch out into the middle of the lane.

Ladybirds are in the stems — black and red and black and yellow — handsome, hypnotic and greedy; and lower down where the grass is still green are the crickets — the great green bush cricket, the field cricket, the oak bush cricket — and the grasshoppers — long-horned grasshoppers and common green grasshoppers; all of them setting up a wheezing rattle which vibrates the stalks and shakes out the seeds. Snails climb up the stalks — grove snails, plaited door snails, white-lipped snails and sandhill snails — each one clinging on with a cold, powerful foot, seemingly unaware of the thrushes hanging from the lower branches of the trees, eyes bulging, heads sideways, wings half open, waiting. A few yards higher up from the stream is a turning on the left which leads to Westwood Farmhouse, Lower Westwood, the Old Smithy — a working blacksmiths until 1953 — and some cottages, four of them thatched. Westwood Farmhouse is a traditional Devon longhouse with a high roof, built on the site of an earlier Westwood, dated 1662 when a family called Snow owned the land. Later it belonged to the Shelleys and then the Lee family,

Cromwell's Cutting.

who have owned it for over 150 years. Lower Westwood Farmhouse is dated 1665. At that time it was a halfway rest house for royalty and the people of the court when they had to change horses *en route* to their summer estates in the West Country. In the meadow next to Lower Westwood is a seventeenth-century tithe barn, where at one time all the produce of the farm was kept before it was handed to the owner of the 'tithe' or tax rights — at this time the royal family — who could then, if they so wished, pass it on to a favoured layman. The payment of tithes was a compulsory law which was introduced by King Offa of Mercia in 794, and it was still in force in England until 1936. One tenth of the wood, corn, milk and eggs, and one tenth of the increase in the number of farm animals, was handed to the owner of the tithe rights until 1836, when the equivalent value in money became payable. No one could be excused payment. Even if the farmer did not till his land, an estimate would be made of the value of his crops and he had to pay the tithe in money.

Beyond the turning, the lane still rises. Tree sparrows chatter in the hedges, chaffinches flutter about and greenfinches are eating corn seeds which had fallen on to the surface of the lane. On the right a farm track edged with low sycamore trees and high banks of nettles and dock leads off to Chiddenbrook Farm. Chiddenbrook is also part of the Westwood Estate and was bought by the Lees in the nineteenth century. Once it was a dairy farm and smallholding, and its traditional farmhouse was set in large orchards. Some of the trees are still there but the house has been turned into cottages.

After the turning to Chiddenbrook, the lane reaches 300 feet (90m). Two rusting iron gates with the letter 'S' wrought into them look over the fields, one at either side, and the grasses here are effervescent and burgeoning, and go on filling the lane with their sweetness until it reaches the top of Pitt Hill where it bends to the north, widens slightly, and then unexpectedly and dramatically slices straight into the startling red earth of Cromwell's Cutting. The walls are fifty feet (15m) high. The soil is tightly packed, dark and damp, and the light is shut out. The earth smell is overpowering and a strange coldness comes from the towering walls. Tree roots are exposed. They point into the lane like the accusing, tortured fingers of some buried goblin trying to struggle out of the earth. There is no sound, only the fluttering of an unseen bird's wing, no movement, save a few pale butterflies investigating the ivy on the jagged rim, and little growth — a few ferns, some foxgloves and a patch of navelwort where the sun slants in.

Cromwell's Cutting was made by Oliver Cromwell's troops during the occupation of Crediton by the Parliamentary forces in January 1646 during the Civil War of 1642-1651. Cromwell was in Crediton preparing to challenge Sir Ralph Hopton and the Royalist army, who held Exeter nine miles (14km) to the south-east, their main objective being to cut off supplies from the Royalists, reduce resistance in the West and to wait for Cromwell to plan his spring campaign.

His men were restless. It was winter. January 1646. They were cold and tired, and they had been away from home for too long. They were not sure at this point who was winning the war, and the harsh discipline and rigorous training which Cromwell considered essential for their survival as a fighting force was hard to endure. Each day they did long hours of meticulous drill going up and down the lanes in full armour, or they practised their battle techniques in the fields adjoining this lane. But as the winter wore on and the cold increased, the men became low in spirits and longed for the comfort of their homes and their wives. So much so, that some of the men began bothering the womenfolk in Crediton. Complaints were made. Cromwell was told, and as a punishment he gave orders for the men to make the cutting. So they heaved the earth out of the top of Pitt Hill with small spades, banked it around the sides and made the walls fifty feet (15m) high and 100 yards (90m) long; a tremendous task which left them totally exhausted — far too tired to chase the women in Crediton.

Oliver Cromwell was a powerful leader who had gained prestige in the first part of the Civil War in 1642. He was a genius at organisation and unequalled in his tactics as a military commander, and because of his legendary energy and toughness he was nicknamed 'Old Ironsides'. Cromwell was tall and rugged, with a red face

Church of the Holy Cross, Crediton.

and a hot temper, and he often spoke his mind, glaring all the time as he did so with his piercing blue eyes. He was a formidable man with a magnetic personality, intensely practical and yet at the same time deeply religious — at times almost mystical. In his thirties he had undergone a profound spiritual conversion in which he had visions of his future greatness and which led him to guide all of his subsequent conduct by prayer and meditation. When he was in Crediton he visited the Church of the Holy Cross — the beautiful New Red Sandstone Perpendicular building where St Boniface, the Benedictine monk and missionary, founded a monastery in 739 — but Cromwell thought it too fancy. At times Cromwell suffered from long and deep depressions, and prolonged bouts of irresolution, and became so physically ill that the whole of his body was covered in terrible boils. But he did not give in to his illness, and became so dedicated to his cause and so persuasive as a speaker that, alone, he raised whole districts to declare against King Charles I and he re-organised the Parliamentary forces into the best professional army in England since Roman times — the New Model Army. This was a mobile army of formidable, fanatical and religious men made up of simple Puritan yeomen — small-scale English landowners who farmed their own fields — and whose profound belief in Cromwell and all he stood for inspired them to take up the task of seeking out their king and destroying his army in the field. On the 8th January 1646, Cromwell assembled his men in Crediton despite deep snow to take the field against the Royalist general in the west, Sir Ralph Hopton.

Cromwell's men in Crediton were the thick-set Cornish pikemen — a privileged class who were chosen for their size and strength. Each man was hand picked, and Cromwell's method of training transformed the God-fearing raw recruits into well-disciplined soldiers. His men were promoted by merit, not by birth, and his 'russet-coated' captains often rose to high rank, much to the amusement of the Royalists who considered them an inferior people. He made sure all their personal needs were taken care of: pay was punctual — twelve and a half pennies a day, even if it had to come from his own pocket; and he saw to it that his men had enough to eat. Moral standards were kept up: 'No man swears but he pays twelve pennies — a whole day's pay — if he be drunk he be set in the stocks or worse.' Their uniforms reflected their beliefs: plain and simply cut with no decoration other than the white Puritan collars attached to their striped jerseys or scarlet jackets. The broad-brimmed metal helmets and breast-plates that they wore were undecorated, and they carried plain swords in plain holders, and pikes — sixteen foot (5m) poles with axes fixed to the end. Their task was to stand and wait for the attack, forming solid squares twenty-five men broad and twenty-five men deep, whilst the musketeers skirmished outside the square. At the last moment the square opened, the musketeers ran inside and the pikemen were left to face the charging Royalist cavalry.

The town of Crediton had been under occupation by both sides of the Civil War at one time or another during the struggle for power between the Parliamentary forces under the leadership of Sir Thomas Fairfax and Oliver Cromwell, and Charles I's Royalist cavaliers under Sir Ralph Hopton in the west. The war had begun as a reaction to Charles's demands for money from his subjects to finance his interests in foreign wars, his persistence in raising it by illegal, non-constitutional means, his growing claims on the sovereign's divine right to rule, and his insistence on settling all the disputed questions in Church and Parliament himself. 'The King is not only glorious, but Glory, not only powerful, but Power', he said. But he was unaware of the unrest in his own country, did not realise that the rift in the English Church was widening, and he chose to ignore the fact that Puritanism was a growing force.

Charles I was a shy and lonely man; short in stature with a bad stammer and a pronounced Scottish accent. This made him a difficult, complex man — introverted, insecure and unapproachable, and as a king he often failed in his duties. He evaded essential matters, did not act when action was needed, was tactless in his speech, he broke all his promises and was faithless to his friends. Men came to realise that his word meant nothing, and eventually his double-dealings and his hesitations brought him to the execution block. By the time he visited Crediton in July 1644, the king had begun to realise just how far events were turning against him. He was forty-seven years old, already lined and haggard; his cheeks sagged, he had heavy bags under his eyes, his black hair and beard had gone grey, and he had not seen his wife, whom he loved dearly, for a very long time. But when he came to Crediton in July with his sons, Prince Maurice and Prince Charles, to review his troops in Lords Meadow by the side of the River Creedy, he seemed the epitome of the regal and dignified king, sure of his power and authority, and convinced of his ability to command the respect of his men.

The Royalist troops made a brilliant show as they stood in their ranks in the warm summer sunshine, filling the meadow with their colours. The smart officers were landed gentry or freehold farmers who enjoyed the best of everything — fine houses, beautiful wives and mistresses, the very best horses and a fine table. Their clothes were elegant and expensive, and reflected their flamboyant attitude to life. Jackets were richly embroidered with gold and silver buttons, loops and silver tracings on the split sleeves, and white or cream shot silk spread out from the splits. They had exquisite lace collars and cuffs freshly pressed and sewn on to their soft jerseys each day, and their silk tunics in clarets, yellows, lovat greens and crimsons fitted each man perfectly. Sumptuous silk sashes were tied across their chests in radiant, contrasting colours, and their soft, felt, large-brimmed hats were adorned in glorious feathers. They wore heavy leather boots with exaggerated wide tops and silver spurs, and their rapiers were narrow and finely cut. The Cavaliers were dashing and charming horsemen, and quite extravagant in all their behaviour, and the 'swashbuckling officers' were the extreme opposite of their adversaries who lived lives of Puritan simplicity. The Cavaliers operated as an army through a council of war with the king as their leader but, although they were excellent horsemen in the field, they were disorganised, insufficiently armed and they lacked discipline. On the 14th March 1646, the Royalists collapsed and Exeter fell. Sir Ralph Hopton's army signed the articles of surrender at Exeter the same day.

At the end of Cromwell's Cutting the walls drop steeply, the overpowering earth smell mixing with the scent of the roses; the silence is broken by the sound of bees, and the sunlight striking the surface of the lane is quite startling. There is a long slope, the lane turns

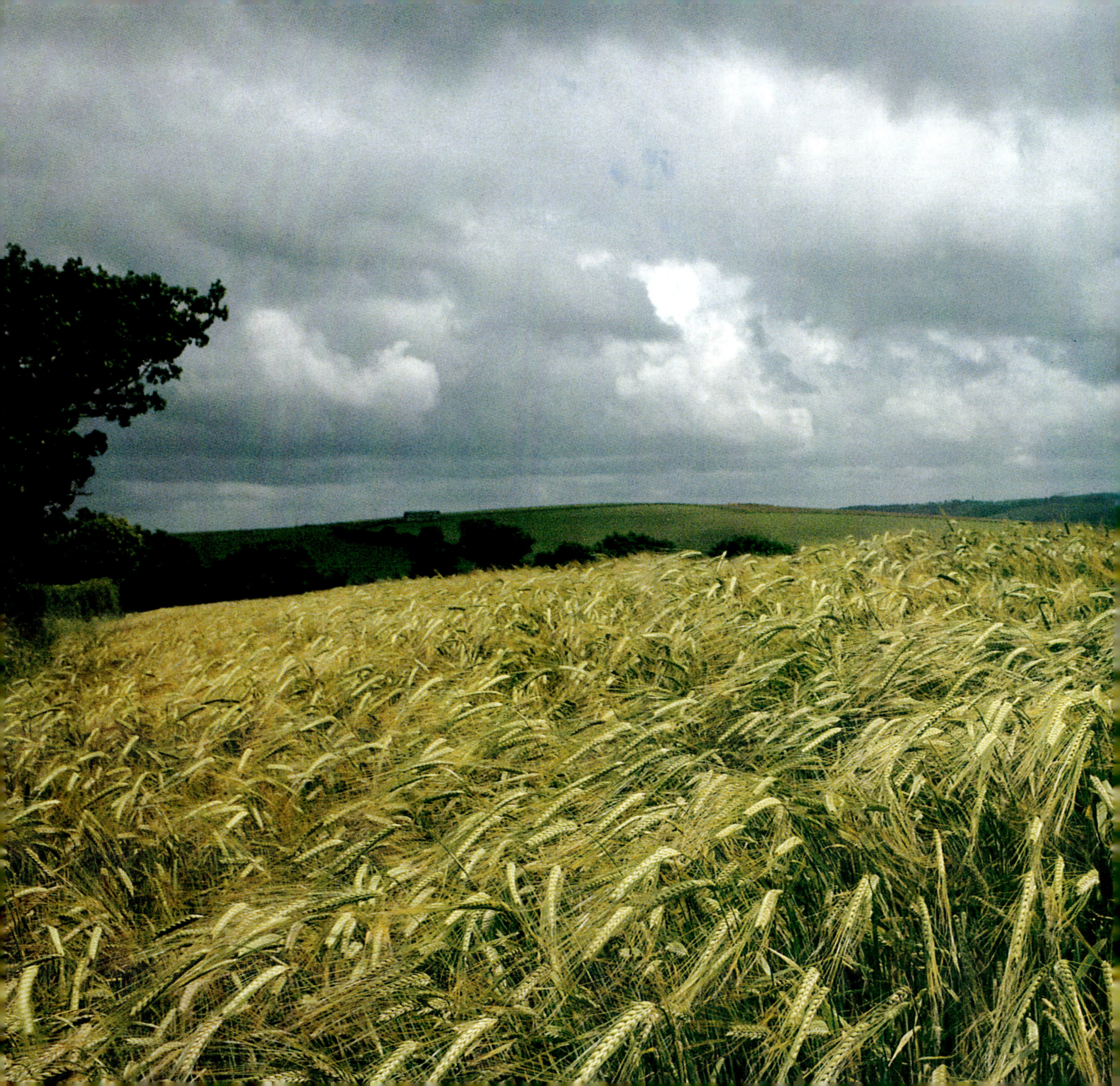

westwards again and all at once, set out in front, like an Arthur Rackham drawing, is a perfect dream landscape. The fields rise like dumplings, one behind the other, some deep red, ploughed and furrowed, some lush green and filled with grass, yet more a gentle brown with barley or amber gold with ripening wheat. Each field is a different height, spread out like a coloured quilt resting on the earth, and in between every one in a hazy frilling splendour are the blossoming hedgerows stuffed with roses, laced with honeysuckle, and thickened with the grasses and the parsley.

    A mixed hedge is on the right. Dog roses and field roses twist upwards, six feet (2m) high in the branches. The pale pink flowers of sweet briar roses are everywhere and the pure white bells of bindweed tumble out from every space. Burdock, sow thistle, cats ear, cow parsley and more go along both sides, soft and fuzzing in the warmth. Hundreds of greenfly squash on to the stems. There are more snails — three or four on each stalk, hidden in the grasses; and more thrushes, still hanging out from under the trees. Two of them stand in the centre of the lane smashing snails on a stray stone. One, victorious, lifts off, and the other, left puzzling over the weight of two gigantic snails, glued together, face to face, heavily into mating — ecstasy in death.

    Now the lane goes into a hollow before rising up again almost at once. Nestling in the bottom is Pitt Farmhouse and barn — two beautiful, ancient, round-roofed buildings 300 years old, and thatched with straw and moss. They stand on the left-hand side of the lane almost covered over by elderberry trees in full flower. The creamy blossoms are lush and full against the red fields behind. There are marigolds and geraniums in the garden, Ralph, the old sheepdog sleeps on the path and a fat black cat sat on the window sill dozing in the sun. The door was open and Mrs Coath, the farmer's wife, came bustling out and stood smoothing down her pinafore with a flour-covered hand.

'My husband likes his home cooking', she said, stroking the cat and leaving a white hand-print on its head. 'Apple pie and cream's his favourite, and roly-poly pudding and herby pie — we make our own cream on the farm and our own butter from the dairy cows. At one time there was cider and malt-making', she explained, 'but that's done now — things have changed.' She came into the garden and looked up at the chimney. 'This house was smaller and had an even lower roof. Half the house was kept for the horses to sleep in so that the men could feed them in the night without going out of doors. There were more people here then; farms were fifty to a hundred acres, now they are six hundred acres. The fields are getting bigger — all machines today. Nothing is the same any more. Except the smell of baking bread and hot apple pies', she said, laughing merrily as she ran in to see to her oven.

Across from Pitt Farm on the other side of the lane is a meadow. A few wooden beehives painted white were scattered here and there. Sheep were in amongst them — Mashams, Skiptons and Mules — breeds with short curly fleeces. Some were on their knees, bottoms in the air, tails wriggling in satisfaction as they grazed noisily on the juicy grass.

Here the lane gives a small but sharp turn north-west. A footpath goes across the field which leads to more fields then other footpaths. They criss-cross the countryside going to Broomhill Plantation, Jews Moor, Western Down Plantation and Slade Plantation. Another footpath on the left, just beyond Pitt Farm, goes to Moorlake and Moor Farm. A long steep rise goes up to Robins Down, a private bungalow, and the turning to Jews Hollocombe is on the right.

The grass verges are narrower now and the hedges grow on the banking, which is higher than before. Butterflies are in patches of nettle and dock — small copper, tortoiseshell and cabbage white, and a single clouded border moth seeking willow. There are house martins and swallows over the fields, and some blackbirds and thrushes shading themselves under the hawthorn leaves. At the corner of the turning are two Scots pine trees, towering upwards, tall and dark, their barks bright with sunlight, their smell strong and sharp. Ivy grows up the trunks as far as the lower branches. Two oaks are below, quite tall, but not very old, and then a beech tree with three enormous green-tinged trunks growing out of one.

Jews Hollocombe is the largest and most ancient farmhouse in the immediate area, and is part of the Westwood Estate. In 1333 it was the home of a Norman, Nicholas le Jeu. He fought with Sir John Sulby at the Battle of Halsdean against the Scots; later, in 1757, Elias Tremlett, a yeoman, lived there. Elias Tremlett was a local rogue full of devilish trickery whose familiar figure was often seen going up and down the lanes with his pack of hunting dogs. Each one had a name — Gypsy, Fairy, Gainfield, Frantic, Charmer, Millers, Faithful and Melody. He hunted foxes and hares, poached game, smuggled and even, it was rumoured, blackmailed, and once he and his dogs chased a stray deer with a besom broom which had wandered here from Dartmoor, across the vale of Yeo, all the way to Dawlish on the coast and right out to sea twenty miles (32km) away with a besom broom. His reputation was so bad that for years the hazelnuts would whisper to the blackberries, 'Luckee zee! Yur comes the ghost of ole Treblett!' And his wicked laugh, they say, still echoes down the lane and around the hedges.

After the turning to Jews Hollocombe, the lane straightens out and stays level at 300 feet (90m). Giant hogweed, wild carrot, plantain, treacle mustard, sorrel, pineapple mayweed, common fleabane and lots of rough chervil grow all in a mixture and spill out from the corner of a field. Red and white clover, chicory and meadow vetchling are underneath, and multitudes of crickets and grasshoppers are still calling in the grass.

This lane has not changed much since the 1700s, except for the red surface which is now thinly tarmacadamed and the types of traffic going up and down — the odd car and tractor today. Then, there were carts and carriages going to busy Crediton market and more people on foot: pedlars, tinkers and traders of all kinds.

Molly Browning and her sisters had a fresh fish cart which they plied over the moors and lanes, coming this way every day. The fish was brought early in the morning by headload runners coming straight from the sea. It was the best fresh fish and it sold so quickly that by mid-morning the Browning sisters had a full purse. One day, in Chiddenbrook Lane they were held up by robbers who jumped out of the hedges with masks on their faces and asked for Molly's money. She shook her head and pointed to the gun hidden in the pocket of her cloak. The thieves fled at once, and Molly and her sisters sat in the lane and laughed. She had surreptitiously slipped a loose carrot from out of her own basket into her hand and had hidden it in her pocket, and the robbers thought it was a gun.

This part of the lane rises again steeply and passes a narrow track going southwards that leads off to Barn Farm, which has pigs and an ancient wattle-and-daub barn, and then to Stairhill Farm and Moor Farm. The track dips down steeply, high hedges cramming either side threaded with honeysuckle and studded with white roses, and crops of sweetcorn standing in even rows are in the fields spread out below. After the turning, the lane goes westwards in a long, straight stretch with blossoming hedges at either side and yellow grasses stuffed underneath. There is another deep dip as the lane curves north-east, a track going to Lower Hollocombe Farm and, at the bottom of the dip around the narrow corner, is Middle Hollocombe, a large, square, white-painted Georgian house which stands directly at the edge of the lane on the left-hand side facing eastwards towards Cromwell's Cutting. In 1796, Middle Hollocombe was the home of Peter Kingdom, who served on the quarter deck of HMS *Pickle*, a ten-gun schooner at the Battle of Trafalgar.

▽ Jews Hollocombe

ENGLISH COUNTRY LANES • 132

133 • CHIDDENBROOK LANE – DAME MARGOT FONTEYN

ENGLISH COUNTRY LANES • 134

The Battle of Trafalgar took place on the 21st October 1805 at Cape Trafalgar, a low headland in south-west Spain near the western entrance to the Straits of Gibraltar, during the Napoleonic Wars. Lord Horatio Nelson, the commander of the British fleet, was the best loved of all the sea captains. He was a slight, spare man who had gone off to sea from his father's vicarage in Norfolk aged thirteen. He had suffered scurvy, fever, and the loss of an arm and an eye in the service of his country. Nelson was a passionate and dedicated man whose vision and naval skill destroyed Napoleon's navy, and made Britain the invincible power of the seas.

At the beginning of the wars, the battle was spread out over thousands of square miles of ocean. English ships hunted the French and Spanish fleets across the Atlantic as far as Barbados and back, but could not close in on them. By the middle of August 1805, Lord Nelson was in Portsmouth. On the 15th September he set sail heading for France and Spain, and soon was stood on the quarter deck of HMS *Victory* watching the advanced squadron of twelve Spanish ships under Admiral Gravina and twenty-one Frenchmen under Villeneuve come into sight. The war had started two years earlier, but this was the first time Nelson had seen the enemy at close quarters.

The British sailing ships were huge. Three-deckers. Painted black and yellow, and bristling with cannons. They neared the French and Spanish fleet, and Nelson's flagship showed a signal flag that said: 'England Expects That Every Man Will Do His Duty.' The seamen cheered loudly when they saw the message, and the sound of their voices rolled across the sea from one ship to the next. A band played 'British Strike Home' as the firing burst from the spread-out French fleet. The great ships came alongside one another. Their rigging became hopelessly entangled aloft, and broadside. The British leaped on to the decks of the enemy and slashed away with their swords.

Nelson lost over 1,000 men, Napoleon 14,000, and Trafalgar became the greatest British sea victory of all time. Nelson was mortally wounded at the height of the battle. He was pacing his quarter deck, wearing a uniform coat and his four-embroidered stars of his Order of Knighthood, when a French sharpshooter up on the mizzen mast of the *Redoubtable* leaned forward and shot him at a range of only fifteen yards. The force broke his back, and the Right Honorable Lord Viscount Horatio Nelson KB, Commander-in-Chief of the British navy, died of his wounds at 4.30 in the afternoon of the same day. The loss of this small, maimed little man of genius stunned the nation and he was deeply mourned. The first ship to bring the news of the victory of the Battle of Trafalgar was the schooner HMS *Pickle* when she sailed triumphantly into Falmouth harbour, along with Peter Kingdom and the full complement of crew.

From here the lane rises once more, then leads on with Dartmoor as a dark backdrop in the far distance. To the west are other lanes, hamlets, farms, houses and villages — each one with a name as fascinating as the next — Appledore, Down St Mary, Furzeland, Frostland, Tuckinghall and Colebrooke.

It was high summer, and there was a whole day of sitting and strolling, of

ENGLISH COUNTRY LANES • 136

day-dreaming and looking, surrounded by the smell of freshly mown hay. Garlands of wild scarlet strawberries wound around the wild roses studded in the hedges, and the honeysuckle plaited the trees with pale yellow flowers like fairy pipes of purest gold, their perfume drenched the lane. Grasshoppers and crickets rejoiced gently in the soft, stilled seas of yellow-green grass, and the snails, mysteriously awake, moved deep down in the left-over dew and whispered their secret laughter. Ladybirds and beetles crusted the slender stems and the greenfly in the hedge parsley were sleepy and full. A hedgehog came out from between the briars and sat in the sun in the lane. It stretched and yawned, and snuffled and washed, and then went in again. The cows grazed on in the painted meadows and the clouds stayed still in the sky.

The day was ending when I walked back as far as the cutting. The shadows inside it were long and cold, and a breeze within blew the echoes from the red soil and seemed to send out the smell of Cromwell's struggle, and the sense of the ultimate futility of war. I turned again, emerging into the sunlight and feasted my eyes on the loveliness of this place. And I lingered once more, resting deep in seas of grasses, saturated in the scent of the roses, listening to the lullabies coming from the hedgerows, counting the greenfly in the heads of the parsley, laughing as a dizzy fly fell out of a flower, and I watched the snails forever climbing, the sheep drowsing and the sunbeams slanting on the farmhouse thatch. The black cat still slept by the window, Ralph was sleeping on the path, the clouds still sailed serenely in the blue sky, and the Earth was covered in an unforgettable abundance which was an everlasting joy.

◁ *Middle Hollocombe.*

Rookery Lane, Sidlesham, West Sussex

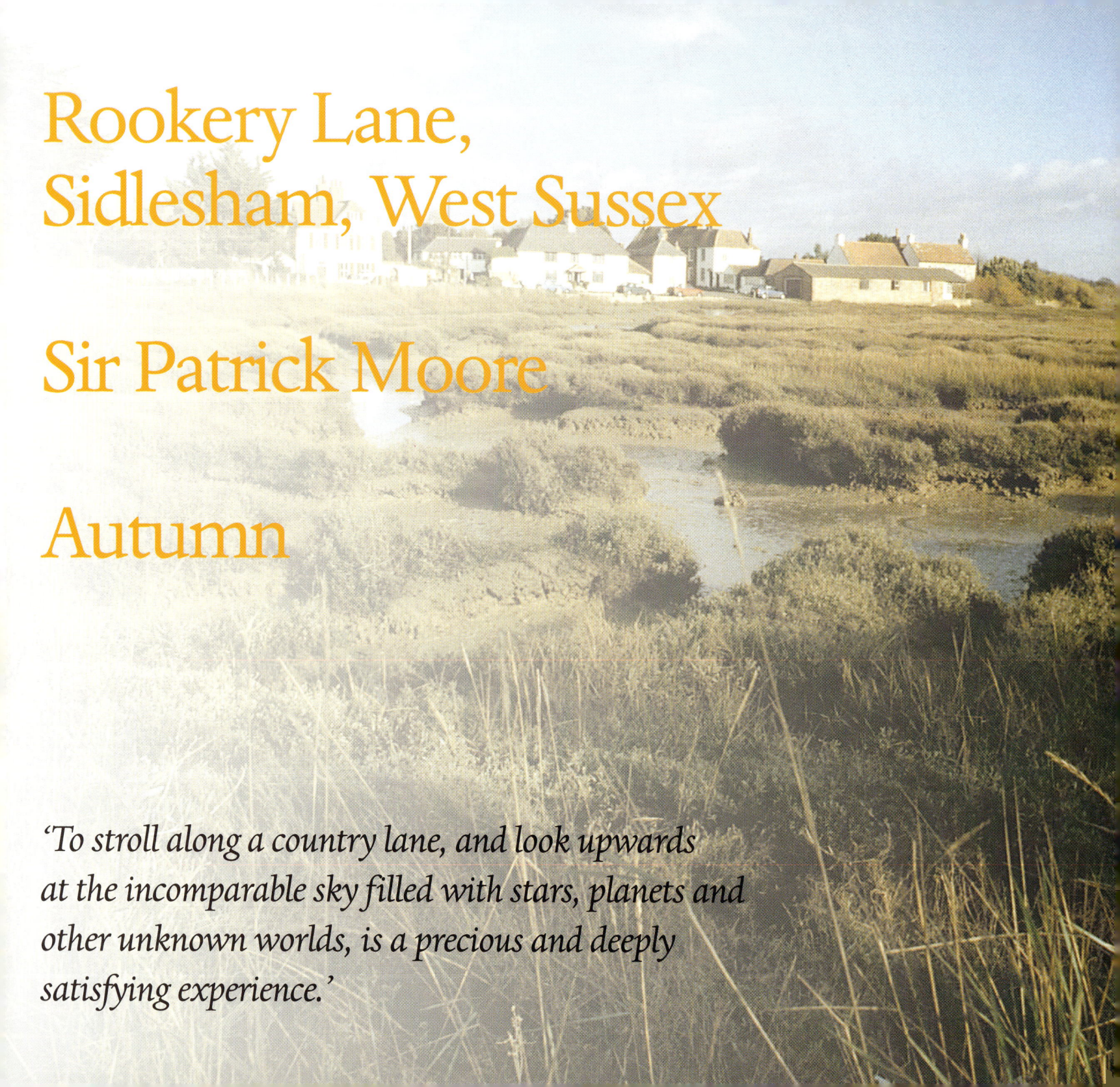

Sir Patrick Moore

Autumn

'To stroll along a country lane, and look upwards at the incomparable sky filled with stars, planets and other unknown worlds, is a precious and deeply satisfying experience.'

Rookery Lane is a busy, bustling bird-filled place — dynamic, dazzling and compelling. Surrounded by salt marshes, shingle, reeds and sedges, and spread out under deep blue, wide-open skies, it wanders through unspoiled farmland, winds beneath sycamore trees and hedges hung with hips and haws, rowan berries and sloes, passes quaint quayside cottages and ends with a flourish on a Saxon shoreline fringed with mud flats, salty lagoons and a harbour thronged with noisy, boisterous, migrant birds. Seals laze on the shingle, sandpipers race the tide, avocets sweep the shallows for shrimps, geese in their thousands darken the sky, porpoises swim silently by and dolphins sneak up near the shoreline capturing mackerel and squid. Toads and frogs doze in damp grasses, slow worms and lizards sleep silent and warm, dragonflies dive over ponds feeding on midges, finches and linnets flock to the teasels and thistles, and house martins feed up before crossing the sea. Here is a place of abundant vitality, radiant and vibrant and brimming with life.

Sir Patrick Moore has lived in Selsey Bill for many years, in a pretty thatched house a stone's-throw from the sea.

'Here, the skies are clear, especially out to sea over the Solent — there is no industry and the air is purer than in the cities', he told me. 'The street where I live is almost a lane, leading down to the sea from my thatched house, which is so near the sea that sand and pebbles blow into

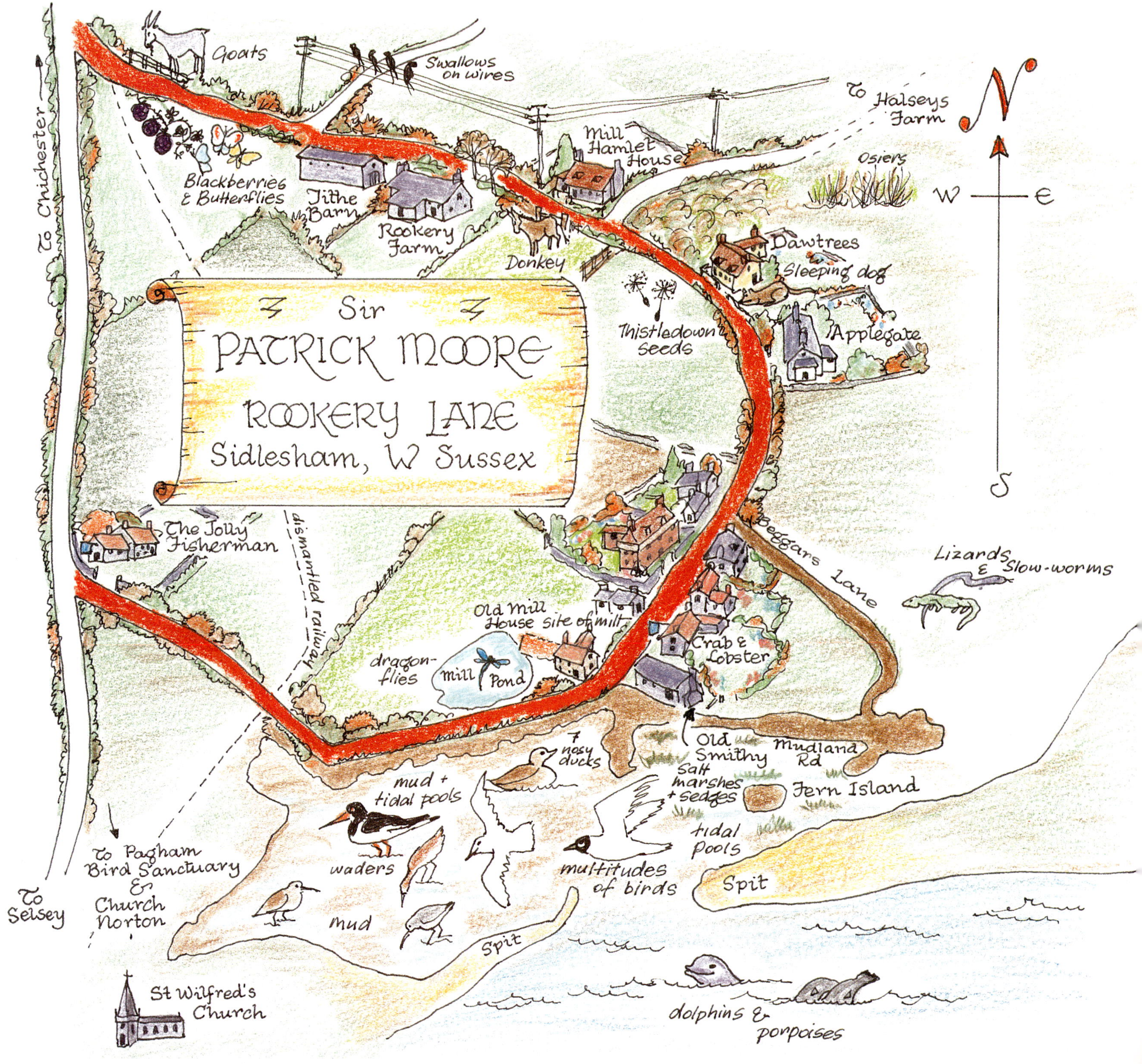
Sir
PATRICK MOORE
ROOKERY LANE
Sidlesham, W Sussex
Goats
Swallows on wires
To Halseys Farm
N
W
E
S
Osiers
Mill Hamlet House
Blackberries & Butterflies
Tithe Barn
Rookery Farm
Donkey
Dawtrees
Sleeping dog
Thistledown seeds
Applegate
To Chichester
The Jolly Fisherman
dismantled railway
Beggars Lane
Lizards & Slow-worms
Old Mill House
site of mill
dragon-flies
Mill Pond
Crab & Lobster
Old Smithy
Mudland Rd
7 nosy ducks
mud + tidal pools
Salt marshes + sedges
Fern Island
tidal pools
waders
multitudes of birds
Spit
To Selsey
To Pagham Bird Sanctuary & Church Norton
mud
Spit
St Wilfred's Church
dolphins & porpoises

my garden and splendid pink patches of thrift grow wild among my flowers.

One of my favourite lanes was in East Grinstead, West Sussex. It was called Worsted Lane and I lived there for thirty-six years until 1965. It was a sandy lane which ran from the road through fields, past a quarry to the Mill Rocks, and it went through two lovely, peaceful woods where I used to play as a boy. Now ... all gone. Quarry filled in, woods cut down and hideous modern housing estates everywhere, using up the so-called green belt. I felt sad that it had been so wrecked. Since moving to this part of West Sussex I have found many pretty lanes leading to the sea — unspoiled, peaceful, full of birds and butterflies, edged by houses with sturdy thatched roofs and flint walls. Among my favourites are Church Lane, leading to the tiny chapel of St Wilfred, overlooking the sea and the mud flats and spit of Pagham Bird Sanctuary; West Street, almost a lane, which leads directly on to a shingly beach and the sea; and Rookery Lane, leading to Mill Lane, which links farmland with the salt marshes and lagoons at Pagham Harbour — places of rest, respite and rich feeding grounds for multitudes of migrant birds. All the lanes run down to the sea, above which is a vast expanse of open sky and at night, millions of stars — perfect conditions for my life's work and accessible from the telescope set up in my garden.

To walk out of my own gate and stroll along a country lane on a warm summer night, the sound of the sea lapping the beach close by, and look upwards at the incomparable sky filled with stars, planets and other unknown worlds, is a precious and deeply satisfying experience. Long may the lanes of England continue to be part of our wonderful countryside.'

Rookery Lane, Sidlesham, leads south-eastwards from the B2145 Selsey road, which runs from Chichester to Selsey Bill on the south coast, goes through open farmland, passes Rookery Farm, bends in a south-westerly direction by Mill Hamlet House, carries on straight and flat to the quayside at Pagham Harbour by the Crab and Lobster pub, turns west by the mill pond and the tidal mud flats and intertidal marshes, the tramway and footpath, to Church Norton and Pagham Nature Reserve, a distance of about two miles (3km).

Rookery Lane turns off from the Selsey road, bears south-west and goes straight through fields at either side. On the left, broad flat fields are marked out with ragged mixed hedges and small trees — their crinkling green leaves have a crisp brown margin around the edges and they rattle in the wind. Yellow-hammers, whitethroats, and willow warblers are in the hedges, and tree sparrows and goldfinches gather on the branches chattering and arguing in hectic, short sharp notes. Multitudes of wing beats vibrate in the afternoon sun. The skyline above the fields is wide and clear over the sea, mud flats and shingle at Pagham Harbour a short distance away. Bar-tailed godwits, brent geese and curlews, here for the winter, are feeding in the fields, pushed on to the land by the high tide. They jab their pointed beaks into the wet soil between the stubble, picking up snails, insects and worms. Two goats are tethered on a grassy patch by the side of the lane sitting down, perfectly still — inscrutable cream-coloured mandarins with short beards, yellow bulging eyes and pupils like narrow, black oriental slits.

On the right is a narrow grassy track and public footpath which was the site of the Selsey tramline.

ENGLISH COUNTRY LANES • 142

The tramway was opened in 1897 by the Hundred of Manhood Selsey Tramway Co Ltd. It was the only rail link from Chichester to Selsey. There were stations at Sidlesham, Chalder, Mill Pond Halt and Sidlesham Mill by Mill Lane, and many other unscheduled stops along the way. Anyone wanting the tram just had to stand anywhere along the line and raise a hand, and the train would stop. At the turn of the century it was a much-needed rail link from Chichester to the agricultural area and 'fine sea frontage' with the 'bracing air' of Bognor Regis, Selsey Bill and Chichester Harbour. The little railway or tram, as it was known, was a light railway, using steam engines, and carrying passengers and heavy goods and children to and from school in Chichester.

The tramway was loved by everyone — whimsical and capricious, it often broke down. The engine would not start in the mornings and, when it did get going, it chugged slowly into Chichester, five miles (8km) away, tooting its whistle at level crossings, slowing to a halt to let the guard jump down, wave a red flag to see if the coast was clear and then beckon the little train onwards. It was a slow process. Children were late for school, 'The train was late, Miss' was an excuse the teacher had to accept.

When the sea broke through the reclaimed land at the harbour in 1910, the tramway could only go as far as the Ferry — a large area of mud flats completely covered at high tide. Then the passengers had to get into a horse-drawn bus to Mill Pond Halt, where another train took them to Chichester. Children loved this irregular form of transport and, in between moves from one type of carriage to the next, would wander off to play or to pick flowers, and further delay the start of the train.

In 1927 the steam train became a Shefflex Rail Car — a little faster, but not much. The tramway closed in 1935, much to the sadness of local people who missed the fun of travelling in the quaint little train and of seeing the engine crossing the flat meadows, blowing its whistle. Now the tramway is a track and a nature trail going from the start of Rookery Lane to Mill Hamlet, along Pagham Harbour, the salt marshes to the Ferry, and is part of Pagham Harbour Nature Reserve.

Rookery Lane continues on towards the south-east. More fields are on the left and a mixed hedge is on the right — blackthorn, buckthorn, crab-apple, hazel and hawthorn, hornbeam and lime. Young oak trees grow up in front; their golden acorns are scattered all over the surface of the lane. Rows of bright yellow mouse-eared hawkweed light up the hedge bottom and toadflax, common ragwort, bindweed and sea-mayweed are at both sides of the lane, and in and amongst are creeping thistles — the seed heads split open, spilling out the minute brown seeds — each one fastened by a tiny slender stem to a thistle-down top that lifts gently in the wind and floats down the lane towards the sea.

There is a bend to the left and another public footpath is on the right, running south-west to the mill pond and Mill Lane. Bramble bushes covered in glistening blackberries are on the right, and blackbirds and starlings are standing on the branches eating the fruit. Above them, on the telephone wires, house martins sit in groups, gathering themselves together before lifting off into the wind, heading south.

A path leads off to the left, going to Church Farm Lane and meeting up with other footpaths ranging over a wide area leading to ancient farms — Honer Farm and Marsh

Farm in the east and then heading south to Pagham Wall, a harbour defence, and Pagham Harbour. Groups of tall brown hogweed stand together, sloping outwards at varying angles, their seed heads almost empty. In the left-over seeds, tiny red aromatic oil glands shaped like crescent moons glow in the afternoon sun. Thin elm trees are on the right and behind them, close to the lane side, is Rookery Farm, a solid, square, eighteenth-century farmhouse. In the 1780s the house and the large tithe barn at the side of it were thatched. The farmhouse, farm buildings and much of the land around was owned by the Rusbridge family for 700 years. Roman cutting instruments, or 'celts', made from stone or metal were found at Rookery Farm, and spear heads, coins, pottery and other implements were found in 1862 on the shores of the harbour.

The Romans landed in Sussex in AD 43, and Selsey was inhabited by Roman colonists and proconsuls for over 300 years. Chichester, the Roman city of Noviogmagus Regnesium, was established as an important base soon after the Romans arrived in Britain. There was an important Roman mint here which, it is said, struck coins from gold taken from Philip of Macedonia, the father of Alexander the Great, and a great number of Roman imperial coins have been unearthed, along with tools for making coins, at Medmerry Beach, Selsey. There is the site of a Roman villa across the Selsey road to the east, and the Roman palace of Fishbourne is four miles (6km) to the north-east of the lane and a mile (1.5km) to the south of Chichester. Fishbourne is the largest Roman building ever discovered in Britain and is believed to be the sumptuous palace of King Cogidubnus, a Briton and king of the Regni tribe. He was a staunch supporter of the Romans who visited Rome and was made a senator. The palace covered an area of six acres (2.5ha), and had gardens and courtyards, and mosaic floors of great splendour. The centrepiece design of a boy riding on the back of a dolphin is the finest Roman mosaic floor found in Britain.

The lane bears to the south-east, stretching onwards and passing a flint barn on the right. There is a yard with bare earth and chaff strewn around. A black and white Sussex cockerel carefully and delicately turns over the chaff with a long, thin, hesitant claw, crowing to himself contentedly, totally absorbed in his task and two hens are taking a bath, flinging dirt all over themselves in a deliberate, accomplished way. They keep their eyes closed, the thin skin lids shut tight in silent, sensuous concentration. A fat donkey leans against the gatepost scratching its rear — the post moves in and out of the ground, squeaking. A long stretch of sun-warmed banking is on the opposite side, and bramble bushes covered in blackberries and butterflies go on as far as the eye can see.

The lane takes a dog-leg curve after Mill Hamlet House, and the lane to Halseys Farm and the osier beds and goes south-west. Two detached houses are set back under the trees — Dawtrees and Applegate. A dog is asleep by the garden gates, stretching out, snoring, twitching and dreaming, his tail wagging half-heartedly, his plump warm body drying up the ground around him after a shower of rain.

After the houses, on the left, comes Beggars Lane, a short, hidden track bordered with ragwort and convolvulus, leading to the mud flats, sedges and salt marshes, and on to Mudland Road. Mudland Road is a sandy, muddy track circling north-eastwards along the intertidal stretches, going as far Pagham Nature Reserve, Pagham Lagoon and Pagham Spit. Mudland Road then goes west along more mud flats to the Quay and the Crab and Lobster public house, eventually joining up with the tramway track to Ferry Long Pools and Pagham Nature Reserve Visitor Centre. Beyond that is Church Norton, where the sea crashes on to the shingle of the spit.

Here, toads, frogs, newts, lizards and slow worms are lazing undisturbed in the damp, warm, muddy soil and the thick grasses leading to the long line of sedges and mud flats: smooth newts, with rosy yellow bellies, spotted throats and wavy crests along their backs; and palmate newts, pale orange and white, with spear-shaped tails and thick black webs between their toes; all stay perfectly still, like lustrous, radiant stones, transfixed and luminous, fat bellies filled up with slugs and worms. Lizards — bronze and yellow, or grey and brown — lay on flat stones, watching grasshoppers and spiders with bulging, hypnotic, greedy eyes. A slow worm is basking in the sun, its close-fitting golden scales reflecting the rays. It slowly blinks its eyelids, then licks its lips with a bulbous, fleshy tongue, savouring the taste of the last juicy snail.

Beyond Beggars Lane are more houses at both sides of the lane, leading straight on in a south-westerly direction to the harbour. On the right-hand side is an elegant red brick house with flint garden walls called Danes Acre — peaceful and still with a pretty parterre at both sides of the garden path.

The house is built on the graves of Danish warriors. At the time of increased Viking raids on the Saxons of the south coast in AD 893, a Danish longship was beached on the mud channels near to the quay at the end of the lane. The warriors were making their way inland when they were separated from their ship by the Saxon *fyrd* or militia, and were surrounded. The Saxon ealdorman, who was in command, offered the heathen Danes their freedom if they would surrender and be baptised into the Christian faith. The alternative was that they would be put to death. The Vikings believed that warriors who died in battle went to Valhalla to feast with their Norse gods — Thor, Freya and Odin. So powerful was the belief that their gods would take care of them in the after-life that

The Old Malt House.

the Danes chose to stand and fight the Saxons, and it was here, in the lane, probably a wide track at that time, that the Danish warriors were hacked to death by the Saxons. The Saxons gave the warriors a ceremonial burial. They dressed them in full battle-dress — iron-horned helmets, chain-mail jerkins, jewelled arm bands and scarlet cloaks. In their hands they held long swords, bright spears and two-handed axes. Many years later their bones were found and returned to the ground.

After Danes Acre, houses are at both sides of the lane, mostly eighteenth-century, old red-brick houses with roses and wisteria climbing over the walls, and lavender and sea thrift in the gardens. Their names reflect their connection with the sea and sailing — Sandpiper, Driftwood Cottages,

Peggoty, Quay House, Newhaven; and with the countryside and the type of work they did — Hawthorn Cottage, Rosemary Cottage, the Old Malt House, near the end of the lane and with 'WC 1738' written into the uneven white plaster walls, Quay House with its ancient beamed wooden porch, and the Old Mill House at the side of the quay.

Almost next to the quay at the end of the lane is the Crab and Lobster, a quiet, ancient inn. The door opens out on to the lane side and a garden at the back overlooks the harbour. There has been an inn here for centuries, serving ale to travellers who tied up their longships to the narrow pier, at that time made of oak timbers driven deep into the mud.

The inn and the quay have witnessed many important historical events. Aella, the Saxon king, who reputedly lived till he was 117 years of age, landed here in AD 477 and pushed the Romano-Britons from Selsey. St Wilfred came in AD 681, and brought Christianity to the south Saxons and founded a cathedral at Church Norton, a mile (1.5km) away across the harbour at the end of the lane, the remains of which are supposedly under the sea. There is a legend that on calm days the bells of the cathedral can be heard under the sea. Knights and companies of archers sailed from the harbour quay in 1415 to fight the French at Agincourt. Then the lane, the inn and the quay looked exactly the same as it does today, except for the tidal mill, now pulled down, and the forge, built next door to the inn by the innkeeper to shoe the horses of cavaliers, coastguards, revenue men and smugglers.

Skirmishes in the Civil War of 1642-1649 led to young men being shot outside Quay House, and at the turn of the eighteenth century there were sailors from her majesty's ships and smartly dressed officers from the men-o-war launches tied up at the quay. On certain occasions, a short, slim, heavily-cloaked figure left his launch and stepped into a private coach waiting at the quayside. This was Admiral Lord Nelson, come from his fleet anchored off the coast and on his way to visit Lady Hamilton, his mistress, who was a guest at nearby Uppark House.

At this point the lane reaches the coastline, and there is an open view of the salt marshes, the mud flats by the side of the quay and, in the distance, Pagham Spit and Church Norton Spit — two points of shingle at the entrance to the harbour. It was here on the 25th July 1588 that the Spanish Armada sailed past Pagham Harbour and the quay at the end of Rookery Lane in full sail, on its way to do battle with the English fleet. Spanish galleons were extremely tall ships and they sailed high in the water. They were so close to the land as they went up the Solent, heading for the English Channel, that they appeared to be sailing through the fields.

The men of Sidlesham and Selsey were ready. For months they had been preparing a forty-ton flour barque which not long before had been used to transport corn and flour to and fro, from the tidal mill at the quay to other places on the South Coast. In the fields nearby they had drilled and practised with muskets and pikes, and any other equipment they would need to repel the Spanish invaders.

The day of the 25th July dawned bright but windy. The prevailing wind was windward — from the west. That very morning, at Church Norton, in the little Saxon church overlooking the sea, a wedding was taking place. The captain of the barque was the best man and the bridegroom was a wealthy farmer from Sidlesham. Just as the marriage had been solemnised and the wedding bells were ringing out, a messenger ran in much haste to the church:

'The Armada is here, sir, just sighted from Selsey Bill, off the Isle of Wight, steering a course up the Channel.'

The captain and the bridegroom left the bride at the altar, ran out of the church, turned to look eastwards and there, in the distance on the horizon, were the Spanish ships. The men of Sidlesham and Selsey, on hearing the news, ran to the quay, boarded the barque, sailed out from the harbour and with great daring made straight for the Armada. They attacked and cut out the *Carthagena*, a huge, high-pooped galleon, achieving a broadside and bringing down the main mast. The captain of the *Carthagena*, seeing his position as hopeless, surrendered and, with 500 soldiers and sailors still on board, the ship was towed into Portsmouth Harbour, where she was repaired and put into service in the English fleet.

The Spanish Armada was the formidable fleet sent by King Philip II of Spain to invade England so that he could seize the throne and return the country to Catholicism. When Mary Queen of Scots was executed in 1587, she left her claim to the throne of England to King Philip. As soon as the king heard news of her death, he began to plan the invasion of England. Such were the magnitude of his plans for the tremendous sea battle that would wipe out the English Navy that the preparations took two years. Money had to be found for warships and troop carriers, for gunpowder and armour.

When the Spanish fleet was ready it had 130 ships, fifty of which were warships, with 8,000 seamen. The commander-in-chief was the duke of Medina-Sidonia, a capable administrator with very little sea experience. He had been brought in at the very last moment when Spain's distinguished marquess de Santa Cruz had died. The crew which manned the Invincible Armada were gathered from the sea-going population of the Mediterranean, and many of them were unskilled at sailing ships in the open Atlantic Ocean.

The Spanish galleons were heavy, cumbersome ships — three- or four-masted vessels having two or three decks with portholes for cannons. There was a forecastle at the bow and a high poop-deck in the stern of the ship where the captain and officers resided in richly furnished cabins. The ordinary seaman, who were the bravest and hardiest of men, had to stay in quarters in the forecastle with hardly enough room to lie down, and which in rough weather was soaking wet. Their food was poor — bread, cheese, salted meat and salted fish with no fresh vegetables.

These towering ships were difficult to manoeuvre, and relied on engaging in combat in line-of-battle formation, where two opposing ships fired their guns at each other 'broadside' — both firing at once. These battles were won by the heaviest ships, and so King Philip of Spain spared no expense in making sure his enormous ships would be superior in every way to the English fleet.

The English ships were different — smaller and more nimble. The vessels were fast and well armed. There were fewer seamen and soldiers, but they had more artillery and ammunition, and English sailors were far superior to the enemy in seamanship and the art of gunnery. The commander of the English fleet was the lord high admiral, Charles Howard, second Baron Howard of Effingham. His second-in-command was Sir Francis Drake, acknowledged to be the 'master mariner of the world'. The English fleet had less than 100 ships, and their magnificent flagship was the *Ark Royal*, weighing 800 tons.

The Armada set sail from Lisbon in May 1588 and arrived at Lizard Point, Cornwall, on the 29th July. The main English fleet lay off Plymouth. The Spanish ships were moving slowly as the wind was light, and it was hard to make the ungainly ships keep their position. As soon as land was sighted, the Spanish admiral ordered his men to take up close formation with the most powerful ship leading. Most of the English fleet were to the leeward sheltered from the wind but, by a series of clever manoeuvres, they managed to position themselves to

◁ The Crab and Lobster inn.

the windward, or upwind, of the enemy — west of the Armada. The strong west wind gave them the advantage in three encounters — Plymouth on the 31st July, Portland Bill on the 2nd August, and off the Isle of Wight on the 4th August.

The Isle of Wight stands out clearly on the horizon, to the west of Selsey, and the cliffs at Bembridge made an impressive backdrop to the battle scene, which took place not far from the end of the lane. Women, children and old men stood on the spit of land at the end of the lane looking towards Selsey Bill, and watched the the giant oak ships in full sail, the Spanish sailors struggling to bring the lumbering vessels around to face the cannon fire of the English.

The lord admiral, Charles Howard, and Sir Francis Drake employed a new tactic that threw the Spaniards completely off guard. Instead of engaging in close 'broadside' action, as was customary according to the rules of war at sea, they harried the Spanish fleet at long range by cannon shot and avoided all attempts to bring them close. Spanish soldiers stood on deck, musketeers in front of pikemen, waiting in vain for the English to draw near, but they did not. The Spanish superiority of size was turned to their own disadvantage. The battle raged for a week, with the Armada holding a snail's pace course in the Channel. The huge ships of the Armada reached the straits of Dover on the 6th August and anchored. The English also anchored, still keeping to the windward side.

It was midnight. The 7th August. The wind was up. The English quietly and surreptitiously set fire to eight large merchantmen ships, sending them out on a strong east-going tide, making sure the wind would send the blazing ships into the host of crowded galleons of the Armada at anchor. When they realised what was happening, the Spaniards ran to cut or slip their own anchor cables so that they could sail out to sea and avoid catching fire. In the darkness the ships collided into one another in the high winds which had begun blowing fiercely. By dawn the great fleet was scattered all along the coast, and the English were sailing in to attack.

All day long the battle raged as the English tried to drive their enemy on to the sandbanks, whilst the Spaniards fought desperately to get into the North Sea. Thousands of the Spaniards were killed and drowned, and their ships horribly damaged. Suddenly the wind changed direction and became gale force, and the Armada fled northwards, trying to make for home in a long voyage around Scotland, Ireland and into the Atlantic Ocean. Battle damage, bad weather, shortage of food and water, and navigational errors caused many of its ships to founder in the open sea. Other ships were driven on to the coast of Ireland and wrecked. Only sixteen ships reached Spain, and 15,000 men had lost their lives.

Charles Howard and Sir Francis Drake had saved England from invasion. When the battle was over, the whole of the country was 'profoundly moved' that a provident God had saved them by sending a high wind at the right moment. '*Efflavit Deus et dissi paverunt*' ('God blew with his wind and they were scattered') became the sailors' motto — it is written on the monument at Plymouth Hoe. Queen Elizabeth I went to St Paul's Cathedral to join with all her people in giving thanks for the 'great deliverance', but the skill and courage of the ordinary men at sea had, without a doubt, changed the course of English history.

During the nineteenth century the harbour — Sidlesham Quay, as it is called — was a commercial port, and every year up to sixty-eight boats of twenty-five tons each would bring cargoes of coal and grain for Sidlesham Tidal Mill, and leave with ground flour.

Where the lane turns into the quay is the site of the old mill. There has been a mill on this site for centuries, the last mill being built in 1755 by Mr Woodruffe Drinkwater, a merchant of Chichester, and it was reputedly the finest mill in the country The mill did considerable business sending out 'vast quantities of flour and taking in much corn'. There were three enormous water wheels, eight pairs of millstones and a large fan for cleaning the corn. The mill could grind a load of corn in an hour. (A load was eighty bushels. A bushel is eight gallons (37 litres).) Most tidal mills had a wheel which was worked by the ebb and flow of the tide, but Sidlesham Mill worked at high tide when the sea water flooded through sluice gates under the mill and was left in the mill pond. The water was let out again to keep the mill working when there was no water in the harbour. The pond was over thirty-six acres (15ha) and very deep.

In 1876 the harbour mouth was closed off, shutting out the sea and reclaiming the land. Rich pastures were made from the mud, and cattle and other livestock grazed on them. Meadow flowers grew in them. Then, in 1910, there was a violent and terrible storm that lasted for many days. Tremendous tidal waves broke through the man-made barrier and the sea returned to the harbour. Around 1,500 hundred acres (600ha) of land were flooded. Siddlesham Mill did not work again. Bricks were needed in the First World War and so the mill was pulled down. All that is left is the mill pond, now belonging to Mill House and made part of a fascinating garden fringed with reeds and sedges, iris and water lilies.

Mallards, coots, reed warblers and sedge warblers nest on the mill pond, and dragonflies and damselflies hunt over the surface in spectacular, dramatic dances feeding on midges and fat flies, then go hawking for more in the hedgerows, under the trees or up the lane: southern hawkers, migrant hawkers, yellow-winged darters, common darters, ruddy darters, black-tailed skimmers, four-spotted chasers, broad-banded chasers, emperor dragonflies, hairy dragonflies, the large reed damselfly, the common blue damselfly and the beautiful demoiselle damselfly. Fabulous, splendid and startling, they light up the lane — sparkling, dancing gems, dazzling in the clear sea air. Seven mallard ducks waddle on to the grassy patch at the side of the quay and promptly all sit down together.

A group of birdwatchers was standing by the quayside in short-sleeved shirts, their sweaters tied round their waist by the arms, too hot to wear in the warm autumn day. Binoculars at the ready, note pads under their arms, they scanned the horizon and made notes.

'A busy time for birds', one of them remarked to me, not taking his eyes away from the mud flats.

'And for birdwatchers', another joined in.

'Such a lot to see and hear — the noise is incredible', said a third. He sat down on the stump of a post and continued looking towards the sea. 'Winter's the best time to be here — there can be up to fifteen thousand birds in the harbour then. They begin arriving in late November and more in December, January and February. Brent geese — more than four thousand come from Russia and the Arctic Circle — and pintail, widgeon, teal, shelduck, dunlin, smew, curlew, godwits, mergansers, Arctic skua, hundreds of turnstones, a few avocets and many oystercatchers.' He made a wide sweep of the shoreline with his binoculars. 'There can be up to two thousand lapwings and sometimes, if we are lucky, the very rare little tern on Tern Island in the harbour. The reserve closes off the Church Norton shingle spit to ornithologists each year so that these rare birds can breed — they lay their eggs on the shingle in a hollow and can easily be trodden on by humans.'

'You can see Slavonian grebes on the sea at Norton, and of course all the gulls, cormorants and other regular seabirds', the first man added. 'You name it, there seems to be every bird imaginable here at some point during the year — it's a fantastic place. The visitor centre in the Sidlesham nature trail keeps lists and reports of all the bird sightings. And not just birds of course — there are important dragonflies here, butterflies and moths, and recently a hairy-winged cone-headed grasshopper was spotted here — extremely rare, you know.' He cradled his binoculars on his knees. 'We all live in Chichester and come here when we can. It's magic — a different, undisturbed, wilderness world. And', he went on, 'if you stand on the spit, you can see harbour seals, porpoises and even, on occasions, bottle-nosed dolphins. Two days ago I saw a pod of six dolphins cavorting and playing around off the spit, beyond the Severels.' He lifted his binoculars once more and scanned the two arms of the spit where the tide was beginning to rush in. The others did the same, standing in a row gazing at the harbour and the birds.

Birds are everywhere, wheeling, circling, twisting and turning, and the sky is full of hooting, honking, piping, whirring, warbling, trumpeting and trilling — all mixed together in a busy, chattering throng. Some birds are on the mud flats feeding eagerly before the tide comes in, others are on the spit, and yet more are on the sea or in the air.

The mud flats are directly in front of the quay and cover the vast expanse of the harbour. A path goes eastwards to Mudland Road — a muddy track going around the east side of the harbour to Pagham, the Little Lagoon and Pagham Spit nature trail. Here there are old sheltered shingle ridges with banks of wild roses, tamarisk, gorse, sea thrift, brambles, thistles and teasels. Greenfinches, goldfinches and linnets are on the seed heads.

The mud flats and salt marshes of the intertidal area is the main part of the nature reserve at Pagham Harbour, which is of international importance and is classified as a 'High Status' reserve. The reserve covers 16,115 acres (6.5ha) and the intertidal salt marshes of the Harbour cover 700 acres (280ha). The rest of the reserve is farmland, kept especially for the birds to graze at high tide, and copses, lagoons, reedbeds and shingle beaches. The two shingle spits almost meeting at the entrance to the harbour are among the most important in Europe due to their length. Sea kale, yellow-horned poppy and the largest colony of the rare childling pink in Great Britain grow on this calcium-rich shingle. The main area of mud is covered by the tide twice a day, and there is a large inlet between the spits with a powerful tidal race. Mud collects here, and countless small creatures — ragworms, crabs, lugworms, shrimps, small snails and more — live in it. Sea aster, cord grass, glasswort, seablite and sea purslane grow in profusion.

St Wilfred's Church.

At the end of Rookery Lane is Mill Lane by the quay, and the tramway track by Island Cottage is the route of Sidlesham nature trail, leading to the Ferry Pond nature trail and the tiny chapel at Church Norton, the shingle on the spit and the open sea.

The afternoon rain had dried up by the time I reached the sea. The sky was teeming with birds, so I sat on the grass by the quayside watching the tide flow in, listening in wonder to the cries of the wild birds as they circled and wheeled above me, below me, around me, and somehow, I became part of the magnificent dance.

Waders came down to the mud and ate in a frenzy, outpacing the tide, printing their tracks in the mud as they moved. The squelching silt oozed up to their bony knees. Sandpipers ran on the shingle, piping in shrill, anxious voices; curlews gave out strange, sharp, warbling cries and a solitary avocet stood in the shallows, silently and hypnotically, sweeping the waves with its upturned bill.

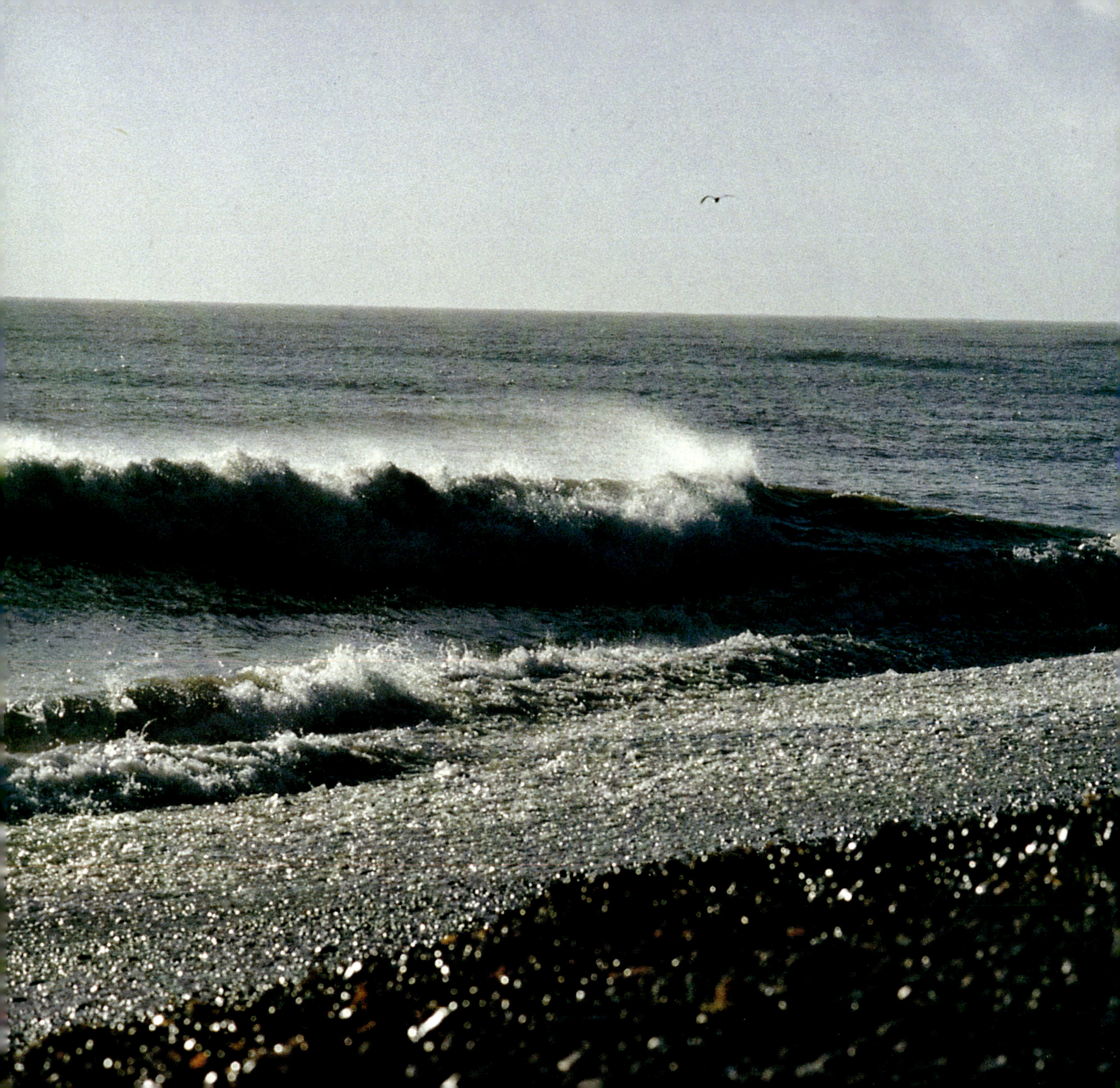

Behind me, the lane, fringed with hedges, red with berries, spread out through the white harbour houses, shining and clean. The sun warmed me as I went to the mill pond and gazed at the dragonflies shimmering over the rushes. Droplets of rain stayed in the sedges and the midges returned.

Then I walked on the track by the mud and the sedges, and sat down, surrounded by tamarisk, bright yellow gorse and pink sea thrift, and I stared at the shapes of the birds as they crowded across the clear azure sky. I stayed a while, marvelling at the noise of the wings of wild geese on the skyline and the sea pounding the shingle as the tide came in.

The day became cooler, the birds were quieter, so I went to the Crab and Lobster and sat by the log fire listening to the slow tick of the old wooden clock, seeing the sky darken through the tiny windows in the ancient walls and then, warmed and rested, I went outside once more into this wonderful place. I walked to the spit as the night came over, looking up at the brilliant stars in the black night sky, listening to the sound of the sea on the shore and feeling the throbbing, ceaseless rhythm of the waves forever returning. The moon shone on the water and porpoises came; slowly, gently, rising and diving, breathing and blowing, in the same endless rhythm as the magnificent sea.

Coombe End, Whitchurch, Oxfordshire

Sir Michael Caine

Autumn

'Every time I walk down an English lane, I expect to find at the end of it some forgotten land, perhaps the very heart of England itself.'

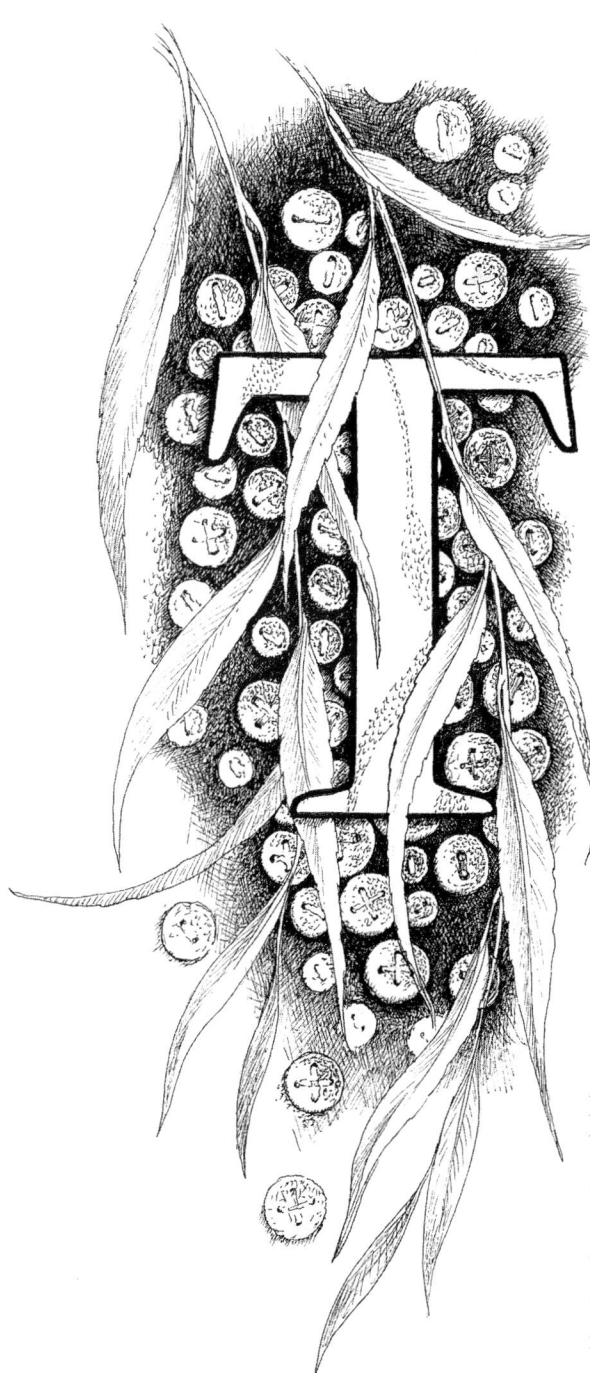

The lane at Coombe End is brilliant, burnished and berry-filled: an incandescent place which wanders through an idyllic bronzed landscape, meanders beneath great stands of gilded beech, winds between sun-filled coombes crested with ancient yew, dips down through sloping, flowering meadows and ends by the side of the slow-moving Thames. It's a glorious, golden, carefree lane. Soft grey herons fish in the busy, bubbling shallows, kingfishers dance like gems in the surf, tall white swans swim over the ripples, water rats hide in the reeds, and plump, tumbling otters play on the banks. There are ginger foxes waiting in wine-red copses, red-legged partridges in scarlet groves; quails call out from copper hedges, and sumptuous pheasants with long crimson tail-feathers feed on rich autumn fruits. Here the world seems easy, and the days are ripe and full.

Michael Caine was born in the East End of London not far from the River Thames. The river seemed always to be part of his life, and recently he had a house in Oxfordshire with grounds alongside the Thames, surrounded by secluded country lanes.

'I was always fascinated by the River Thames', he told me. 'It has been an integral part of my life since childhood. Often I had to cross the Thames for some reason or other, and I would stand and watch it going by,

Owl Cottage
Stapnalls Farm
Wilderness
Primrose Hill Shaw
The Great Chalkwood
Cockpit Plantation
Brambly Corner
Partridges
Trees & berries
Gatehampton
Hattonhill Shaw
Pauls Grove
Cows
Purple elderberry & white butterflies
Beech trees
Nature Reserve
Wildflowers
Ancient Yew Trees
Gatehampton Bridge
barge
swans
Badgers
Coombe End Farm
Water rat
To Goring
Coombe Court Farm
Fisherman
The River Thames
N
W
E
S
Sir
MICHAEL CAINE
COOMBE END
Whitchurch, Oxfordshire
Whitchurch Hill
To Whitchurch & Pangbourne
Hartslock Island
otters
Hartslock Cottage
Ratty's Boathouse
Coombe Park

Gatehampton Bridge over the River Thames, towards Oxford.

at that time a great stretch of shining water full of fish — salmon, eel, trout, tench, carp, barbel and chub — and busy with barges, boats and ships. I loved to watch the big ships sail past, hooting and easing their way towards the estuary and out to sea. The best time to see them was at sunset when they were all lit up and London was a dark silhouette all around, like a stage backdrop over the wide, shining river which moved silently below.

The river filled me with a sense of longing — I wanted to travel, to see the places the ships were sailing to, and to experience the world which I knew lay beyond the sea. In the summer I used to go and watch the bargemen working their beautifully decorated barges filled with coal, cement, bricks and other types of cargo going up and down the Thames. They were always singing or whistling as they went, their plump wives hanging out the washing on the stern or watering the red geraniums which seemed to be at every window. Sometimes, if the barges were moored, I was able to talk to the bargemen and their wives, and they held me spellbound with their stories of life on the river.

I used to wonder about the Thames, where it began and what it would be like in the upper reaches, and I knew that, one day, I had to go up river and see for myself the 'silent, silver kingdoms, the meadows wide spread . . . the brown snaky tree roots which gleamed below the surface of the quiet water . . . the silvery shoulder and foamy tumble of a weir', described so vividly in *Wind in the Willows* by Kenneth Grahame. So as soon as I could I went to Oxfordshire, found Pangbourne and Whitchurch, and walked the towpath to Goring. I, like Mole, was overcome by the beauty of the river, its backwaters and deeps, its water rats, otters and toads, its wildfowl, weeping willows and its elegant royal swans — so very different from the riverscapes in the East End of London. How I loved it!

Whenever I could, I returned to this part of the river and as I began to walk or bicycle in the surrounding countryside I discovered the country lanes. I came to care deeply for this small corner of England, and wherever I was in the world my thoughts always returned here. I had a house in Oxfordshire where the river ran alongside the grounds. I could see the white swans go past my window, the weeping willows waving in the current and if I was lucky an otter or two. When time was available, I walked the country lanes surrounding my house, perhaps going as far as the Ridgeway at Streatley or into the deeply-wooded coombes near Goring. But always the River Thames was beside me, a symbol of idyllic peacefulness, and yet at the same time a tempting and intoxicating reminder of those faraway places filled with excitement and adventure. Later I moved to Chelsea Harbour, living once again close to the Thames.'

The lane at Coombe End lies north of Whitchurch Hill and east of the B471 road from Pangbourne to Woodcote, and this part starts by the turning to Coombe End Farm and the lane to Owl Cottage, Wilderness, the Chalkwood and Stapnalls Farm. Coombe End goes east past Coombe End Cottages, Cockpit Plantation and Booths Shaw, edges Hartslock Nature Reserve, winds down through steep-sided coombes, passes close to the River Thames, and ends by Ferry Cottages and Gatehampton Farm; a distance of about two miles (3km).

The lane begins at the National Trust sign, just where the lane from Brambly Corner meets the lane from Owl Cottage and Wilderness. On the right is a small sloping

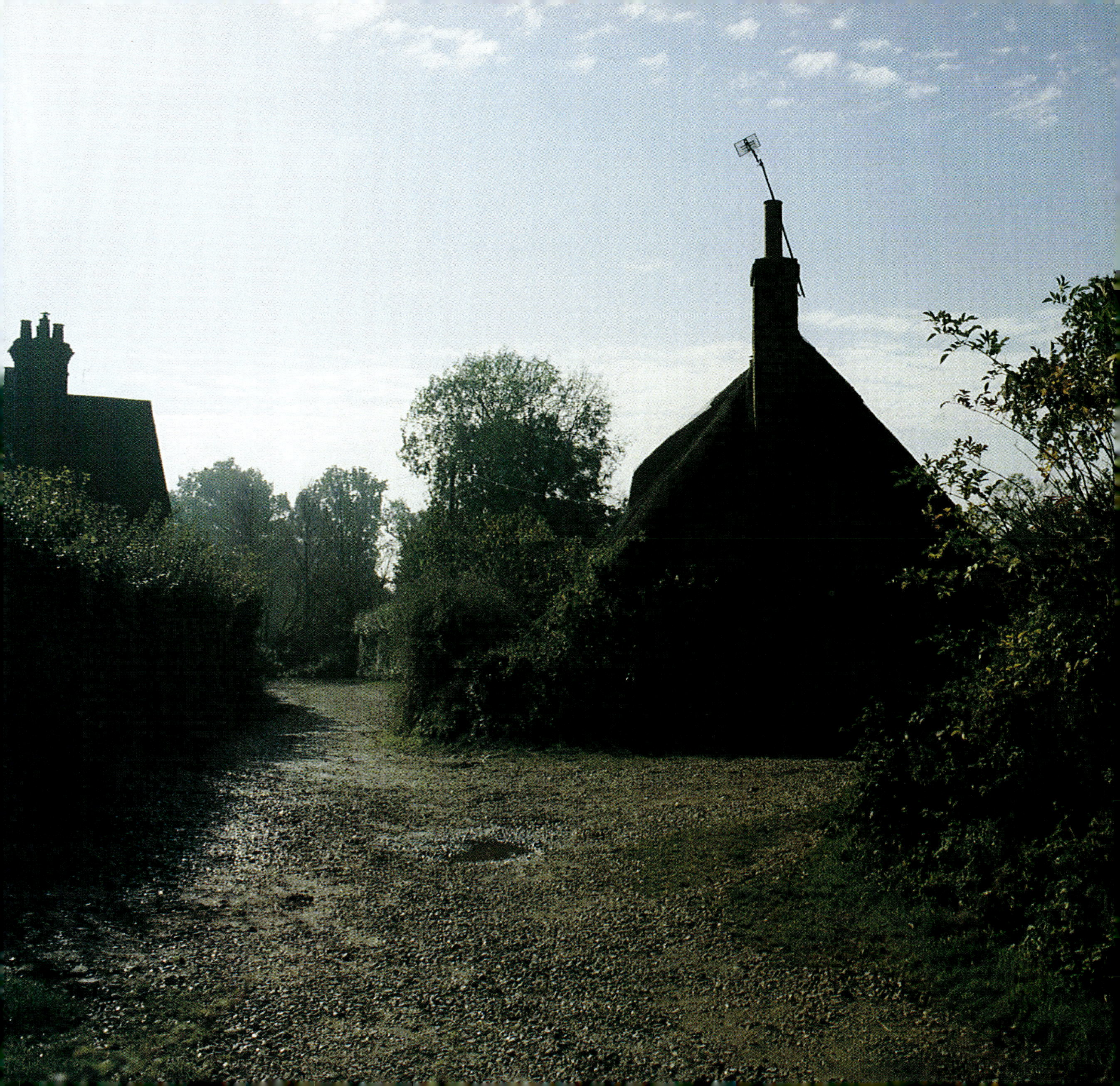

ENGLISH COUNTRY LANES • 164

meadow. A herd of Friesian cows crush close together in the corner, stretching their heads over the fence to eat the long, lush grass at the other side. They munch and chew, lick their wet noses with long sweet tongues, shake the flies from their ears or gaze out into the lane with their large dark eyes.

At the back of the meadow, almost out of sight, is a tiny thatched cottage, so pretty it belongs to a fairy tale. Honeysuckle grows down the side of the roof from the chimneys, covering the thatch and hiding the door. A wisteria hedge curls up to the eaves and swallows nest in the roof. On the other side of the lane are a few sycamore trees, then oak, ash, hazel and birch, and a long line of magnificent beech trees covered in copper leaves curves away to the south and Coombe End Farm. In the branches are greenfinches, goldfinches, chaffinches, mistle thrushes and jays. The sound of a pheasant echoes through the trees, a partridge flies over, and a fox moves off from behind the hedge, its white tail brushing the grass as it goes.

Coombe End Farm house is an old farm homestead which belongs to the National Trust. Four hundred years old, it has flint walls, a tiled roof with seventeenth-century oak beams, and there is a well-preserved cruck barn with a sloping roof which stands at the side of the house. Beech trees are all around the farmhouse and barn, and along the edges of the fields. Their crisp leaves lie scattered on the paths in a fading mosaic of glossy colours — rich browns, rubies, ochre, magenta and maroon.

Sir Rickman Godlee retired to live here in the 1920s. He was a brilliant Victorian surgeon who was the nephew and pupil of Lord Lister, the pioneer of antiseptic treatment in surgery. Sir Rickman was the honorary surgeon in ordinary to the king, Emeritus Professor of Clinical Surgery at University College, London, and in 1917 he published a book about his uncle, Lord Lister, who lived at Coombe Park, the fine mansion house set in the meadows next to the River Thames a mile (1.5km) below Coombe End Farm to the south.

After the beech trees, the lane curves slightly to the south-west. Here the surface of the lane is broken and stony, and covered with leaves. The white chalk soil shows through. Coombe End Cottages are on the right. Coombe End Cottages were the farm cottages belonging to Coombe End Farm Estate. They are red brick and flint, with tall Tudor chimneys, and their gardens are filled with ripe fruit trees and bushes — cherries, blackcurrants, quinces, apples, plums and pears. Larkspur, dahlias, marigolds and phlox fill the gardens, and the cottage called Trees has a row of huge sunflowers staked up, nine feet (3m) tall, the flowers fading, the heads hanging down, standing next to a few well-grown buddleias — their flowers all dried up and drooping.

Beyond the cottages, the lane divides into two. One path turns south towards Coombe Court Farm, another small farm which was once part of Coombe End Farm Estate, and the other goes east and passes Booths Shaw and Cockpit Plantation, a small copse of mixed trees on the right which was the site of an old cockpit where fighting cocks were set against each other to fight to the death for a wager.

Further on Coombe End lane, there is a straight stretch which continues westwards along the top of a ridge in between two fields. The hedges at either side are hawthorn, blackthorn, birch and hazel, with brambles, briars and honeysuckle growing up among them. Where

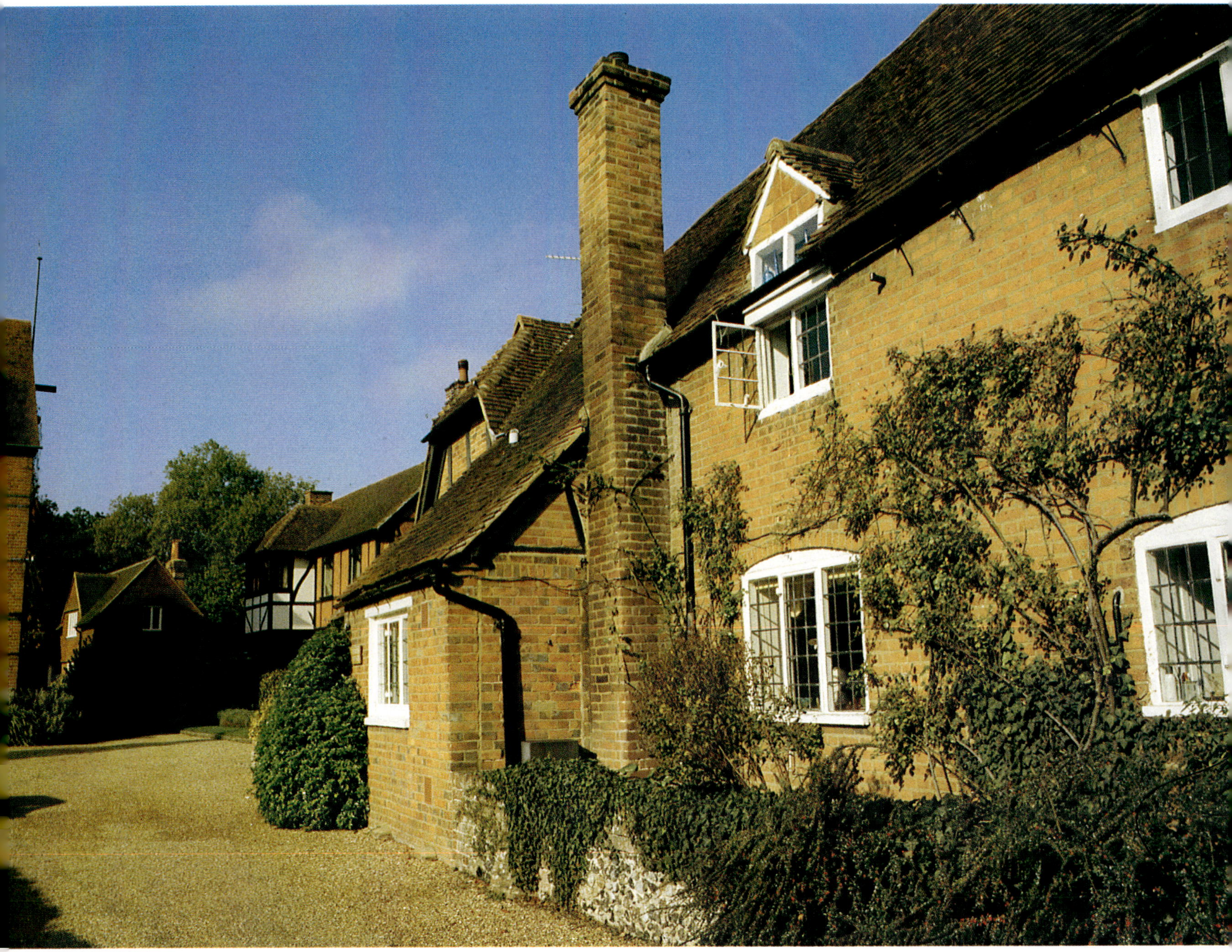

the hedges are taller, fruits and berries are knotted in the branches — elderberries, rose-hips, haws, the lush orange globes of rowan, crab-apple, wild pear, blackberries and the succulent but deadly deep-red fruits of the guelder rose. Cabbage white butterflies surge in a streaming foaming mass around the purple elderberries, and greenfinches gather on the tops of the bushes, then drop down on the leaves gobbling the berries and dribbling the juice on the ground. Game birds promenade along the lane in a haughty dazzling splendour picking at the choicest fruits: red-legged partridges with bronzed bodies and bold black eye-stripes, Hungarian partridges with lavish chestnut tail feathers, and pheasants with glorious golden tail feathers touching the ground. A soft brown, shy and secretive quail bobs in and out of the tree roots looking for snails.

Here the lane is quite straight and continues going westwards between two long meadows before taking a slight turn to the north. The top of Pauls Grove is on the left and a path goes down through the trees, splits into two, rejoins and leads to Lower Hartslock Wood. Other tracks lead to a Neolithic standing stone almost hidden in the wood, and the north bank of the River Thames.

Pauls Grove is a large area of ancient yew fixed in the Chiltern Scarp. Tall, stout and immensely old, the trees grow in a thick dense area sheltered from the wind on the side of the coombe. Some of these trees are a few hundred years old and they were once thought to be magic. Yew trees can live up to 2,000 years of age — there is one as old as this in Perthshire, Scotland — and because these trees outlived many generations of men, they were regarded in ancient times as a symbol of everlasting life and held special magical significance on earth. When men or women died, small sprigs of yew were placed in the folds of their shrouds and the strong red heartwood of the tree was scattered on their graves to ensure the continuation of life after death, and when the first Christian missionaries came to Britain they worshipped under the yew tree before their churches were built. Many country churches have yew trees growing next to the church itself, showing perhaps the original place of worship on the sacred ground and, more than this early man's reverence and connection with nature as being part of God.

The yew trees in Pauls Grove come right up to the edge of the lane in a narrow stretch on the left; lower down the side of the coombe they spread out, and where the canopy is more open the yew is bushy and much shorter, and it mingles with beech, hazel, holly and ash. The tops of the trees below are hazy smudges of golds and greens; they shade the folds of the coombe into softly floating disconnected shapes which reflect in the river below. There are stoats and weasels sneaking in the spent dry grass along the edges, foxes linger in russet groves, fallow deer and roe deer graze undisturbed in the dappled shadows, and somewhere under the trees are the badgers tucked into their sleeping chambers deep inside the banks. After Pauls Grove the lane curves northwards, the hedges at either side go along

◁ Church Cottage, Kenneth Grahame's house.

167 • COOMBE END – SIR MICHAEL CAINE

as before, until the lane narrows and then comes out through some trees which meet overhead at the top of the coombe — here a large, sloping stony-harrowed field with the chalk showing through. Beyond are the Berkshire Downs, stretching out to the far horizon; a warm and waving landscape with hazy golden fields and copper trees and the River Thames below looping through the valley like a liquid amber thread. At the entrance to the field are teasels and thistles with fluffy heads, and the tall, gaunt skeletons of hedge parsley and giant hogweed are behind. Rose-hips glow in the sun and blackberry bushes with dazzling, juicy fruits billow into the lane. There is no sound other than some great tits 'sawing' in the woods and the occasional broken call of a pheasant from the thickets. On the right is a carefully ploughed field which rises away northwards towards Stapnalls Farm and the Great Chalkwood just visible behind a line of beech and elm, and at the end of the lane leading to Wilderness and Owl Cottage.

Stapnalls Farm is a small farm of thirty acres (9ha) with a thatched, picturesque farmhouse. The house is flint and brick with oak beams, and is over 500 years old. There is an open farmyard, byres and barns, cattle in the meadows, and ducks and hens in the yard.

In 1187 the land at Stapnalls was given to the nunnery at Goring by King Henry II; in 1325 the farm came into the possession of William de Stapenhulle, and in 1355 John of Stapenhulle was granted the mill and land at Gatehampton, which later became part of Stapnalls Farm. Sir Thomas Pope lived there in 1555. Sir Thomas held high court posts in Chancery, the Star Chamber, the Mint and the Royal Court of Augmentation. During 1555 he had joint charge of Princess Elizabeth at Hatfield House

169 • COOMBE END – SIR MICHAEL CAINE

and in that same year he founded Trinity College at Oxford. An ancient packway starts near the house and goes southwards to Hartslock Woods and the river.

A little way on, past the ploughed field, the lane divides. One track goes right and enters the private land belonging to Gatehampton House, and the other skirts the field at the top of the coombe, and then suddenly sinks down and changes into a winding path which goes down the side of the coombe through a grotto of trees.

Until recent times this part of the lane was much wider and was a coaching track from Goring to Whitchurch Hill and beyond. Now it is almost overgrown, remote and silent, a speckled tunnel of dense brown leaves and very dim. Mixed woodland is at either side and the branches of the trees are wound round with the rope-like stems of traveller's joy. They climb to the crowns of the trees and their hairy white fruits make a soft showering curtain down both sides of the narrow track. Lower down, another coombe, pale and grassy, a crest of evergreen on its top, comes down to the edge of the path.

The path widens, turns to the south, then dips down between soft, sun-warmed banking. There are milk thistles, spear thistles, blue scabious, common mallow and burdock in the margins, and above are hips and haws with dark red leaves. On the left are more yew trees, a meadow with a palomino pony in it and, lower down, a wooden gate and stile which leads to Hartslock Nature Reserve, Hattonhill Shaw and the River Thames, which is quite close across the next field.

Hartslock Nature Reserve goes from the edge of the lane, along the side of the coombe to Paul's Grove and Hartslock Wood, and along the riverbank as far as Hartslock Cottage and the boathouse. The nature reserve is part of the Buckinghamshire, Berkshire and Oxfordshire Naturalist Trust, and it was bought with the aid of the World Wide Fund for Nature to preserve the rare species of flora and fauna found in the rich chalk downland of Hartslock and the good alluvial soil alongside the river. There are butterflies — the chalkhill, adonis and the small blue; wild herbs, grasses and sedges; some very rare wild flowers such as bastard toadflax, chalk milkwort and the extremely rare downy fruited sedge; grasshoppers, among them the rufous grasshopper; many uncommon moths, beetles and trueflies; and a well-established colony of badgers under the trees. Other more common species of grass and flowers fill the meadow on the sloping side of the coombe above the wood: sheep's fescue, dodder, downy oat grass, horse-shoe vetch, cocksfoot and rock-roses. The trees are beech, ash, oak and yew.

▽ *The River Thames towards Pangbourne and Goring, with Hartslock Island.*

ENGLISH COUNTRY LANES • 170

171 • COOMBE END — SIR MICHAEL CAINE

From the top of the coombe, one can see the River Thames, beautiful, 'full-bodied', sun-drenched and slow moving, flowing southwards a full five miles (8km) from Streatley Hills and Goring Gap in the north, under the elegant Gatehampton Bridge and past Ferry Cottages — where the eastern section of the ancient Icknield Way meets the prehistoric Ridgeway — then continuing on, past the church at Lower Basildon, Basildon House and Park and the Childe Beale Wildfowl Reserve on the south bank. Beyond that, the river flows onwards and southwards by Hartslock Wood on the north bank, Hartslock Island, Hartslock Cottage, the boathouse, the magnificent and stately Coombe Park and grounds, and the wharves, weirs, mill race and pretty water mill at Whitchurch and Pangbourne.

A fisherman sat alone in the meadows along the south bank, his fishing tackle on the grass beside him. We talked about the river.

'I like the tranquillity of the river', he said. 'Here is peace and quiet. Old Father Thames flowing on in just the same way as he always did, curving and flowing through the landscape as if the world had never changed — timeless — the trivialities of human life put into perspective.' He gave a sardonic smile and I asked him if all fishermen are philosophers.

'I suppose so', he answered. 'It's all the contemplating that we do whilst waiting for the fish to bite.'

I questioned him about fishing in the Thames.

'Anglers have taken over from the professional fishermen who have fished this river since the thirteenth century. This is one of the finest rivers in the country for coarse fishing. Plenty of perch, pike, roach, chub, eels and trout, and sometimes salmon — and plenty of other

ENGLISH COUNTRY LANES

are here too. They breed on Hartslock Island, and when I am fishing they always come up investigating and disturbing the fish — but I don't mind, for they really are the most beautiful and serene creatures.'

He moved his fishing stool a bit closer to the water's edge and peered into the water.

'And of course, there are the swans. Richard the Lionheart brought the first swans into England from Cyprus. They were eaten in this country until turkey became popular. There are said to be 600 swans on the river.' He lifted his fishing rod and re-settled it in the water. 'The swans in England are owned by the queen', he continued, 'and the Vintners' Company and the Dyers' Company — the swans here', he pointed to a pair of swans further down the river, 'belong to the queen. Each year, on the third of July they catch the swans and mark

wildlife too', he added as a whooper swan flew overhead. 'There are Canada geese, teal, tufted duck, mallards, pochards and terns, and occasionally there are crested grebes. And in the backwaters, deeps and eyots — small islands — are moorhens, coots, water rats, toads, sand martins and kingfishers.'

'There's a lot to look at', he said as he stood up to recast his line. 'See the old grey heron over there, waiting under the willows?' He pointed to a large grey bird with a blue and black waving crest and a bright yellow beak which stood poised in the shadows staring solemnly down at the river. 'Like me, he's been fishing this same stretch for years. Looks as fit as ever — perhaps it's because to survive he has to be alert the whole time. But there I go philosophising again', he joked. 'There are kingfishers shooting up and down the river, almost too fast to see. Just flashes of turquoise low over the surface — and otters

173 • COOMBE END – SIR MICHAEL CAINE

them. It's called Swan Upping and it takes place at Henley a few miles down the river. Crowds gather to watch all the ancient pageantry, brass bands play, the men wear swan's feathers in their hats, much beer is consumed and it's all very jolly.'

A big brown water rat poked its head out of the opposite bank, looked around and then disappeared under some reeds.

'Did you see that?' he asked. 'Water rats are really called water voles and they are delightful creatures. Spent hours watching them. The water rats, toads, otters, moles and badgers along this stretch of the river were put into a book — *Wind in the Willows* by Kenneth Grahame. He lived just nearby, and just across from Hartslock Island is the original thatched boathouse — or what's left of it — which gave him the idea for Ratty's house on the riverbank. He used to spend his days in a rowing boat on the river with a picnic hamper, a bottle of port and his writing pad, thinking up his stories, and this stretch of river from Cookham Dene to Pangbourne, Whitchurch and Goring was the inspiration and setting for his story . . . a wonderful book. And talking of food — it's tea-time.' He bent down, opened a willow basket and offered to share his tea.

Cookham Dene was where Kenneth Grahame spent his childhood. He left and went to work in London for thirty years in 'a blue-pencilled nightmare', became secretary to the Bank of England, then retired and came to live at Church Cottage in Whitchurch in a house with a splendid garden and a ship's bell at the front door.

Grahame was always quiet and withdrawn, yet a kindly man, innocent and naive, who had a mystical attitude towards life. He needed to be free to find the peace and tranquillity of natural life, and when he came to live by the River Thames he found what he was looking for.

Often he would row upriver to find remote stretches of the Thames, or tie up his boat and spend long hours in the backwaters and deeps, watching water rats, moles, otters and toads go about their private business, or, he would wander off in solitude crossing the high ridges of the Downs.

The River Thames and the quiet lush landscape was the 'still centre' from which the story of *The Wind in the Willows* evolved. The river islands, the weirs, the backwaters and deeps, the paths, the lanes and the Downs, and the animals were all woven around and set in the pagan, golden and lyrical days of times gone by. The

ENGLISH COUNTRY LANES • 174

Ridgeway at Streatley was the Open Road where Mole, Ratty and Toad rambled over the grassy downs, then took to 'strolling along the high road'. Grahame wanted to show how life should be. He believed passionately that rural society should defend itself against the industrial world and remain a perfect Arcadian place. When he died in 1932, his grave was lined with thousands of sweet peas.

Other famous writers lived here, were charmed by the river and found that it encouraged them to write: Edward Thomas, Jerome K Jerome, Miss Read and William Penn. The poet Robert Bridges spent long years of his life here writing, and Lewis Carroll recognised the magic of the river whilst out boating and had the inspiration for *Alice in Wonderland*.

The River Thames has been used as a highway since very early days — primitive people, Romans, Saxons, Vikings and medieval man all sailed up the Thames to gain access to the middle of the country, and in Tudor and Stuart times, when sea-going trade increased, boats and barges would come up river carrying goods from abroad.

At that time there were also great pageants and triumphal processions on the river in celebration of special events, and kings and queens would often be carried up from London in their magnificent and highly decorated barges to visit the palaces and mansion houses built alongside the river. Queen Elizabeth I especially loved the Thames, and Henry VIII would often go up to London from Windsor in sumptuous barges.

The 93 mile (150km) convoluted river journey from London to Oxford took three days, and the barges would be rowed upstream by oarsmen, working hard, pushing their craft slowly onwards, fighting the strength of the current all the way. Royalty sat under a golden awning at the stern facing the oarsmen, who were dressed in the finest livery. An heraldic flag flew at the prow, and a small orchestra would play rousing marches and fanfares — corontos, rondos and other lively music on sackbuts, crumhorns, shawms, oboes and drums — and the ebullient and joyful sound would bring the workers from the fields and the millers from the mills to the river's edge to stand and listen and watch in awe whilst the resplendent barges sailed past.

Not only kings and queens had splendid barges specially built for them — dukes, barons, earls and the new rich merchant middle classes had ceremonial craft to display their wealth and circumstance.

Later, other boats crowded on to the Thames. Skiffs, gigs, punts and seventeenth-century Thames wherries — all light craft for carrying passengers. Then there were flat-bottomed Thames lighters — used for cargo — and, during the Industrial Revolution, there were barges which were bow-hauled by men or pulled by horses along the towpath, and later came the steam tugs, barges and working narrow boats carrying cargoes of coal, cement, timber, bricks, malt, grain, flour, cheese, paper and hay for London's markets.

Before steam engines arrived, a 200-ton boat required twelve to fourteen horses or fifty to eighty men to pull it, and could travel twenty-five miles (40km) a day upstream or thirty-five miles (56km) downstream, with overnight stops for men and horses. The men looked after their horses better than they looked after themselves because they were their means of livelihood, and every day they were groomed and fed, rested, and dressed in shining horse brasses with coloured bobbins wound into their manes and tails.

The men who steered the boats up and down the river were called bargees. Proud and independent, they were a law unto themselves. They mixed only with their own kind, intermarried, spoke their own dialect, could neither read nor write, and were a rough and tough people who were often accused of robbing orchards, stealing chickens, breaking down fences and leaving women pregnant wherever they went. But their life was their own. They were their own bosses, and they loved the simple life on the river and stayed to work on it generation after generation.

The barges were their homes and their prized possessions, and they painted them with loving care in bright colours and decorated the panels with gold lettering displaying the boat's name. The cabins inside were cosy and had little seats covered in pretty material, a small stove or polished black range with brass rods above it; and there were more panels with painted castles and knights, cavaliers, roses and sunflowers on them, and buckets painted black with garlands of small flowers and roses intertwined. Shelves of plates, lace curtains, brass knobs and pots of geraniums were everywhere.

Their life was poor but picturesque. The highly coloured boats would chug down the peaceful waters on a summer's evening, or perhaps stop at one of the public houses alongside the riverbank. The children would play on the banking or sit on the prow, watched over by their mother with a baby in her arms and the father leaning against the cabin door smoking his pipe or drinking his pint of beer, and always the peace and beauty of the river was around them, a central part of their everyday life.

After the gate leading to the river and the nature reserve, the lane sweeps south-west and becomes wider. Hips, haws and sloe berries at either side are swelling and bursting, and an ancient elderberry with marbled red leaves squeaks in the breeze. Further along are high, wild pear trees, crab-apple, hawthorns and more travellers' joy winding around their branches. The lane divides into two again: one path leads to Gatehampton House, and the other goes southwards alongside a flat river meadow with some swans paddling near the willows, then turns into a tarmacadamed road, and ends by the Icknield Way and Gatehampton House.

September had touched the purple-tinted woods spread out below me as I walked along the lane in the late autumn sun. The river flowed easy and amber into the backwaters and deeps, and the Downs in the distance lay still and quiet, spread out and burnished brown.

Beech, elm and chestnut trees grew on the crests of the coombes — their great leaves a radiant mixture of red, yellow, garnet and gold, and as I walked beneath them the light was fused inside and each splendid tree was changed into a soaring flaming canopy so startling that it almost hurt to look. And the coombes were round and grassy, and set like soft warm breasts beside the Thames. Deep within, the trees were hung with fruits and berries — luscious apples, wild pears, dusky cherries and erotic sloes.

Boats cruised by on the water, the swans paused and dipped their heads, herons waited in the willows, otters stayed to sunbathe on the banks, while all along the ridges, the dark deliberate yew was undisturbed and marked the place where badgers slept in ancient setts.

And later in the day, as I sat by the side of the lane watching the sun go down and the river below me melting from bronze to silver, the grassy coombes smelled warm and rich, and the gurgling song of the water, the fragrance of the flowers in the meadows and the murmuring creatures in the trees lulled me and calmed me. Badgers were busy above, cleaning out their setts, and their lazy good-natured grumbling and grunting carried across the dusk and echoed around the great stands of beech and the ancient yew.

As I watched, the wind moved in the willows, the soft mewing of an otter sounded somewhere beyond, and the old brown water rat came out of his hole and, with a soft and gentle sigh, twitched his nose and tested the air, then swam upriver, leaving a trail of silver bubbles behind.

Millfield Lane, Highgate, London

Lord Menuhin

Very late autumn

'The buried English lane is that typical and blessed English compromise, neither jungle nor road'

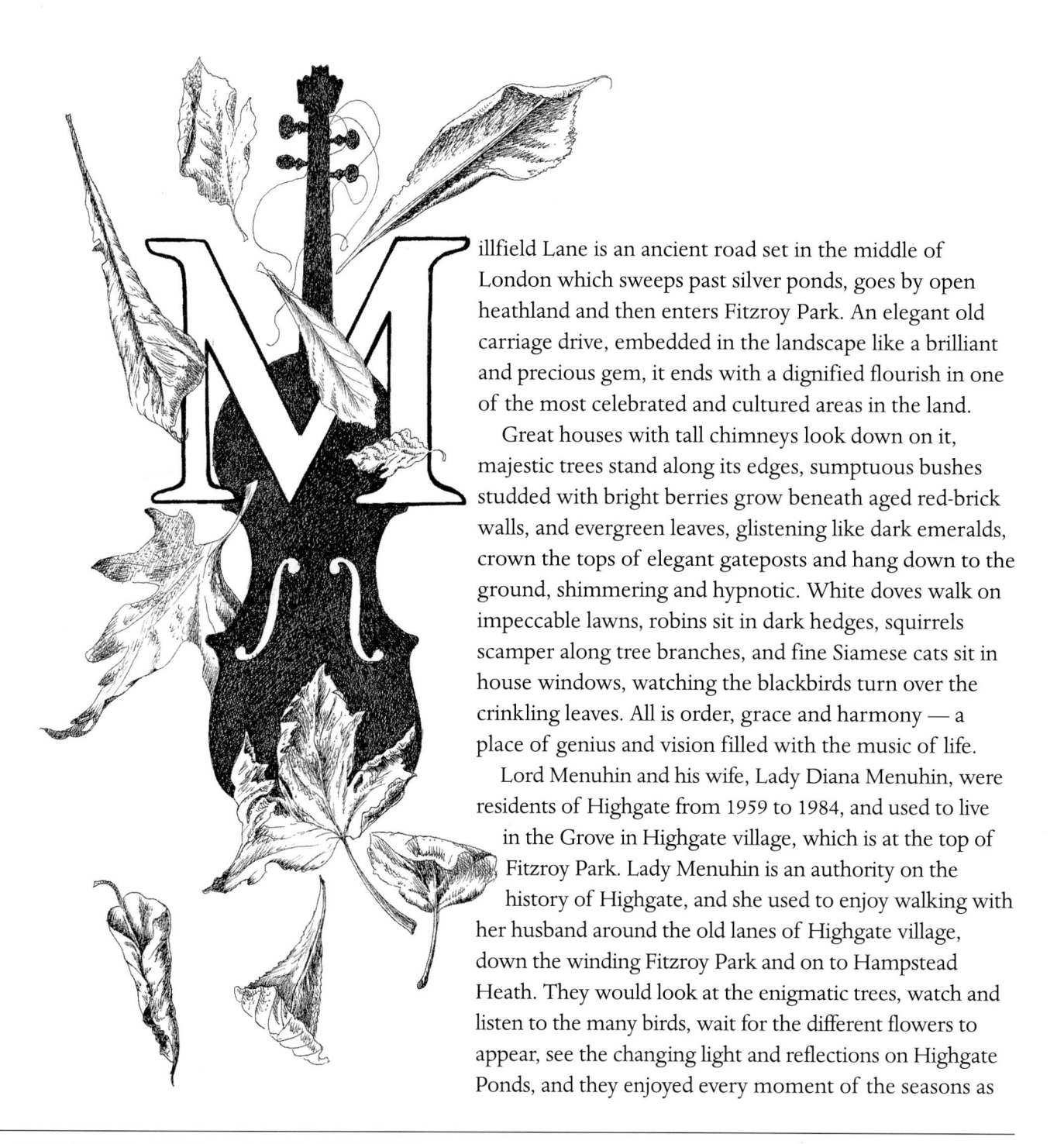

Millfield Lane is an ancient road set in the middle of London which sweeps past silver ponds, goes by open heathland and then enters Fitzroy Park. An elegant old carriage drive, embedded in the landscape like a brilliant and precious gem, it ends with a dignified flourish in one of the most celebrated and cultured areas in the land.

Great houses with tall chimneys look down on it, majestic trees stand along its edges, sumptuous bushes studded with bright berries grow beneath aged red-brick walls, and evergreen leaves, glistening like dark emeralds, crown the tops of elegant gateposts and hang down to the ground, shimmering and hypnotic. White doves walk on impeccable lawns, robins sit in dark hedges, squirrels scamper along tree branches, and fine Siamese cats sit in house windows, watching the blackbirds turn over the crinkling leaves. All is order, grace and harmony — a place of genius and vision filled with the music of life.

Lord Menuhin and his wife, Lady Diana Menuhin, were residents of Highgate from 1959 to 1984, and used to live in the Grove in Highgate village, which is at the top of Fitzroy Park. Lady Menuhin is an authority on the history of Highgate, and she used to enjoy walking with her husband around the old lanes of Highgate village, down the winding Fitzroy Park and on to Hampstead Heath. They would look at the enigmatic trees, watch and listen to the many birds, wait for the different flowers to appear, see the changing light and reflections on Highgate Ponds, and they enjoyed every moment of the seasons as

Lord Menuhin
Fitzroy Park
&
Millfield Lane
Highgate, London
Hampstead Lane
Beechwood
The Grove
Highgate
Fitzroy Park
Shops
The Flask
South Grove
St Michael's Church
Rembrandts
Turners
Kenwood House Museum
Sculpture, Henry Moore, Barbara Hepworth
oak trees
The Elms
Squirrels on lawns
Allotment Gardens
trees
London plane trees
Horse Chestnut
site of The Limes
site of Hillside
The Thousand Pound Pond
Open air stage Bowl
Bathing house
W
E
S
Oak Trees
woods & meadows & grassy paths
Blackbirds, Robins & Hollyberries
reeds
Heronry
Hampstead Heath
Mallards, herons,
Highgate Ponds
Canada Geese, Cormorants, Goldeneye ducks
grassy places & paths
Millfield Lane
Berries & Ivy
West Hill
Holly Gardens
Millfield Cottage
Bandstand
people & dogs

they came and went. On their walks down the lane, they marvelled at the graceful architecture of the magnificent houses all around them and rejoiced in the fact that here, almost in the centre of London, near to their home was the perfect peace of an English country lane.

'Over the years', Lady Diana writes, 'we have watched as masses of simple families came up from the dreariness of Hornsey and Holloway with their picnic baskets and their children to go on to Hampstead Heath or to tend their allotments higher up the lane in Fitzroy Park. Of course, in an earlier period, 1925, when Kenwood was made public, they used to go over to Kenwood itself.'

'It was lovely living in Highgate', thought Sir Yehudi Menuhin (later Lord Menuhin), 'which, being on a hill, finds its lanes not altogether flattened out, even if in some cases, old brick walls serve the seeds with crevices and the many-fingered plants with something to crawl over. The pattern of the lanes sometimes penetrates into the heart of cities, sometimes even denuded of trees — as at Brighton: but even then, window fronts, little shops, people, convey and retain something of the organic character of the plants and the many various-legged creatures, winged and belly-bound to earth, which animate the country lanes. How far removed from the wastes of cement, so crushing of life and its very spirit. The car is certainly an intrusion on the lanes, for they belong to feet and, at the very most, to bicycles. Yet even the little car — for buses and trucks are for the most part unviable — is kept in its place, for we are made aware that nature would soon, however gently, close ranks, probably for our benefit.

The buried English lane winding between a celebration of life, vegetable, insect, bird and worm is that typical and blessed English compromise, neither jungle nor road. It is born of a benign climate, sufficiently wet, warm and sunny to clothe the earth in green, yet not so much as to prevent a clear path through the thickest vegetation, a path which, however meandering and whilst remaining browsing, does eventually reach its destination. It is so very English.'

Millfield Lane begins at the bottom of West Hill, Highgate, goes west, and climbs north-west past Hampstead Heath and Highgate Ponds. This part of the lane ends and enters Fitzroy Park, bends north-east, runs alongside the Allotment Gardens, then rises up higher and ends in the Grove, Pond Square and Highgate village, a distance of about one and a half miles (2.5km).

Millfield Lane starts at the bottom of the steep West Hill and bends abruptly, going north-west and rising up at once. At the corner of the bend is Millfield Cottage, a quaint, sixteenth-century red-brick cottage with white plaster and green shutters, secret looking and secluded. Ivy tendrils, some of them in flower, tangle over the chimney stacks and twist down from the low roof, almost covering the leaded windows and the black-painted door. Behind the cottage, on the left-hand side of the lane, the unexpected expanse of Hampstead Heath opens out and Highgate Ponds — five large freshwater ponds — follow the curve of the lane close by. Highgate Ponds were small ponds originally fed by the head-springs of the River Fleet, but were opened up in the sixteenth century to create reservoirs for the residents of London.

Multitudes of birds are on the ponds. Moorhens and coots, constantly quarrelling and flicking their tails, swim around in small circles, swans sit cleaning their feathers or moving gracefully on the water, their black-webbed

ENGLISH COUNTRY LANES • 182

feet paddling slowly and methodically, river gulls chase and dive, and ducks are everywhere — teal with handsome chestnut heads and green shining stripes around their eyes, mallards with glossy emerald heads and smart white collars, all-white smew with a touch of black, and goldeneye flying low with whistling wing beats.

A whole flock of Canada geese with fine black heads and fat chests potter about the water's edge or paddle across the surface, twisting it into finely traced silvery patterns. A number of them sit down, packing together, posing and preening or stretching out their necks, honking regally into the fog. The sound softens slightly in the heavy air. Higher up on the next pond are more swans, almost hidden in the tall rushes, and crested grebes glide in and out and distract the heron from its fishing. The leaden sky is vibrant and noisy, alive with the sound of calling birds and fluttering wings as they skim over the water, make soft landings on the banking or cruise slowly in great arcs choosing a clear place on the water to touch down.

The third pond is the men's bathing pond and the fifth is the ladies' bathing pond for outdoor swimming, and were much used in Edwardian days. They are still in use today.

After the second pond, a path leads off to the left going over the heath, past a tumulus or round barrow, and on to Parliament Hill and the Victorian wrought-iron bandstand by the café. Parliament Hill is the spot where in 1605 some of the conspirators involved in the Gunpowder Plot waited to see the Houses of Parliament blown up.

The Gunpowder Plot was a conspiracy by the Roman Catholics during the reign of the Protestant King James I to blow up the king and queen, and the leading men of the country when they assembled for the opening of Parliament. The leader of the plot was Robert Catesby, who, together with six other conspirators, Thomas Percy, Thomas Winter, Robert Winter, Christopher Wright, John Wright and Guy Fawkes, were angry because the king refused to show religious tolerance and allowed the Catholics to be persecuted, imposed heavy fines on them for following their religion and banished their priests. The conspirators were all fervent Catholics, and in the spring of 1605 they plotted to blow up the Houses of Parliament.

Guy Fawkes was a Yorkshireman who had been in the Netherlands serving with the Spanish army as an explosives expert. He found that he could rent a cellar storeroom that extended underneath the House of Lords, and he was able to bring thirty-six barrels of gunpowder which he hid under coals, firewood and bars of iron in the cellar. Robert Catesby decided that more conspirators should be involved in the plot as he felt there was a need for more support for the cause. One of these men, Francis Tresham, sent a note to his brother-in-law, Lord Monteagle, who was a Catholic, warning him not to attend the opening of Parliament but 'to retire into the country for they ... shall receive a terrible blow'. The letter was passed to the lord chamberlain, who searched the area around the Houses of Parliament and came upon Guy Fawkes guarding the fuel in the cellar. He was arrested and the plot was foiled. The other conspirators waited in vain, here on Parliament Hill, for the great explosion which never came.

Guy Fawkes was taken before the Scottish King James and he shouted at the king that it was his intention 'to blow the Scottish back to Scotland'. Under torture he

The Victorian bandstand, Hampstead Heath.

refused to betray the others, and would not give their names until he knew for sure that they had been put to death. Then, so badly tortured that he could not walk to the gallows, he went stoically to his death. In January 1906 Parliament established the 5th November as a day of public thanksgiving. Guy Fawkes Day is still celebrated in England with fireworks and the burning of effigies of Guy Fawkes on huge bonfires lit in public places.

Hampstead Heath covers an area of 825 acres (335ha) and reaches 423 feet (129m) above sea level. Once it was part of the great forest of Middlesex and was the bishop of London's hunting ground. Later there was a clearing made which became the bishop's parkland. The heath has always been a refuge for the people of London. In the winter of 1603, when the Black Death ravaged the country, people flocked to the heath and up to Highgate Hill, away from the cramped, closed conditions of London; and later, in 1666, when the Great Fire of London swept through the city, they fled here again and lived in tents, huts and hovels with no comfort, having no clothes to wear or good food to eat while they waited for the fire to burn itself out. On the heath there were circles of tents stretching over several miles. Pepys's *Diary* of 1660–1670 tells of the misery of that time and of how even the wealthy people with stately furnished houses were reduced to misery.

There is a gentle slope, a curve to the right, and the lane sweeps northwards running along the edge of the heath. The grass comes up to the lane side and the fog, thinner here, hangs on each blade and changes the green to a pale grey. Wild lupin, teasel and some shaggy, fading goldenrod stand together in a thicket of beech saplings — their empty seed-heads faintly etched against the light. A large burdock wilts from the cold.

On the right is Merton Lane and the grounds of Merton Lodge. Opposite, another path leads off eastwards and downwards, going in between the third and fourth pond, and joining with the other paths running in various directions. Millfield Lane ends, and a wide sandy track leaves the last section and goes through enclosed trees with black iron railings on the left, and leads to Fitzroy Park Farm and Kenwood House.

Kenwood House is a magnificent, white neo-Classical villa filled with important works of art and bequeathed to the nation in 1927 by Edward Cecil Guiness, first earl of Iveagh and the second-richest man in England at that time. Bordered on three sides by Hampstead Heath, it stands on the top of a high ridge overlooking the grounds, landscaped by Capability Brown.

King Henry III confirmed by charter the gift of land to the Holy Trinity Monastery known as Caenwood (Kenwood) in 1226. The house was built in 1616, and before that Kenwood was a woodland estate growing and selling timber. From 1764 to 1779, Robert Adams and his brother James remodelled the whole house, encased it in white stucco and added to the building. There is a breathtaking library, or 'Great Room' as it is called, in which the famous and stunning late self-portrait by Rembrandt hangs. Other works of art are by Gainsborough, Van Dyck, Frans Hals, Joshua Reynolds and Turner, and in the grounds along the Lime Avenue are sculptures by Henry Moore and Barbara Hepworth. There are gardens — the Formal Garden, the Picturesque Garden and the Thousand Pound Pond, where there is a concert bowl across the water and concerts are held on summer evenings. People bring picnic hampers filled with champagne, and strawberries and cream, listen to the music and watch the firework display which finishes the evening's entertainment.

Attached to the west side of the house is an orangery — a long gallery room with large high windows used for promenading in wet weather. It dates from 1694 and was named after the Dutch Royal House of Orange. To own an orangery filled with exotic fruits was a status symbol in the seventeenth century. The long gallery was filled with orange trees, peach trees and myrtles, crowded together with geraniums and sweet lavender, and the colour and scents cheered people up in the gloom of winter weather outdoors. Robert Adam wrote of Kenwood that:

'It was most magnificent, beautiful and picturesque and one could see London, Greenwich Hospital, the River Thames and the ships passing up and down, framed by the hills of Highgate and Hampstead.'

In 1753, John Stuart, third earl of Bute, tutor to King George III, prime minister of England and one of the founders of Kew Gardens, was proud to own Kenwood. In 1757 he told a colleague that he could see the whole city of London with sixteen miles (24km) of the Thames from every window, and when William Murray, the first Earl Mansfield, owned the house, he expanded the estate to 1,500 acres (600ha) stretching south past Highgate Ponds and Millfield Farm to Parliament Hill, Hampstead Heath and beyond. Lord Mansfield was lord chief justice for thirty-two years, he reformed court procedure and was the greatest British judge of the eighteenth century.

Successive earls have lived at Kenwood and in the late 1800s, Grand Duke Michael of Russia lived there and left two gravestones in the grounds, one with the inscription 'sleep old friend' marks the grave of Bill, his beloved dog, and the other stone reads 'An old and faithful friend' and is dedicated to Mac, another favourite dog. These stones are all that he left as mementoes of his life at Kenwood. In the early 1920s an American millionairess, Nancy Leeds, lived there and then in 1925 Kenwood was opened to the public by King George V. Eventually the house and grounds were bought by Edward Cecil Guiness to house his famous art collection.

After the sandy track leaves Millfield Lane almost next to it, on the right, a dark archway marks the entrance to Fitzroy Park. Berries are everywhere — purple laurel berries, black-cherry-coloured laurel berries, vermilion japonica, scarlet cotoneaster, blood-red holly berries and pure-white snow berries. Some are set on crimson twigs or fine-spun leaves with silver veins, more grow up in pearl-like bunches — brilliant ornaments in glistening green. Behind them are the trees going up each side of the drive, one behind the other, tall, beautiful and utterly compelling: limes, elms, poplars, London plane trees, horse chestnuts, sycamores and beech covered in shining brown seed nuts set in left-over shrinking prickly cases, twisting skins, bobbling green knots or papery wings.

At first there are a few detached houses at each side of the lane hidden from view behind wooden fencing, laburnums and fir trees. Here the tinselled shapes of greater plantain grow in rich neat rows coming from beneath the edges of the tarmac, some fat hen, fading and fallen over, is next to it, common chickweed, nettles, old goldenrod, rosebay willow-herb withered up and wrinkly, and left-over lupins heavy with hairy seed-pods split open and empty.

The Allotment Gardens are on the left. A few empty Brussels sprout stalks poke up out of the black dug-over ground. Ivy is threaded on the railings and on the low roof tops of the garden huts. The lane narrows, the huge trees close in and a gate on the east side looks over the grounds of the now-demolished mansion house called the Limes. Tall stands of poplar, limes, Scots pine, ash trees, willow, hornbeam, oak and elms grow clear to the skyline with no sound save that of the rooks and the quick, white fluttering doves.

There is a long straight stretch which passes sculptured gateposts and splendid drives. Old brick walls are covered in spiky autumn carpets of scarlet and cream Virginia creeper laced here and there with deep red leaves. Impressive lamps sit on the top of each gatepost, and thin, pale cushions of wet moss soften the square edges and corners, and smudge down across the bricks. Each empty spore capsule at the top of the minute stems shines like a frosted pearl.

Beyond the gates at each side of the lane are the mansion houses and villas of Fitzroy Park standing here and there concealed in the trees. From the sixteenth century onwards, Fitzroy Park, Highgate and the surrounding area was the centre, in England, of wealth and culture. Writers, philosophers, musicians, poets, bankers, scientists, politicians and the paramount rulers of the land have lived and worked here or been guests in these magnificent houses.

Beechwood, a huge white mansion house with six tall white chimney stacks, square chimney pots and

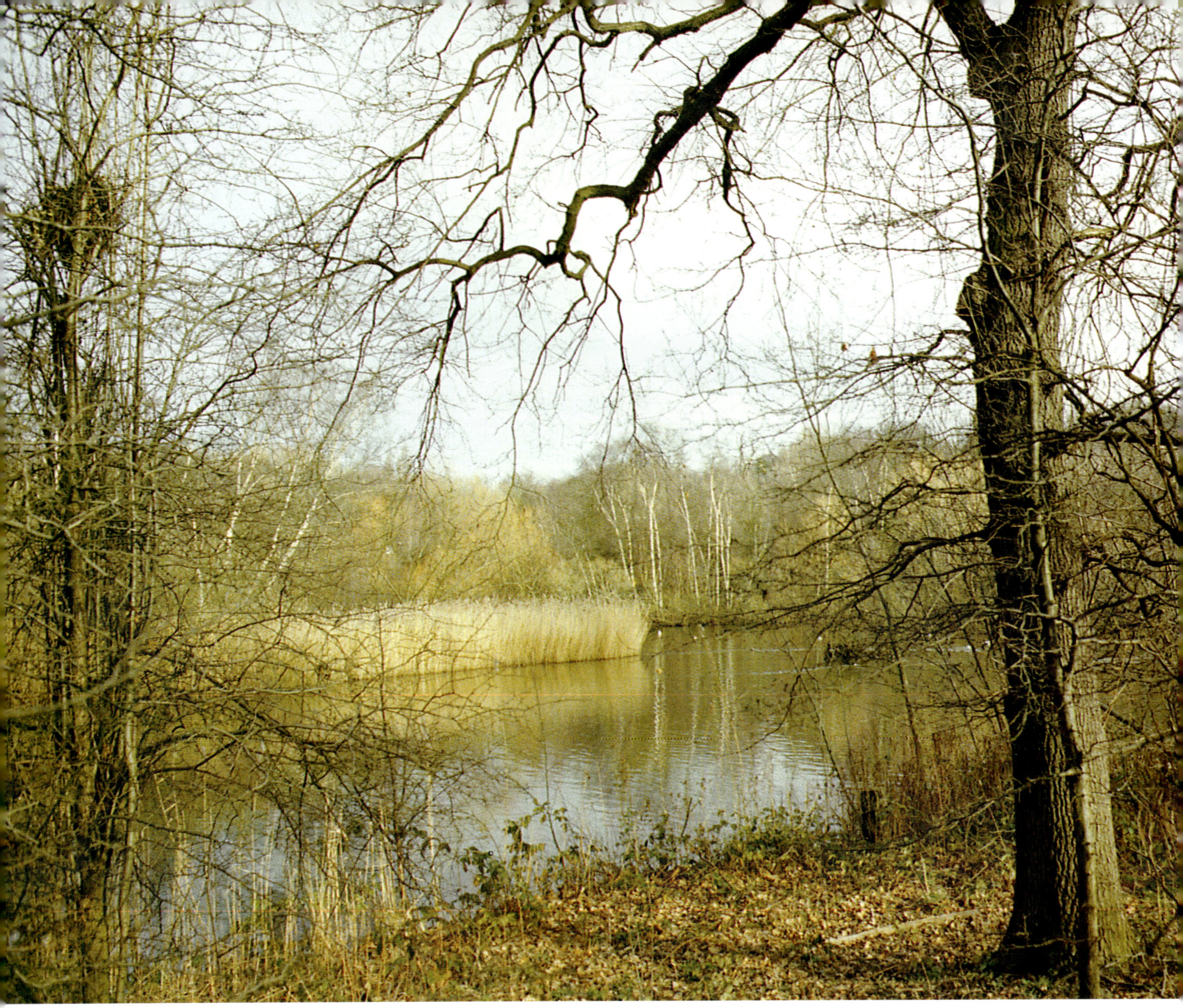

glass-topped skylight rooms, stands on the first bend in Fitzroy Park. Beechwood was built on the site of the old Fitzroy House, then a fine red-brick house, almost a palace, which was the home of Charles Fitzroy in 1768. In 1780 he was raised to the peerage because of his estate. In 1811 Fitzroy House was the home of the earl of Buckinghamshire, and when Mr Robartes, the banker, owned it, he had literary dinners, and Lord Byron, Keats, Samuel Taylor Coleridge and Thomas Carlyle were among his guests.

The Parkfield, now Witanhurst, was built in 1665, has Georgian additions and is at the top of the lane and looks down over Fitzroy Park. This sandstone mansion house has sixty-five bedrooms and is the second-largest privately owned house in London. (The largest is Buckingham Palace.)

Some of the big houses which stood in the park have been pulled down and only the grounds remain. Southampton Lodge stood further down Fitzroy Park on the right, the Limes was higher up on the same side and in between was Hillside, the elegant home of Mary and Margaret Gillies. In 1847 Hans Christian Andersen was a guest at the home of Dr Southwood Smith next door. He was staying with William and Mary Howitt at West Hill, Highgate. They welcomed him and showed him an English home 'full of poetry, sincerity and affection'. He thought they were 'charming intellectual people', and he helped with the summer hay-making and at harvest time rode on decorated wagons with the children carrying flags. He made them pretty posies of flowers and sat with them on the heath telling them his fairy stories whilst they clustered round, listening in delight. Hans Christian Andersen was born in a slum in Odense, Copenhagen, in 1805 and struggled to achieve a place at the university of Copenhagen. There he began to write his famous fairy stories 'The Tinder Box', 'The Princess and the Pea', 'The Snow Queen' and many more. His fairy tales are compelling and enduring for he used folk legend, the belief in the ultimate triumph of goodness and beauty, and he identified with the unfortunate and the outcast.

George Eliot, the writer, spent long summer holidays at Hillside and sat in the landscaped gardens working at her writing. The Elms was built in 1839 by the architect George Basevi. The actor Ronald Shiner lived at Elm Cottage on the left-hand side of the lane, and Dr Jacob Bronowski, the scientist and writer, lived at the Hexagon, a very avant-garde house further up the lane on the right-hand side.

The lane climbs up past a red pillar box and becomes wider, then dips a little, getting narrower. There are houses on both sides set back. After the houses, the lane turns left and rises again. More wooden fencing closes off the houses, but tall trees with wide trunks and blue tits in the branches, and rough grasses here and there give the lane a feeling of rural peace.

The topmost section of the lane is very steep. On the right a curving brick wall shores up the banking. There is a row of tall holly trees, more laurel and an oddly twisted sycamore. A robin looks out from inside the dark branches of a fir tree, and down below, in the dim light, a small grey squirrel patiently turns over some damp leaves with delicate pink fingers. Wilting grasses bending on to the surface of the lane fringe the bottom of the walls. At the top of the lane are the stables which belonged to Fitzroy House, now a private house. There is a leaning gas lamp painted black — one of the original gas lamps which have been changed to electricity — and then Fitzroy Park comes out into the Grove, Pond Square and Highgate village.

The Grove is an elegant row of Georgian houses, some four storeys high. Other houses in the Grove were built between 1680 and 1690 and were the first semi-detached houses in London. Two of these houses were for the children of city merchants who had fallen on hard times. Many famous people have lived there: the actress Gladys Cooper, Sir Yehudi Menuhin and his wife Lady Diana, Lord Justice Fry and his son Roger Fry the painter, and in 1939 J B Priestley was there.

Samuel Taylor Coleridge, the poet who wrote *The Rime of the Ancient Mariner*, *Kubla Khan* and other great narrative poems, moved in to the house of James Gillman, a surgeon, in 1816, remaining there until his death in 1834.

Other famous people have lived in Highgate. A E Housman wrote *A Shropshire Lad* in Byron Cottage, North Road, after walking on the heath, a 'beer from The Flask Pub', the fifteenth-century inn across from the Grove, 'frothing up inside of him'. William Hogarth, the eighteenth-century painter, would spend his Sundays in the Flask drawing the amazing faces which a 'quart pot had made distorted and hot'; and Dick Turpin, the highwayman, hid in the cellar. Andrew Marvell, the seventeenth-century poet and 'fine singer of green shades', lived in a pretty cottage in Swains Lane, which is off South Grove, just behind the Flask, and entertained Nell Gwynne here. Nell Gwynne also stayed at Lauderdale House on the far side of Highgate Cemetery with Charles II. It was here that she threatened to drop their son from the window unless the king gave him a title: he became the earl of Burford.

Highgate Cemetery is in Swains Lane just east of Fitzroy Park and here there are thirty-seven acres (15ha) of woodland, 2,000 selected trees and over 1,000 species of wild flowers. It is a special place, with the tombs of Karl Marx, George Eliot, Michael Faraday and many more.

Francis Bacon, the philosopher and lord chancellor, stayed with his friend Sir Thomas, earl of Arundel, at Arundel House — now the beautiful Old Hall in South Grove — in 1626. One day Francis Bacon decided to prove his theory that meat would keep as well by freezing as by salting, and so he went into the garden and stuffed a

Highgate Ponds.

191 • MILLFIELD LANE – LORD MENUHIN

chicken full of snow. It was so cold he caught a chill, was offered an unaired bed and died of pneumonia.

T S Eliot taught at Highgate School, which was founded in 1562, and so did Gerard Manley Hopkins, the Jesuit priest and poet. Sir John Betjeman, the poet laureate, lived in West Hill, and Charles Dickens was a frequent visitor to the wealthy Baroness Angela Burdett-Coutts' house, Holly Lodge, which is across West Hill from Merton Lane. In the nineteenth century Baroness Burdett-Coutts was the richest woman in England next to Queen Victoria.

Highgate was one of Charles Dickens's favourite places. He would come before breakfast. Alone. Walking fast. Covering as much as thirty miles (50km) in a morning. Thinking. Planning. Ordering his tightly meticulous day. Sometimes he would walk again in the evenings, going through St Giles' to Seven Dials, the city slums near St Martin's Lane in Westminster, and he would be saddened by what he saw.

Dickens was a brilliant man who cared deeply for humanity, and especially children and their poverty appalled him. Poverty he himself had not long left behind. There were rag-and-bone shops everywhere, pawnbrokers' shops, and tumbledown houses with their windows patched with paper and rags. Dirty clothes were hung out in the streets to dry, slops wetted the streets, mothers slouched about in the doorways, swearing, drinking and fighting, and the children with their matted hair played in the filth of open drains or walked barefoot in the gutters, dirty and hungry.

So he brought the sad-eyed children of the slums to Highgate and the heath, and showed them the flowers, the trees and the animals, and he saw their fascination and

△ *Fitzroy Park.*

ENGLISH COUNTRY LANES • 192

their curiosity, but was upset by 'the foulness of their talk, the death of their sensibility, their substitution of the love of horror for the love of beauty ... "are there bears and wolves?" they asked'. As he stood with them collecting buttercups, he looked across the heath and saw 'the long curved line of trees in their first gold-green, a mist of blue in the distance', and realised that 'this place made one feel with deep awe the pollution of these young spirits'. And so he wrote about them, spoke about them in public lectures and helped them change their lives.

When the dark nights set in, he would come here again going to a ball at Baroness Burdett-Coutts's. This time he would come in a carriage and pair — a lean, lithe man, dashing, handsome and dark, dressed in his evening suit and fine silk shirt with ruffs at the collar, pure white gloves and a black top hat. He adored finery and enjoyed dressing up immensely. Occasionally his wife and sister would be beside him in their long muslin gowns, garnets and rubies around their necks, fur wraps around their shoulders, mufflers on their hands and pretty poke bonnets on their heads. Dickens loved to dance, listen to music and attend the theatre. It was the other side of his life. In 1851 his father died and two weeks later his baby daughter, Dora. He was heartbroken and spent much of his time walking, going up and down Millfield Lane, Fitzroy Park, on to the heath and back again, walking until he was exhausted, and then he would go and sit in solitude by their catacombs in Highgate Cemetery.

Charles Dickens was born in Portsmouth in 1812, but from the age of ten he lived in London, and then in 1860 moved permanently to his country house, Gads Hill near Chatham, a house which he dearly loved. He is regarded by many as one of the greatest influences on English literature. His novels were popular in that they appealed to everyone from the simplest person of the working classes, who could read at that time, to the sophisticated, educated upper classes. Major novels such as *The Pickwick Papers*, *Oliver Twist*, *Nicholas Nickleby*, *Bleak House*, *A Tale of Two Cities*, *Great Expectations*, *David Copperfield* and his Christmas stories among his many other works are compassionate, perceptive and humorous.

He wrote about the lost, the oppressed or the bewildered. He had first-hand experience of the images of prison life and the workhouse when his father went to a debtors' prison and he used the privations of his early life

ENGLISH COUNTRY LANES • 194

in his writings. Dickens attacked social evils, and gave public fundraising lectures and readings from his works, both at home and on two hectic lecture tours of America. He was considered to be one of the best public speakers of the age.

He gave his time to many benevolent causes and for over ten years he directed, with great gusto, a reformatory home for young female delinquents financed by his benefactor, Baroness Burdett-Coutts. Poor, humble and simple people had, he believed, the most human decency, and he avoided close contact with much of high society, believing it to be corrupt and superficial, but he did have lifelong friendships with some members of the aristocracy and with other authors, journalists, artists and actors.

Charles Dickens was a man who valued his house and family in his early years, and was a 'proud and efficient householder'. He had nine children and was a devoted father. A lively and energetic man, his friends called him 'the human hurricane'. He was 'charming, his laugh was brimful of enjoyment, his enthusiasm was boundless … a large-hearted man, unpretentious, un-literary, sensible and not too intellectual'. He was one of the great forces of nineteenth-century literature whose influences on his own time was 'extensive — pleasurable, instructive, healthy and reformatory'. Charles Dickens died in 1870 and was buried in Westminster Abbey.

At the end of the lane, across from the Grove, in South Square is St Michael's Church with its high single spire. This church was dedicated in 1386. A poster outside gave notification of an evening concert given by the children of the Menuhin School of Music: 'Elgar Violin Sonata, Mozart Duo in B Flat and a Mendelssohn Octet'. Starlings sit in the eaves of the church giving their pre-winter whistles; the cherry trees by the side of the church are bare, the trunks glistening a deep reddish-brown, and the laurel hanging over the wall tops and growing by the church walls is thickened with luscious deep-blue berries standing up in clusters like antique glass beads faintly powdered in the mist.

Highgate Scientific and Literary Society Library, established 1839, is north-east of the church, and beyond that is Highgate village. The shops are lit up, their windows lighting the streets: bookshops, antique shops, fruit shops and sweet shops. A dried flower shop sends cascades of colour from behind bowed and mullioned windows, and a coffee shop exudes a rich brown smell which drifts across the square.

It was November when I came here, and the great trees in the lane were almost empty. Early fog darkened the day and the lights were on in the houses. Ladies in fine dresses and precious jewels chattered beneath glittering chandeliers, gentlemen in smart suits sipped sparkling champagne from tall cut glasses, sophisticated cats sat on window sills with upturned noses staring out at the sky, and musicians tuned their violas and violins, and began to play 'We are the music makers … we are the dreamer of dreams'. Sir Edward Elgar's music. The sound filled the gardens, and I stood beneath the gently breathing sleeping trees gazing at the windows of the staggering white houses, watching squirrels on the lawns and pale doves on the tall white chimneys, listening to the afternoon drawing-room sounds.

When I had walked in Fitzroy Park from Millfield Lane, I came into the Grove and stood by the trees. It was tea-time, almost evensong time, the beginning of cocktail hour. I stood looking at the beautiful, opulent houses,

Kenwood House.

ENGLISH COUNTRY LANES • 196

excited by their history and overawed by their memories, and I thought of the men who had lived there — their great minds, their music, their words, their work and what they had achieved for themselves and others. Closing my eyes, I could see the carriages coming along the lane and up the drive, hear the horses hooves clattering on the cobbles and the long rustling gowns of the Victorian ladies, and I saw Dickens striding here, broken-hearted and caring, thinking up his stories.

Then the street lamps came on, the shops seemed brighter, a chestnut vendor stood warming his hands by his brazier in Pond Square and the solitary bong of St Michael's Church signalled the end of the afternoon, and there in the churchyard, waiting by the cherry trees, were the small, neat children of the Yehudi Menuhin School of Music, chatting and happy, anticipating their evening concert and their afternoon tea. As they passed, their merry laughter echoed through the fog. And deep in the lane where the city was muted, a Canada goose called from the still, silver ponds, the rooks grumbled, the starlings roosted early and the melody was changed.

◁ *Witanhurst.*

BIBLIOGRAPHY

The Street

Baker, J H, *The Ipsden Country* (William Smith and Son, 1959).

Bloxham, Christina, *Portrait of Oxfordshire* (Robert Hale, 1982).

Small, H G, *In and Around Ipsden* (Albury Printing Co, 1978).

Reading Mercury, 24th Nov 1962 & 30th April 1996.

Thames Valley Countryside Magazine (nd).

Peddars Way

Ashbee, Paul, *The Bronze Age Round Barrow in Britain* (Phoenix House, 1960).

Baker, M, *Folklore and Customs of Rural England* (David and Charles, 1974).

Beedell, Suzanne, *Windmills* (David and Charles, 1975).

Beresford Ellis, Peter, *H Rider Haggard: A Voice from the Infinite* (Routledge & Kegan Paul, 1978).

Blake, P W, et al, *The Norfolk We Live In* (George Nobbs Publishing, 1958)

Brown, R J, *Windmills of England.* (Robert Hale, 1976).

Burrell, R E C, *The Romans in Britain.* Wheaton/Pergaman, 1963).

Chadwick, Nora, *Celtic Britain* (Thames and Hudson, 1963).

Delany, Frank, *The Celts* (Hodder and Stoughton, 1986).

Dorman, B E, *Norfolk* (Batsford, 1986).

Forman, Joan, Haunted East Anglia (Robert Hale, 1974).

Fry, Somerset, *Roman Britain* (David and Charles, 1984).

Longman, C J Ed, *H Rider Haggard: The Days of My Life* (Green & Co, 1926).

Glyde, John, *Folklore and Customs of Norfolk* (E P Publishing, 1973).

Grinsell, L V, *The Ancient Burial Mounds of England* (Methuen, 1973).

Helm, P J, *Exploring Pre Roman England* (Robert Hale, 1973).

Higgins, D S, *H Rider Haggard: The Great Storyteller* (Cassell, 1980).

Hiller, Henry, *The History of the Borough of Kings Lynn* (1907).

Lawson, Andrew, East Anglian Archeology Vol 2 (1976).

Rendall, Caroline, *A Norfolk Anthology* (Boydell Press, 1972).

Rider Haggard, H, The Days of My Life: an Autobiography (Green & Co Ltd, 1926).

Robinson, Bruce, *The Peddar's way and Norfolk Coast Path* (Countryside Commission, nd).

Seego, Michael, *Birds of Norfolk* (Jarrold, 1977).

Scott, J M, *Bodicea* (Constable, 1975).

Vince, John, *Discovering Windmills* (Shire Publications, 1981).

Wailes, R E, *The English Windmill* (1954).

Wagg, Gina, *Full Circle: History of a Windmill* (Peacock Press, 1993).

Webster, Graham, *Boudica* (Batsford, 1978).

Yaxley, David, *Portrait of Norfolk* (Robert Hale, 1977).

Tacitus, *Annals, XIV 33* (Bristol Classical Press, 1992).

Marly Lane

Gausden, Rev P J, *Hoath & Herne.* (K H McIntosh, 1984).

Rupp, Gordon, *Thomas Moore* (Collins, 1978).

Williams, Rob, *Chislet Parish Magazine* (nd).

Crummack Lane

Brumhead, Derek, *Geology of Yorkshire* (David and Charles, 1979).
Cowley, Bill, *Farming in Yorkshire* (Dalesman Books, 1972).
Craven Muster Roll of 1803.
Crowther, Arnold, *Yorkshire Customs* (Dalesman Books, 1974).
Duerden, Norman, *Portrait of the Dales* (Robert Hale, 1978).
Foote, P G, & Wilson, D M, *The Viking Achievement* (Sidgwick & Jackson, 1970).
Hartley, Marie, & Ingilby, Joan, *The Yorkshire Dales* (Smith Settle, 1991).
Hartley, Marie, & Ingilby, Joan, *Yorkshire Village* (Smith Settle, 1991).
King, Alan, *Early Pennine Settlement* (Dalesman Books, 1970).
Magnusson, Magnus, *Vikings!* (Bodley Head, 1980).
Mitchell, W R, *A Dalesman's Diary* (Souvenir Press, 1980).
Mitchell, W R *Haunted Yorkshire* (Dalesman Books, 1969).
Pevsner, Nikolaus, *The Buildings of England* (Penguin Books, 1961).
Raistrick, Dr Arthur, *Ice-Age in Yorkshire* (Dalesman, 1968).
Scott, Harry J, *Yorkshire Heritage* (Robert Hale, 1970).
Sledge, W A (ed), *Naturalists' Yorkshire* (Dalesman Books, 1971).
Williams, Ann, *Country Crafts in Yorkshire* (Dalesman Books, 1980).
Wilson, A A, *Geology of the Yorkshire Dales* (National Parks Publication, 1975).
Yorkshire Facts and Records (Dalesman Books, 1968).

Castle Lane

Bede, Cuthbert, et al, *Fotheringhay and Mary Queen of Scots* (Kent and Co, nd).
Bloe, J W, *Warmington: an Architectural Des. of Church & Village* (1937).
Fraser, Antonia, Mary Queen of Scots (Weidenfeld & Nicolson, 1969).
Hunt, S J (ed), *A History of Fotheringhay* (Hillison Printers, 1987).
Ireson, Tony, *Northamptonshire* (Robert Hale, 1974).
Lightfoot, Miss F, *The Chronicles of Fotheringhay* (The Library List, 1933).
Mee, Arthur, *Northamptonshire* (Hodder & Stoughton, 1977).
Muntz, R A (ed), *Some Ancient Interests of Fotheringhay* (1958).
Page, William, (ed), Victoria History of Northamptonshire Vol 2 (nd).
Smith, Juliet, *Northamptonshire and Sole of Peterborough* (Shell Guide, 1968).
Steane, John.M. 1974. *In a Northamptonshire Landscape.* Hodder & Stoughton.
Webb, Peter Graham, *Portrait of Northamptonshire* (Robert Hale, 1977).
Mary Queen of Scots (Pitkin Pictorial Guide, 1996).
Richard III (Pitkin Pictorial Guide, 1994).

Chiddenbrook Lane

Angel, Heather, *The Countryside of Devon* (Jarrold, nd).
Bennett, Geoffrey, *Battle of Trafalgar* (B T Batsford, 1977).
Durrane, E M, & Lansing, D J C, *The Geology of Devon* (University of Exeter, 1982).

Howell, Roder, *Cromwell* (Hutchinson, 1977).

Fraser, Antonia, *Cromwell, Our Chief of Men* (Weidenfeld and Nicolson, 1973).

Pettit, Paul, *The Country Life Book of Cornwall and Devon* (Hamlyn).

Sellman, R R, *Illustrations of Devon History* (Methuen & Co, 1962).

Watson, Dr, *Life and Times of Charles I* (Weidenfeld & Nicolson, 1972).

Wedgewood, C V, *The Trial of Charles I* (Reprint Society, 1964).

Whitlock, Ralph, *The Folklore of Devon* (B T Batsford Ltd).

Rookery Lane

Haynes, Rev H W, *Sidlesham Past & Present* (Southern Publishing Co Ltd, nd).

Heron-Allen, E, *Selsey Bill* (1911).

Knapp, Stephen, Pagham Harbour Nature Reserve (Warden's Report, 1992).

Knox, A E, *Ornithological rambles in Sussex* (London Press, 1855).

Newbury, K M, *Sidlesham Mill* (local notes, 1980).

Ogden, P, *Discovering Selsey* (Village People Publication, 1998).

Simpson, Jaqueline, *The Folklore of Sussex* (London Press, 1973).

Wallis, Tony, *A Sussex Garland* (Godfrey Cane Associates, 1979).

Pagham Harbour Reserve Leaflets, *Pagham Spit Nature Trail* (1996).
    Plant Check List (1994).
    Sidlesham Ferry Nature Trail (1996).
    Butterflies of Pagham Harbour (1992).

A History of Sussex, The Hundred of Manhood (Victorian County Histories).

Coombe End

Gladwin, D D, *The Waterways of Britain* (B T Batsford, 1973).

Gladwin, D D, *The Canals of Britain* (B T Batsford, 1976).

Green, Peter, *Kenneth Grahame 1859û1932* (John Murray, 1958).

McKnight, Hugh, *Shell Book of Inland Waterways* (David and Charles, 1975).

Squires, Roger, *Canals Revived* (Monahe Press, 1979).

BBONT Naturalist Trust Leaflets.

Fitzroy Park

Bryant, Julius, *Kenwood* (English Heritage, 1990).

Hattersley, Roy, *Nelson* (Weidenfeld & Nicolson, 1974).

Norris, Ian (ed), *The Heathside Book of Hampstead & Highgate* (nd).

Norhcote-Parkinson, C, Gunpowder, Treason and Plot (Weidenfeld & Nicolson, 1976).

Richardson, John, *Highgate, its History since the Fifteenth Century* (Historical Publications, 1983).

General

Angel, Heather, *et al*, *Book of the British Countryside* (Drive Publications, 1973).

Dowdeswell, W H, *Hedgerows and Verges* (Allen & Unwin, 1987).

Encyclopedia Britannica (1999).

Hadfield, John (ed), *Shell Guide to England* (Michael Joseph, 1973).

Hippisley-Cox, R, *The Green Roads of England* (Michael Joseph, 1973)

Lee, Christopher, *This Sceptred Isle* (BBC/Penguin Books, 1997).

Trevelyan, G M, *History of England* (Longman, 1973).

Wilkinson, T W, *Pilgrim's Way: From Track to By-Pass* (Methuen, 1934).

Unstead, R J, The Story of Britain (A & C Black, 1969).